# IOVIS

ANNE WALDMAN

# IOVIS

ALL IS FULL OF JOVE

COFFEE HOUSE PRESS :: MINNEAPOLIS :: 1993

Cover art: Wall painting from Villa at Boscoreale—*Lady Playing the Cithara*. Used with permission from The Metropolitan Museum of Art, Rogers Fund, 1903.

Parts of this poem have appeared in the following places: *American Poetry Review, Bombay Gin, Big Rain, Conjunctions, Exquisite Corpse, Human Means, Kaimana, New Directions 52, New Directions 55, Notus, Stiletto, The City Lights Review, Exit Zero, Patterns/Contexts/Time, Tyuonyi, American Standard, The Little Magazine, Scarlet, Big Scream, High On The Walls (Morden Tower Anthology)*, and in *Helping the Dreamer: New & Selected Poems 1966-1988*, published by Coffee House Press.

For contributing words to *Iovis,* I thank, especially, my son, Ambrose Bye. Also John Waldman, Bill Bamberger, Red Grooms, Douglas Dunn, Reed Bye, James Laughlin, Brendan Ritcheson, Dan Mage, Duncan McNaughton, Andy Hoffmann, Robert Masterson, Tom Kretz, Jason Wahlberg, Clark Coolidge, Clint Frakes, Lewis Warsh, Nate O., Rene Depestre (tr. Anne Waldman), Joseph Richey, Ronnie Burk, Martin Ramstedt, Joe Brainard, Ed Foster, C. E., Andrew Schelling, Fred Denny, The Qu'ran, Gilgamesh, Shakespeare's King Lear, The prophet Amos, Aeschylus & Nebuchadnezzar II.

Gratitude for help with the machines to Judy Hussie, Randy Roark and Paul Rubin and appreciation of Claud Brown for collaborating on the John Cage performances. The Sang Hyang Semara is Balinese hermaphroditic deity, primal energy source of all existent things.

The publishers would like to thank the following funders for assistance which helped make this book possible: the Bush Foundation; the Minnesota State Arts Board; the Dayton Hudson Foundation; General Mills Foundation; and the National Endowment for the Arts, a federal agency.

Coffee House Press books are available to the trade through our primary distributor, Consortium Book Sales & Distribution, 1045 Westgate Drive, Saint Paul, MN 55114. Our books are also available through all major library distributors and jobbers, and through most small press distributors, including Bookpeople, Bookslinger, Inland, and Small Press Distribution. For personal orders, catalogs or other information, write to:
Coffee House Press
27 North Fourth Street, Suite 400 Minneapolis, MN 55401

# CONTENTS

for Ambrose Eyre Bye

&

to the

SANG HYANG SEMARA

I was a hidden treasure and I loved to be known
so I created the world.

> — *Hadith gudsi,*
> attributed to God
> by Mohammed

*"Give it a rest Zeus."*

> — Hera speaking
> Lucan

## Both, Both: An Introduction

Today I write in the context of 4 white walls. I woke to overcast sky. I stayed up late last night. The night was still. I could think clearly again extracting myself from the child's voice: demand & interruption. & yet I had the notes of his contribution to the long poem which he had sung out in the car outside Telluride. It was a list for the guardianship of plutonium, all the coverings to encase it: "one of every single stone in the world, pennies, quarters, everything" or "play-dough—dried & dead peoples' bones, & then there's plain dead people with nothing on them."

Last night I had nibbled at the psychotropic mushrooms & was lying in the grass in the yard waiting for the near-full moon to rise. I was counting the "fathers" I had known in consideration of the long poem which among other things male, celebrates them. How many of them were dead now? How many of them had become stars in the sky? In any sky? I invented a list of questions for my father about World War II. What were the names of all the towns in Germany he passed through? Had he met any women in those travels? What had he told me years before O tell me again about the dead arms reaching to heavens near the Maginot Line! "Imagine O" I heard then & now. I experienced the dread of the act of making this poem for seven years & of all the men dead & alive going into it & saw them beckon to me to speak of my relationship to them in a language perhaps only I could understand. & I heard lovers, grandfathers, brothers, father-in-law, students, husbands, son, and the friends of my son, boys, speaking to me. And a persistent sound too was the sound of a bigger vatic voice inside any myth, classic archetype, any ritual sacrifice.

Then I tried to imagine my great-great-grandfather Thomas Hand, a sea captain, shipwrecked—no—lost at sea between Cape May & Liverpool delivering the south Jersey oak & pine they craved abroad. Who was he? What was the vocabulary of that boat & occupation & what tempest rocked him dead?

I feel myself always an open system (woman) available to any words or sounds I'm informed by. A name. A date. Images of war. Other languages to which the ear attunes. What you said in your letter about the praying mantis: "I brought it right up to my face and opened my mouth and it wasn't afraid" or what words go on between the nouns & verbs you choose. What phoneme exists there.

I get up & dance the poem when it sweeps into litany. I gambol with the shaman & the deer. It is a *body poetics*. I am in the context of those before me who worshipped a goddess whose eyes were mirrors. One eye reflected the "inside," the other the gorgeous & dark phenomenal world. Take your pick. Both, both. She, the muse, puts an invisible protection cord around my neck to protect me from ego. She exceeds my aspiration to disappear.

I write with the disappearing coral reef in mind & the total extinction of the dusky sparrow.

I exist in a community of my own choosing & making which is attentive to language & poetry before language. It harbors the secret wishes of all my tears and predilections. Community is "voice." It strides the blast. So many have heard these words in earlier form, recrudescent though they be, and felt the heat and Zeus's juice. They asked this book to be. I thank them.

In the dream of "Friedrich Hegel" later the same night, Hegel, a father, was 88 years old, with copious red hair & crisp spectacles. He was to perform his latest piece in a bright green meadow & he let it be known that all the women present were invited to fall in love with him. He was philosopher-patriarch, often irresistible. He could mouth the plan or structure of a stable, composite world but would he take it apart again?

"Iovis" literally *of Jove* is the possessive case, *owned by Jove.* As well as about him, a weave.

"Iovis omnia plena" from which Iovis springs is a phrase from Virgil—*all is full of Jove.* & I wanted that sense of filling up: "plerosis." How that is both a celebration and a danger. And how complex is the relationship of this poet to the energy principle that does that. In Sanskrit the masculine energy principle is "upaya," skillful means. See it everywhere. How skillful is a war in the Middle East? But how sweet is the grandfather bidding his wife purchase a sweater-coat his size in 1908. All the life I want to make things happen. Stop explaining I have to say.

I honor & dance on the corpse of the poetry gone before me & especially here in a debt & challenge of epic masters Williams, Pound, Zukofsky & Olson. But with the narrative of H.D.'s *Helen in Egypt* in mind, and her play with "argument." I want to don armor of words as they do and fight with liberated tongue & punctured heart. But unlike the men's, my history & myths are personal ones. I want & need the long poem. In one doctor's description I've "too many male hormones." Let them sprout & spurt off the page. But let it not be said she wanted to be a man. Point of view: both accommodation and scorn. And don't forget Wit, a dark fairy. She teaches balance, redress, how to face the end of the world with dignity: make a space for her entourage. Sisters of beauty & seduction with no truck in the male poems these past years. Come out of exile, something still a real person we hope, welcomes you in.

Each section in this poem is a "take" on the last: strands, leitmotifs come back around. One friend notes—as if to see the "questions" from many—not points of view—but on many scales, as in sizes/proportions. There is a structural constant how the sections evolve: cumulative, wave effect—each self-organizing as it proceeds, thick with sperm that binds them. Fragments built on other fragments, finally organizing, one hopes, each other toward some kind of cohesive landscape. The field of Mars. May I be so bold to say these things? Narrative tags at the beginning of each section track the poet's steps as they thread through a maze.

Words are used here with awe, dread, submission, humor, cheek, as if they were sacred creatures—pulsating, alive, mocking. As such they are little mirrors. For this poem I summoned male images, "voices," & histories as deities out of throat, heart, gut, correspondence & mind. Call them *dakas* as they set off, like seed syllables, into the sky. They are semi-wrathful messengers, protectors. They're the heroes, thought forms of the theistic father and the pagan shape-shifter or boy-child-trickster of the poem. Every epic requires them. And she who sits at desk under dark spell and dances out under hot moon names them to release them.

A.W.

Autumn Equinox 1989 — Winter Solstice 1992

## Manggala

*The poet invokes the familiar Judeo-Christian patriarch who is seductive in his humility. Her own magisterial power competes with his. He comes as sorrowful one, infects humanity with his lowness & passion. She has often felt this as "trick," as ruse designed to inspire pity which turns to subjugation, because it is harder for they-who-think-themselves-guilty to rise again. But she remembers the gnostic dream within the dream and the human potential for resurrection. Moment to moment the mind turns. She gets out of bed each day to greet & study the phenomenal world. And her investigation is the highest art she imagines. Moses staked a claim and held up one of the first books as emblem of rule. She will imitate, play prophet & tell allegories on judgement day as only a woman might. These are the words of a meditator, a lover. She declares her poem, the "book" — by implication, holy — as a new doctrine. The world's resources depleted, too many people on the planet, how to respond? Keep writing & hope to alleviate some of the suffering.*

A man of sorrows
comes in lowness
comes to me in lowness
& this humiliation becomes passion
lamb into lion
then I am in lowness
& He is the great King
& he is the bridegroom
Time, O time is at hand
& I am in lowness
& He is the great king
& I am in lowness
The dragon is Pharaoh
& I am in lowness
I eat the book in this oral philosophy
Tell old Pharaoh to let my people go
The time is at hand
(& I am in lowness)
The time is at hand in lowness
I will take his sorrowful past into my future
I will take both testaments
& transmute the mundane into heavenly music

& eat the book
The scroll is my number
& do not destroy my temple
I sing within & without the temple (it's this book the temple I speak of)
The male gods take over as electricity & dynamite
& let me preach these allegories for the last day
& we, goddesses, giddy on the last day
will preach these allegories on the last day
I speak out of my lowness
but the messiah is a man of sorrows
& O he is the great King
But I am in my writing
& in my richness
I speak a new doctrine to an old form

\*

old
    a yard of it
word
      go flame
to scroll of it
holy form
    no harm
say book of it
    burden, down
its glory
      made holy
writ of it
    words to
"good augury"
    but doom abound
on earth of it
      *aqua benedicta*
      splash
not brag
    this hag's tongue
      in *genus femininum*
*be blessed bride to book*

# I

ALL IS FULL OF JOVE

*The poet positions herself in the cosmos, already Wlled with the sperm of Jove who "peoples space." She challenges his infusions. She lays out the page as battleWeld, honors her ancestors, her family, and lovers past, present, future, & in all ten directions. Conversation in a taxi with Red Grooms — a painter of wry vivid eye — refashions her childhood streets. Her ear pricks up to major voices & obsessions that will return again to haunt & radicalize her poem. Her son who is willing to magically grow up to her as she grows down to him will be her guide. He is trickster, shape-shifter who both interrupts her & goads her on.*

He catches my eye, my fancy
    October
    I ride an orange car
    The radio is sad & hopeful
    "Don't Turn Your Back on Love"
    Clouds lift higher
    & clutter the mountain
    It's in the weather everywhere
    I am helpless
    Ex Stasis
    I'm Gaia
    Father Sky look down on me
    Stars are his eyes
    He enters me
    All is full of him

What's true by excluding nothing (I can't really do this): the birthplace, the rain (40 days & 40 nights) observed from a screen porch. Cradle me in memory and make me a goddess-fearing Titan. I didn't resist & pulled my weight, a firecracker to be born in this world. And swept in the tide of this post-war boom, the child of such & such a divine mother and a father, the soul of gentleness. A plain kind of basics weep now to think of modesty in financial matters & hard facts of life, the fanatical enemy war that made sense, the war that hoped to be brought into a safer place, the letters and photographs, you can imagine, & description of dead soldier limbs lifted out of rubble (he saw this, they saw this, they all saw this) the unmitigated trouble of it, and it a mighty cause, and the children everywhere of it now, in my life, of survivors, prisoners, dead ones, tortured or heroic, what could come after this in the nuclear sense? Yet how it "ended," what is the payoff, the result of any way you look at it, those survivors too, the Japanese, and now we live in the combined karma, if I might use that word, dear sister Yoshiko, dear reader dear student, in the sense of what continues, a thread of energy perhaps is all. Which is why now I can say the poet must be a warrior of the battlefield of Mars, o give me a break, thank you very much.

No one will sign on this dotted sky line. But what is perceived is the vast body, the sky itself, coupled with earth and someone (Virgil) said: IOVIS OMNIA PLENA. All is full of Jove (his sperm presumably to people Chaos).


Whole the moon, whole the year
  *tuliz U tuliz hab*
whole the day, whole the night,
  *tuliz kin  tuliz akab*
whole the breath when it moved too, whole the blood too
  *tuliz ik cu ximbal xan  tuliz kik xan*
when they came to their beds  their mats, their thrones;
  *tu kuchul tu uaob tu poopoob tu dzamob*
rhythm in their reading of the good hours,
  *ppiz u caxanticob yutzil kin*
as they observed the good stars enter their reign,
  *la tu ppiz yilcob yocolob yahaulil utzul ekob tu yahaulil*
Everything was good
  *Utz tun tulacal*


But this is way after the feminine principle is making her mark on universal time equals space. I don't know anything, I know it all. The war is full of war and Levite laws, not tamed by laws of mercy, and Ashtoreth goes underground, as women are dragged into caves. And later a cruel Gentile world. Research: intercourse with mothers & daughters (as beasts do) a dream:

This was after the fall of the mother earth & giants
I said this already about sweetness

I said My Father, like a small lake
"Creators" as in Greek for poets, yet nothing is created from          limitless
mind
but
but this


The famous artist takes me to a hotel in a city like Portland. I'm a real red-
head now, but am concerned about the Dharma test I had to take earlier &
I have the distinct feeling they'll say I was being too literal when I wrote the
phrase "Things as they are." I was thinking, then, on the phrase, how I
wouldn't have a daughter now that I had all these "I"s. Two boy children,
where did the second come from? Red is now pulling the black slip strap
down. I am excited but worried about his exotic girlfriend who is brewing
Vietnamese coffee in the next room. "Wait don't move!" He says as we're
about to kiss. "Hold that stance!" He pours a bag of cement in the robin's-
egg blue porcelain sink, mixing it with hot water the way you do henna.
Then he picks up a little shovel in front of the fireplace and proceeds to
dump the mixture over my head. It feels good and quells desire.


But this desire
is a weekend
a mere idea
I think "50 labels self-sticking"
I think how life is compounded by paper
I think how sleep tonight tomorrow you suffer
I think I'll fall in love with him all over again
Me a Woodswoman from the City of the Mill
Grandfather John a glassblower, sedate in the wind,
spectacled, pale, works hard in the Protestant ethic

Millville, New Jersey, which was the epitome of a place small
& human and at the lake the motorboat coming in at dusk.
There was a swing piano style (my father's)
& the chimney he (a father) built on the house never to
be owned ours

— 9 —

Millville, Feb 4, 1902

My Darling,

Yours at hand — and I would certainly have been disappointed if I had not re-
ceived it. I have been resting a little since supper — as I am real tired tonight it is
now nearly seven o'clock and we got to German lessons at eight. I hope you
have spent two real nice pleasant days and hope the remainder of the week is or
will be just the same and also that you derive lots of good from them. Now my
first two days have not been so pleasant I have had some real trials nothings has
went well and I feel real out of sorts tonight. I hardly know what I would have
done had I not received a letter from someone very precious to me. Well our
orders have been running very bad lately. I think things will come better here-
after I hope so anyway. Well this is too much grumbling for you I won't com-
plain any more.

   I went out to Church last night. James wanted me to help him sing Well they
had a very good meeting. I think there were two conversions. The young man
who they tried to get Sunday night his brother was converted, he was there but
would not go but they think he will tonight. May McLaughlin's father was up
last night. Mr. Hunter asked that the men invite all the men in the factory
tonight and I think there will be a big time there. Mrs. Hunter is going to sing
Memories tonight.

   Well I am going to finish up on scolding. Now who said it would be good to
be apart awhile I would like to know did I ever say that and mean it? Oh yes! You
ought to see my mustache it's a beauty. Well darling feed up well and when you
come home Sallie will soon kill the fatted calf. Don't worry about me going
skating. No more for me. Remember me to all I will close and go learn a little
dutch

Yours only and truly

John W. Waldman


Admonishing students to avoid writing the grandmother
in the attic, for example, or mother too, think of Creeley &
that respect & ease
To ease the distant dead one
But the mother was hard on the father, dominating 47 Macdougal
Street you must say "below Houston"

A: So talk a little bit about your neighborhood.

R: We're passing the new Golden Pacific National Bank which is kind of a out-standing piece of Chinese architecture, very brand new. And it's already begin-ning to flake off on the red columns. And they've got outside marble Chinese dragons and we're heading now past the old Centre Street main police station which has been abandoned for ten years, but is about to be opened up as a con-dominium. And I think it'll be quite a landmark. Now we're, as we get to the corner of Broome and Centre Street, we're looking across to what I believe to be a German-sponsored project which seems also to be some sort of condomin-ium, I . . .

A: . . . are wacky . . . this green . . .

R: Yeah, well that's the old stuff. The building itself has some kind of, it's kind of nice, it looks like . . . I don't know what it looks like, but . . .

A: Yeah, but the windows could be a little?

R: Yeah, but the new design is, for some reason, somebody chose his kind of aluminum siding . . .

A: Look at that chandelier, I mean, it's so odd . . .

R: Right. And they didn't put anything over their awning there.

A: Germans you said?

R: For some reason, I don't why, I heard that Germans had taken over the place. Now we're getting up to Cleveland Place and we're passing Eileen's Cheesecake which is a very distinguished product, I certainly sponsor it.

A: Where? Not this.

R: No. We just passed Eileen's. Now we're getting up past the old methadone center, which is now moved up here, which was kind of an outrage in the neighborhood. We're passing Jennifer Bartlett's loft. She was very much against the methadone clinic. Now we're getting even to the fire station and past PIM magazine, a very cute little miniature gallery, which is also publisher of proba-bly the smallest publication in New York. And we're heading now past the illustriously renovated Puck Building.

A: And what's the story on the Puck Building?

R: Well, the Puck Building was for years and years like a printed ink building. They manufactured printing ink. And it always smelled very nicely. But since some big entrepreneur has taken it over and done a nice job, it looks pretty glamorous. They've got green trees out here, anti-bum fences and I think they rent out the ground floor to benefits, big dos, you know. I think Williwear had a do there or something. I don't know who else, but lots of things and probably there's some terrific spaces there. Now right here we're on the corner of Houston and Centre Street or Lafayette Street as it turns, it turns into Lafayette and then turns into Park Avenue, and we're in what I think is filling-station land, where all the cabbies gas up at the gaseteria here, it's an Amoco station on my left. And across the street is the fast parking, gas-and-wash emporium, which is probably the best place to get your car washed around here. And then there's the attractive Lafayette Tire and Auto Safety Center, sporting a Michelin tire sign and looking pretty jazzy. And there you see the remains of an old City Walls mural. It looks kinda like from Byzantine days. And now we're just passing Houston Street and there's many — Houston Street still is holding about the same pattern with some slight gentrification to the west here, with some new stores on the SoHo side. And now we're heading down, we're heading west on Houston Street, just passing the car wash place. Not much to say about that I haven't already said. Across the street you see the billboard for the Semaphore Gallery which I think is quite interesting, they are changing it every month and doing a nice presentation with a new billboard by the artist they're showing at that, concurrently. That's pretty interesting.

A: That's one of a kind, isn't it?

R: Yeah, I don't know any other gallery that does that. I mean, they, and they only do it one billboard. And I saw an artist there for the first time that I liked a lot, and then I went to see the show, so it worked on me. Now we're we just, we're just almost in the heart of SoHo, we're just about to pass, we're passing these new stores. The first of them seems to be called Fuel Injection, which I think is a Japanese, sort of fast-food clothing boutique. And, what's happening, this is the old Lilien Hardware and Supply Co. on the northwext corner. That's been there forever.

Cabbie: Forget about that fifty cents, I hit that by mistake.

R: Right. Thank you. Now, this part of Houston, oh this is a very interesting natural park by I think the artist's name is Sonfist, What's his name, Alan?

A: St. Anthonly's.

R: Yeah, St. Anthony's. So, I mean, food festival.

A: It's where I grew up. Right here.

R: Thompson Street?

A: Two houses down. The grey house, the red one. I grew up on the top floor.

R: Wow. Doesn't look like it changed much. Are you Italian?

A: No. I wish. No, I'm a Protestant, a Huguenot.

R: And you grew up there?

A: Yeah. I grew up there. My father still lives there.

R: Wow. I didn't know that.

A: My brother's living there now. Forty-seven MacDougal. The St. Anthoy's parochial school is across the street, I grew up in the festa and I went to school right on King Street.

R: . . . Canal Street, it's like a forty-dollar number or something.

A: Really. I'll go get one. I have about three at once. They're broken down.

R: Yeah. Go to Canal Street.

A: Which place?

R: It was near, well, they got so many of them. This place happened to be near Centre Street on the north side, very near the corner. On the street, like out at, you know, on a table outside. Now we're into what is really kind of a backwash. I mean, we're near a Martin's bar and I think almost all -

A: (can't hear) bar.

R: Oh, yeah, the SOB. Actually, I've been in there, have you?

A: No.

R: Is that like a club, nightclub? Music loft?

A: Yeah. Music loft.

R: But I know this Martin's bar across the way, which is at Varick, and is this Houston?

A: Yeah.

R: Has been there from year one. And I think almost all Martin's bars were, used to like, be all over the City, or have been torn down or changed.

A: There's a loft for rent.

R: That loft, that loft has been for rent for twenty-five years. I have for years, I have speculated living there for years. Because it's always for rent.

Cabbie: (can't hear)

A: What's that?

Cabbie: They open after-hours places in these lofts now.

A: Open air . . .

R: They're after-hours clubs.

A: Oh, after-hours clubs.


The cabbie hinted no subject matter but the experience of that father going to school on the GI Bill, studying that beautiful language of literature, & that was that & could attain right livelihood in such a manner of speaking, and nailed on the oilcloth to the black table my mother's first husband built with half-Grecian hand upon which we had countless meals and struggles. And Glafko surfaced once to defend a poor Mexican, be beaten up alive still, hospitalized, too gentle in this New York world.

Welcome in this world, Met Opera broadcasts and hiding places behind awkward chairs and fear of oranges from the little brother who came into this world to make me jealous & wiser. My father on the post-war dream, recovering, come on get with it, not a Catholic in me, although we are surrounded and informed and made alive by these visions and rituals & food. I did too see the Devil with the rest of them in the girls' room at P.S. 8! I swear, Mrs. Mulherne! He was red with horns & a tail & a sneer & he smelled like the devil too, all spermy & peppery. You could say he was a sex symbol, a voyeur (we were so little, prepubescent in the long lunchroom hour). The older half-Greek half-brother confused me with his little black box, Pandora's he called it, a box of woes, the accoutrement of the diabetic. How many relationships to break a heart? This is for fathers & brothers. A younger golden boy who usurped the breast, the remote father, tamed by war, the mysterious half-Greek, a dark musician. I honor & obey these first men in my life who were to repeat in a swirl of patterns & combinations of other men so dear to me. Should I go on?

President Ronald Reagan
The White House
1600 Pennsylvania Avenue, N.W.
Washington, D.C. 20500

Dear Mr. President:

On November 19 and 20, when you meet with General Secretary Gorbachev in Geneva, the hopes of not just all Americans, but of the entire world, will be with you.

Mr. President, I believe that we must take steps to limit the nuclear arms race.

I recognize that the Soviets are our principal adversaries in the world. They are tough, determined negotiators. Nevertheless, each of your last five predecessors – Presidents Kennedy, Johnson, Nixon, Ford, and Carter – has been able to work out important nuclear arms control treaties with them – treaties which have helped reduce the threat of nuclear war.

The Geneva summit provides you with a real chance to break the current negotiating impasse–to reach the kind of agreement between leaders which is needed to obtain significant arms control.

As you yourself have said, "A nuclear war cannot be won and must never be fought."

Mr. President, now is the time to put the power of your high office behind those important and telling words. Now is the time to take positive steps to limit the nuclear arms race.

The Geneva summit represents an opportunity to break the arms control stalemate of the last five years and to enact new arms control limits which will *strengthen*–not weaken–our national security.

I encourage you to seize the opportunity the Geneva summit offers.

Sincerely,

Anne-Who-Grasps-The-Broom-Tightly

June 1, 1904

My Dear

I just finished reading your letter and I will say you are rather late in the day to have a bouquet holder made by Saturday. Why tomorrow is Thursday and it would be Sat. before it would come out of the oven. You should have thought of this sooner. You can get one later if you wish. I am very sorry I did not send you the measure for those windows right. But I will get them for you tonight and will mail this letter when I return home. The number on the house is 419. I am very sorry you are having such bad weather but I think it will be clear to-morrow. I understand Mr. Ware to say you told him about the carpet. I will give Mr. Sithers your note tomorrow. Will finish this when I return home tonight. Well it is now nine o'clock I have been uptown I went out to the house The measure of the windows from centre to bottom of casing is 39 inches. I hardly think the number I told you above is correct It is 417 but I will explain. The double house next to it on the west side is 411 & 413 so I think ours should be 417 but the single house on the east side is 423 There is no number on the house as yet. You have them printed 417. They have 2 rooms papered downstairs — they look real nice Well I will close now hoping that I have everything alright

Ever your John


November 21, 1985

Dear Anne,

You tell all and remain mysterious. You've got love to burn. The poem floors me, the words cut me up. Ardent and mute, yes, I am. The dancing does it, but I can't tell, can't speak; I worry, a conscience violated? Afraid of loss, so always losing. Patterns emerge: the legs, a certain shape, the butt, breast, firm, propor-tion, most important, but aura, it's everything, inseparable. The temptation of one who wants more attack.

In La Jolla, the Pacific is Mediterranean blue. The museum's windows look out on it, and the art isn't as good. George Trakas, know him? he's renovating a hill there. We dance in the theatre. We flew over you, both ways, and I wanted to stop and ask you how to make life-enhancing love out of this passion-pain.

Your son's becoming a demon perhaps? I and my son, possessed by demons, must become them.

Thanks for the passionate communication. I love you.

Son: We are lovers & Daddy is a wolf
　　　How old are you Mommy? 44? 29?
　　　Mommy you are always 21. Come
　　　down to 21 Mommy. Stay 21 forever
　　　& I'll grow up to 21. You are
　　　not as loud as Dad. You have no
　　　scratchy face. You are my most
　　　beautiful Mommy.


I get out & am not a sneaking Madam
Not a silhouette
Not a dreamy housekeeper
Not writing the modern Arcadia
Tangibly not at home
The copy on this page, on my shelves, in my heart
　　in my room is not a lie
Not mere loneliness, not slipshod
Not metrical, but operating
as pioneer, as trust, as Woman
as Passion, as Champion of Details


My older brother's wife rips up the photograph of his earlier daughter. I struggle in heart with the little godchild my lover commands with him into my world. The male makes us suffer for his heart of hearts. I sleep with my older brother's brother not my blood but who yet resembles him, after sitting on my brother's lap in what seems like a long taxi ride (it was raining) home. My mother is trying to keep us apart. We go to Hotel Earle with old-man lobby, whore at the door and make illicit love something like incest, unskilled in a burning urge to forge a link. The beautiful god is in town a few days, heading out west. Can I really make love to this yet again another Greek? Too cerebral, unsatisfied. It's the dark connection in this one. I always wore a black turtleneck then. I speak confidently.

　　The blond on the telephone is a long story, like my younger another brother who confesses desire for drugs & men. He takes my virginity as we used to say and we are cheerful in a sullied bed. Because my mother died I can speak these things I state again this is for fathers, brothers, lovers, husbands, son for that is next of kin alive & changing in a fluid world. It is a palpable motion toward them from one who slumbered many years in the body of a man and in herself a turf of woman becoming Amazonian in proportions (I grow larger even as I write this) as she spans a continent takes on the wise mother as she dies. I gave birth to a son to better understand the men whose messages pour out of me.


Dear Iovis:

Thinking about you: others in you & the way
You are the sprawling male world today
You are also the crisp light in another day
You are the plan which will become clearer with a
     strong border as you are the guest, the student
You are the target
You are the border you are sometimes the map
You are in a car of love
You are never the enemy, dull & flat, dissolving in the sea
Illusion lays its snare, you resort to bait, to tackle me
Our day is gone
To name a place steeped in legend it tempting
To name now and then Nambikwari, Arawak, Poona, makes
     them appear
We go as far as possible, any old town disappears
We look at the globe from vantage point of sun
The clouds under us are rich with
For manners for trouble for passion we do this to each other
     & forces us back into not-so-terrible childhood
     & forward to old age sickness death you know it
The lines translate to Sanskrit as I say this to you
Exhaustion with phenomena at last
As I say this to you the furniture is rearranged in a sacred text
The room is now long, the room is tall, the room is male
It is a cathedral after you have named them all for me
Or Theodora, a lusty woman
It is All Hallows' Eve & many dead lovers walk tonight
The wind goes through us, we aren't so solid

All you could hold onto I'm knocking out of you
The wind did this when I wasn't looking to me too
Your conscious eyes compel us together
A game of guesses
What is in the gentleman's mind?
Something in you reminds me of a magnate, a planet, a small prayer
A little girl is trapped inside trying to get out of you
I make a new plan every day to ride your mind
Drugs are inconvenient & stand outside the room
In the other room, the "she" carries it off, waving goodbye
The great thing is to love something
the land, the sea, the sweep of a hand, the way something boils
Man is the arm gesture of the woman or something like that says T.
The battle with the "Ugly Spirit" is not to be discounted says D.
A. needed a woman and caressed a tree
B. knows maximum intensity is best in this life
A world of heredity quiet in R.'s syllables
A woman's mockery is strong & hearty
She's fond of knowledge learn something about her
The large heart scans the future
Vague unrest I tell you so
You contradict your many selves
Your mind spills out, the page holds on
"You make a man of me" sings radio, gruffly
All is full of Jove, he fucks everything
It is the rough way to prove it
The male gods descend & steal power
How does it happen
How does it happen Blanche Fleur & Heart Sorrow?

     Here's how:

I lie back & take him in. He wounds me after a fashion. A new sensation of art & stimulus, for I watch them both & participate after a fashion until they are spent & the man is melted in arms, and no longer to do battle on this bed stage. The bed is the book is the bed is the book where sheets record every muscle tear sweat ooze of life & groan. It is the playground of the senses for this artist as sweet rehearsal for the nonexistent pages that will honor this rumbling & panic and lostness. I want to say to dear male lovers living & dead not anger made this but with due respect in spite of the crimes to which your sex is prone. I honor the member who is a potential wand of miracles, who dances for his supper, who is the jester & fool and sometimes the saint of life. But she, me, who takes it, who responds clasping with cunt teeth, the receiver, the mountain, whatever it could be called, the emptying, the joining of this most radiant sphere where the chakras glow under the sheets or else they are fucking in water, she is witness in this brave act. It feels like the great sperm whale entered me.

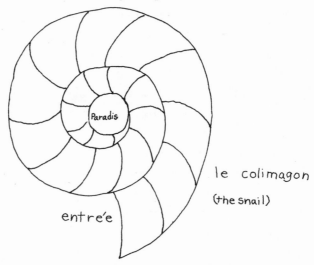

"You are done for in the labyrinth"

# II

## SOME KINDA ANIMAL

*The poet receives letters from an advisory elder who complains about Jove, from a misguided inventor, and also a prize student, which change her mind's atmosphere. She is moving out to confront the Desperado, most difficult challenge perhaps as he worships her & takes her as teacher. This turns the poet weak. Desperado & son meet as aspects of her attention, catching her ear with quirky syntax & desire. She sends bulletins into the void as she sweeps the battlefield, grasping the broom more tightly now, nervous about her own animal nature. Men are by nature aggressive. And women?*

Mature love you say but my wounds come out through inner temple

which are participants containing a statue of . . . female personnel,

not subject matter, a tableau of outerspace, concubines?

where we had countless meals and struggles with any father.

What is the mature and conditioned space O Jove?

Dear Anne,
Please advise how I may develop a scintillating poetic presence. Last time I read most dozed off. I dislike Virgil. Result of having to construe 40 lines a day at Choate — those endless similes

> As when at dawn the ducks
> from out the marsh
> Curdling their pintails in
> the early starch
> etc etc etc

Sorry, that's clammy armpit . . .

Very best to all,

JL

Never liked Jove either. Wd prefer to be inhabited
by Αφρωδιτη or some nifty Olympian girl.


It is a play or way to amuse the girl or is it? A way to talking
is another to journey to never abuse but wounds are fake and
are the scourge of me and they are real scourge of me. Where
to leave off talk of all these brothers and leave it here.
Dear Man-Who-Rends-My-Table-And-My-Hearth: SCRAM!
I am a ruined table because
I met a maiden good
I walked into an explicit house
and was a trait of forefathers
They could arrest me in my cunning
But they are not the boss of me
They are not the actor in a new phase of history: horse & chariot
They are not a grimace in this old gal's boot
We are like one city and another
And another comes along soon
the shape of Neptune's face
or Saigon, a sight for the broken
heart of anything
It is the ancient place of Ur
It is your own place won in fair fight
giving the lie to property tax
and the language of my people
O Male Civilizations!
I am not a party to my gold
but relate what has gone past
once the sufferings are over
Are they ever? I doubt it
But they are done to a crisp
and die in cold light
I am a regular next winter
I am a vestal in my propensity for service
I stretch my neck with music
but I doubt the way The Prophet

goes about bringing them to the Mount
Not doubt but a kind of wonder
It is a fiery night
and proud Maisie stalks the wood
She is the maiden of me
She is the good of me
I am a timetable for anything wet,
for anything with star and waxing moon
I am the dream of me, mere
illusory scales & fins, webbed toes
I grow into the scout of me
the densest one who reports back
to the head of me and sprouts
the garden you put your mind to
one sunny day
It glows like a pregnant thing
and grows the seed of any Art
It is alive nor is
the heart of me dead
I go so that a windless bower be built
So that I go quietly, I go alone
I am alone and delight in how speech
may save a woman
How speech is spark of intrusion


LETTER TO MISS IDONA HAND

Washington July 15, 1903

My Dear

I suppose you rec'd a postal from me by Tuesday noon – I thought you would
be anxious to know weather we arrived safely or not. We have had a splendid
time. I cannot describe the beautiful sights we have seen it is something won-
derful. I and the boys are sitting in the Pennsylvania depot. They are waiting
while I write this small message. We just saw the house where Garfield was shot.
We have covered a good bit of ground since arriving but we have several places
yet to visit. I am trying to make a note of everything so I can explain it to you.
But next summer you must see things for yourself. This is the most beautiful

place I ever saw. Everybody is feeling well we have a few jokes on one another. When we first arrived we walked down Sixth Street and we wanted 452. Charlie looked and saw the number 859 and called it out. It was sign saying established 1859. You want to ask him if he stopped on Establishment Street. This morning I awoke about six o'clock there was a bell ringing it rang twice and then commenced ringing harder. I said Boys there is a fire. I lit out of bed in a hurry. They are having fun about that. Well Dear I must close now hoping this will do you some little good. I will be home about Saturday and tell you all about it.

Yours

John


What are you you are what are you are you what seems lady?
Idona's seamed stockings in the attic, John a Protestant
never protesting on the porch, a gentle man outside any
war, born in the gap between worlds in collision.
All the lovers getting out of the army for one sane reason
or another, generation skipped. The grandfather in white,
father in khaki I won't skip over them to what you are
You're a pistol eye a mistletoe a missile man a Marxist
You're a sword eye a job queen a devil-may-care
You're a conch a knob you guys are slobs
We're playing ticktacktoe you're a sticky glue-stick
but a stick-in-the-mud too are you
You're spaghetti-hair Dad, you crazy old man
You woman Daddy you *New York Times* reader
You *New York Times* reporter
You're a suitcase What? What are you?
You're east of the sun & west of the moon
Are you are you are you are you What? What are you?
You slob you rubber band nose
You're a bully and a mean-shoot a paper clip a peppercorn
You've stuck in my teeth
You're a European walrus
You're a blue muscle you're a red tomato
You crossbow you arrowhead you man-of-me

You're a bellow of church
You're a bump thump bump dummy
You're a broken-down hospital
You're a cracked people
You're a craggy rock cliff
You're Michael Jackson you're Jacky Frosty
You cup nothing
You're a hundred thousand bristle blocks
You're a peony—means you're a broken-down housebell
You are my wife Mommy you are the dream of me

> The keep & key of an unruly person
> absorbed everyone & you realize he's
> only wild since noon

You're just out there looking at the moon

> So great my love on my male partners
> I have to leave town

(When you look into it on any person's desk
the town appears small)

> so now

I RISE BEFORE ISHTAR IN THE EAST
I RISE BEFORE ISHTAR IN THE EAST

Moon disappearing
all's sluggish, dull
What's the color
Pronounce it windless
A shroud song is sad
sword cuts who?
Some wicker man staggers
Listen to the peregrine fall
I try, towered upon a short stretch

Seeing Mother meshed with herself
O dire is her Mother need
She's shortened loose
She's in the fittings
Windows iced into dark holes
are quiet
but I think of a dream
in green jasper
It goes like this:
something shattered in chips
sailing down     (was it?)
long canals
cut channels
Something like Hawaii
for the craft
Need sharp eyes here
for a pagan sea

Lights stand up
in a dark wood
I'm now swimming in night green
"I shall paint my body red & dance"
she said I
will wear antlers or a
bone blooded with Earth-Time
I will
I will

In sets, sets in with her
holding tight slips
Those Martian canals are
cracked ice
I cut to the Andromeda movie
"Venus" is here too
I thought my body green or faun
& dropped the sexual stick
Shadows showed the crater

to be a new moon
a story-book pomegranate split
She's got a myrtle whip
She made her name in whips
& made me worship her
Me, a mere shadow of sight
standing in the shell of the dream
eyed back into dark ovals
Of all the Pagans I was One
what oath is mine?
Who wouldn't bend to a
Virgin standing on the moon?
Can't resist
I'll paint myself white
You paint yourself red
We'll dance to a
Low Eastern Bright Eye tune
& follow that song
Our bedsheets will be like fire & ice
& I'll have to walk out
the next door
to close out the smell of you


THE CREATIVE IS SPEAKING   It is a large you-name-it-machine made
of words to show you O Princes what's the side of He-Who-Risks
all for me, he the Bull leaper for in Bulls does the Earth-shaker
delight for in bulls does she know her truth & set down this
soft earth bed too grosse for Heaven upon which I end where
I begunne. (His loincloth will be immaculate and bright,
his bracelets will be costly, his hair curled, his face painted
red & black for a night of love)
THE CREATIVE IS SPEAKING to write a nuclear warhead, to
walk inside itself circumscribed as an obtrusive lope. The
man wants to play the music loud to think he's some kinda animal
some kinda some kind some kinda animal
Douse him or send him into the next votary's mind

He's some kind some kinda animal
Not that he's untamable but ancient you know like a
tryseerotops which is not to say it died by living
out its need

& needed more than one of us

Touched him she thought he thought
Some space between
He said about sex all over again
She said Here I go again
A couple mentions the "you" factor
you know then
She's ready too
We hold out our hearts
So what's the suffering all about?

THE CREATIVE IS SPEAKING   How the sons of immigrants go back
to fight in the ancestral homelands. Now you know you are American
Now you know how this is preserved in memory

You know how memory is cunning
That sex is early on the girl's mind
Now you know all manner of speaking openly
The myths are alive for a time
I come out full-grown out of my father's split head
and am armed for the battle of love
These words are in answer to an assignment to make sense of
three and five
I represented my mother to Greece
Poo EEE Nay stah sohn ton lay o for EEE on?

There is not more hope than this: to find the right bus
Athens, which is a city built on the extension of Hestia's hearth
The head split in two and something is noticed in the duality
of city life: in and out, the inner and outer working daily
for the virgin spinster who would like to make sense of all
these trade routes, know who went where when and the little
amphora handles are clues to great travelers with goods who
plunged ahead to carry with them their genetic structures

among other things, & all the manifestations of all the senses:
color, texture, taste, smell, sight
The spice of night
the silk of midday
The clear soup of morning
A way of studying stars
A photograph of a kind
The queen's proclivities
The way people might decide on a crime & so on
On returning from Egypt I had
1 hookah
2 scarves of silk, red as my fantasy of the red in Red Sea
& 1 Mediterranean blue
1 scarab pin (imitation)
Another scarab was lost in England in the room of the lady
who said "Scarabs always get lost around me"
And from these places I brought a new appetite for a
particular olive


It was the olive branch and owl which symbolized the way men
lived before they were civilized and somewhere out of darkness
I went to meet them.


Dear Lady,

I am an ingenious amateur inventor. For five years I meditated on trying to produce as many new good invention ideas as I could. I did think up about 50 of them. After checking patentability I discarded 12 of them and had 38 left. When I tried to sell some to a few businessmen, I got two of them stolen. I got them witness and disclosure documents on the rest. I then sold one to a lady and then am now offering any or all the 35 inventions for sale to you now. I trust you enough to take a chance anyway. Many of these are cheap and easy to build and make. All have good money making profit potential, some many millions profit potentially. I am not at this time financially able to afford getting any patents because I am getting by just barely. I hope to sell 10 or 12 of my new Inventions and then patent two or three then myself. I did get your name from the Who's Who book in America and address. Rest easy though I'm only sending a few letters to a few ladies to try my luck and will not advertise my invention or write to any men at all about any inventions. Read the next page for more details and bless you regardless of your decision.

from Kenneth Alexander Walker

Brief Indication List of Invention Ideas of Kenneth Alexander Walker

1.  Device for air improvement in homes.
2.  New type of pet bird cage. Should be liked by bird lovers.
3.  New type of child's tricycle.
4.  New type of ladies watch band.
5.  New type of stylish sun protection for eyes.
6.  New type of loud noise control hearingwise.
7.  New type of eyeglass frames. Should make people feel better.
8.  New type of outdoor bird house. Bird lovers should like this one.
9.  New type of barometer.
10. Improvement for safer night driving.
11. Burgler catcher mechanism.
12. New type of life raft.
13. Improvement for all replacement car door lock knob.
14. Method of getting massage while driving vehicle.
15. New type of food freezer. Should keep food frozen quality longer.
16. New type of refrigerator. Should keep food fresher longer.
17. New type of fish aquarium. Pet fish lovers should like.
18. New type of small animal cage for pets pet animal lovers should like.
19. New improvement for pet bird water dishes.
20. Method of improvement for men's briefcases.
21. Improvement on photo grey sun protection.
22. A camera and film picture improvement.
23. Improvement for teachers' blackboard pointers.
24. Improvement for telephone handles.
25. New type of scalp massage
26. New type of wax candle. More light for its size compared to others.

27. Improved clothing iron women will like.

28. Light increasing lampshade electricity saver.

29. Directional light increased electricity saver.

30. Shark repelling life jacket.

31. New type of stove that is an improvement.

32. Flexible light aimer improvement.

33. Auto window washer improvement.

34. Drinking water cooler improvement.

35. TV commercial alternative improvement.


To His Excellency Mobutu Sese Seko
   Head of State

Citoyen President:

I appeal to you for the immediate and unconditional release of Tshisekedi wa Mulumba, a lawyer and former member of the Zairian Assembly who was arrested last October.

   I believe that Mr. wa Mulumba is a prisoner of conscience, held solely for his nonviolent exercise of fundamental human rights. He is reportedly held at Makala Prison in Kinshasa.

   Thank you.

Anne-Who-Grasps-The-Broom-More-Tightly


IOVIS OMNIA PLENA The world is full is full of you my lingering
one, lingam of any century of this old papa's realm of this
sweet love & sweat. Dear Father who made me so to be a poet
on the battlefield of Mars, whose seed got dipped, got used
& cannibalized to be this witness such and eke out her income
her life her light on a bed of love, earth is my is my number
O earth is the number to be joined by you old grandfather
sky and harking back to he who is the genetics to any plump
German girl, or any paranoid Huguenot daughter. I can take
him or leave him, juiced out over many wars:
               & all these messages
                 are the light

of me

the life

of me who receives them in the guise

of anyway you want

hemmed in . . .
lost
willful
prepubescent in the long lunchroom hour . . .
I conquer you


A PERSONAL MESSAGE:

Dearest Anne, there is so much more I wish I could say to you. This test has been
enjoyable and frustrating in equal amounts. Sometimes I wonder why I bother,
but when I hear you and certain colleagues of yours read, it at times seems
worthwhile.

Looking at you, I see a romantic, an idealist, and a revolutionary. You seem to
call it the way you see it, and have no qualms about nailing the "jello faced
abominations" (My line) to the wall. You don't have any aversion to graphically
describing sexuality, pain, life, death, the reality of what it means to be men and
women.

If I seem nihilistic and cynical, it is because I am a heartbroken utopian
dreamer and romantic who has slammed up against the grey wall of reality a
considerable number of times. I live for vengeance, a sort of "poetic justice."

I admire how you with your greater experience of years and life than my own
can still see so much "basic goodness." But you are still willing to call a cat a cat,
a dog a dog, a man a man, and a woman a woman. And blame few indeed for
what they inherently are.

I really would like to be a successful novelist, and my audience response at
this most recent reading was better than usual, and I got positive feedback from
Rick Andy Tom. Poetry is even more fun than drugs, you were right about that.

I got Bill Burroughs (Sr.) up on my wall smoking a joint and looking right
through you. There is beer in the fridge, Joan Armatrading on the radio. What-
ever you would tell me, I probably would take it seriously.

The battle with the "Ugly spirit" is not to be discounted. Me and my whole
little faction of friends and lovers wave at you, smile, flip the bird, blow a kiss
from '77 '81 '83 '84. Here in exile I wish to know how I can best serve all those I

left behind.

Gregory Corso said something to the effect of "If you take your shit and show it to some guy and he says THIS SUCKS you gotta say, fuck you man, you're full of shit I'M A POET."

Burroughs said "There will be no self-pity in the ranks."

I would really like to have THE DEFINITIVE QUOTE from you. And if you want to tell me I have the whole damn thing wrong, I'll listen.

Fer-ever yours, your hopelessly sentimental and incompetent warrior in disgrace—

D.M.


D'accord that is the place to be, D'accord with him a place
to go down down on him with no music to prop this boy love

I extend to boy

It is the truth of me when I needed him and I was hard on him
& he in me, hard on me

to stay to prop this boy love
to be this fast hard boy love in me
I be it
in me, in me
to fast this love to fasten as I was hard on him to prop
his love

a violation & a forgetting    to prop all love

for I was hard on him to be a boy & love of the boy to be
a boy
go by, boy
yours in the ranks of any promise of manhood
& you are no music
you are no manhood yet

you are wonder I am spectator once      O boy!

Yet Guelfs, listen! This makes sense . . .

# III

## HEM OF THE METEOR

*The poet travels in dreams, skirting the hem of Zeus's robe which sways like an orbit of sexual prowess. She moves through the lives of particular men as a kind of sympathetic magic to catch experience. She wants the men to do the same: change into women. She travels to Berlin & into narrow annals of literary & military history which take her to certain conclusions about how to call the name of war. Her friend the Priest writes from Rome in a kind of conversion experience. She listens to the young boys & records a conversation, anxious they will survive & writes in a twilight language, intoxicated, typing quickly now. Marginal expressions, the speech & aspiration of gay men, transsexuals need to be heard. Pondering this, she continues to honor the hermaphrodite as the ultimate mental state, although she cautions it to have no expectations at the gates of heaven. Because it is an intolerant Christian heaven on the base level. She ingests magic mushrooms to prove a capricious point. Possibly about the other gateways — the ayatanas, literally the doors of the senses. She expands further into the universe through ritualized thinking, tells more stories. Desperado left behind, languishing on the banks of the river, he could not fulWll the writing assignments.*

Dear Hermaphrodite: *Lasciate ogni speranza voi ch'entrate*

*Cómo está el arroz?*

*está frito,* mon

bloodshot stars in a void

eyes off, shot from a gun

hem of the meteor, Zeus

no sleep

lines between two eyes

aim carefully: scent of human realm

First sex, a dark room in Nogales, Sonora, like Jack lost it in a whorehouse, five dollars even, 16 years old, sixty miles south of Wilmot Avenue, Tucson. Taxi driver laughed, "Zona Roja! Sí!" And the father pimp chuckled, guiding my friend & me, laughed even harder when we asked if we could do it in the same room, "No, no! Thees is no good idea! Follow me, let me show you Maria!" And it stunk like urine, the room, and she was probably about twenty, twenty-two, chunky, and, here, I start to undress her, every romantic notion, a dream to undress a woman! (We used to talk about screwing our friends' mothers!) and she laughs, says, "No. Five dollars." The bra took me awhile. And I could not believe how luscious her skin was, women were for me, this was good, I climaxed immediately, felt proud and cold and nervous about syphilis . . . . I did not love her, had this odd respect for her . . .

My hair was first
covering
my brows
(child's method
of wearing hair)
breaking flowers
I was frolicking in front of yr gate
When you come riding on bamboo stilts
(you–ride–on–bamboo–horse–come)

astro-physics lapsus memoriae
loves & penetrates
my hope through a dense forest

& was taken, a virgin
by all of you
to find the way
rather spotted than dead
& do I breathe
& do I, do I breathe?
& does he move?
He is a current in me
& does he move the current in me
Snake lore!

Penetration of trouble
hissing in the ear
the song of Love me, love me
Good, Good, Love me, Love me
it's good
speaking of him O speak of it
convivial & persuasive
O is a thrust
is O a thrust
curling & striking
My Carmelites, do not desert me!


        dear Anne,

You & Allen Ginsberg & I are standing outside some
kind of old back-East-type brick near-tenement apartment
where I just moved in. He's wearing a bright & slightly
tattered orange wool sweater that looks scratchy but is
really very soft. Everything he says to me you re-phrase
in order to be certain that I understand it thoroughly.
This is not annoying.


I speak as Hetaera
unraveling birth & death
I'll give you pleasure, okay mister
I give you pain
living on the parameter of the chthonic
"Here you can see every sort
     of person
       as if
       you had come to
the underworld" (Plautus speaks)
    & *Lasciate*
I'll send
*ogni*
take a peek *speranza*
Odysseus go down

*voi ch'entrate*
( a boundary for the post-titanic order)
Sing how you men are weapon-prone
How you are prone of heat & battle
Sing Odysseus, men are weapon-prone

Again:

Come then, and put yr sword
in my sheath
Sing, O,
how you men are prick-prone
Let us two go up to bed
(Show me the other sword,
Lying together in this bed of moan
we'll be sweet in each other's flesh)

      Here the streams flow with ambrosia
  by Jove's bed of love . . . .

        he who gathers the clouds
           clean white sheets
          etc.

— *cocinando* —

Now I have to tell you how offering up a hamburger probably saved my life. On December 27, I went to the Rome Airport to pick up someone. I got to arrivals at 8:50, saw on the TV monitor that the TWA plane was 20 minutes late, so I sauntered on up to departures to look at the faces in the crowd, as I love to do. I walked past El Al and TWA booths. At the far end of the terminal building there is a small bar with a number of tables (no seats) for a quick snack. There was a sign saying HAMBURGERS 3000 LIRE. (Well, ole Tom is always hungry, loves Hambies, and they are not easy to find in this city of pasta and wine). So I thought: maybe a quick hamburger while I wait. Then I thought: no, too early in the morning. I watched the faces happily eating and chatting, looked at my watch which said 9:02, turned and headed out the door and down the steps to arrivals. Well, you probably know what happened at 9:06 — handgrenades and machine gun bursts, 13 dead (now 16) and 70 wounded. I heard the bombs from

downstairs, saw a large mass of people running, panicked, some with blood
flying from them. Police forced all of us out into the parking lot. A few hours
later I found my shaken passenger and returned to Rome. I think the Goddess
whispered in my ear: No, Tom, no hamburger this morning, because eating one
I would certainly have been standing in front of that bar; and that bar was the
first place one Arab turned his machine gun.

("be careful, be very careful")

They are my tides my tides a blameless I thank you
They are against my tides or sides a blameless I thank you

      Not what the foreigners arranged when they came here:
           *May bay tun u mentah dzulob ti uliob lae*
      then shame and terror were preferred
           *zubtzilil tal zahob ca talob*
      carnal sophistication in the flowers of Nacxit fluchit
           and his circle;
           *ca cuxhi yol nicte cuxhi tun yol tu nicteob N.S.*
           *tu nicte u lakob*
      no more good days were shown to us . . .

the hazel corpses green
      no more be seen

madre, madre

& as a writer a green light to reorder my world
to fasten this male's mind to a star
& today we're seeing an event in time 55,000 years ago
& scoundrels spooked by their own shadow so thick
a striking grasp of opposites
nova

      through the keyhole of his eye

        I hear you, I hear you
you residing here I hear you
I hear you you here I hear you
    shift in my being too I hear you

                              here it's you
                      I said it: you
                                      Here you, I hear you
                  (Ambrose's Light Years)
                a child's Younger Lightfoot
              tread the meteor, Zeus


& you walk past me in the hallway & as I turn to look back
at you I start to gag & a large mucusy creature about
2 feet long & 6 − 8 inches wide looking somewhat like
a human snake or salamander, comes out from my mouth &
dissolves on the floor. I am stunned but also relieved
to be freed from this demon. I know you have helped
to heal me of this blockage & it has to do with the throat
& expression
                        variant linguistic tongue, to whom this power granted?

my throat, his passage
throat : a daughter of memory
beauty of my thought, out!

out!      hem the meteor
    curl vowel flame
not break the house


                  Nov 10, 1914: Ezra Pound writes a prospectus
                  for a new College of Arts and proposes schooling which stresses
                  "contact with artists of established
                  position, creative minds, men (sic) for the most
                  part who have already suffered in the cause of their
                  art"
            speak sagely through the deathless mouth
cause of the meteor, Zeus
            to break the pentameter, first heave, first rumor

religion at the gates, ether's invisible flame: conversion

rumor has it Christians have
a secret spray
that makes crosses appear
on Moslem women's veils . . .

They are speaking, the two 8-year-olds
in the garden
center stage:

— I'm really sick
I'm wounded

— Get some mint leaves
They'll cure you

— It's too late almost
I'm shot bad

— We have medicine
in the wagon

(dresses his wound)

— Feeling any better?

— Twist it up more

— I'm gonna get some new weapons

— Who's the en. . en . . en . . en. . enemy now?

— The new religion

— Yeah, pray to a dollar bill
— Muslims got some fancy weapons

— Allah ate a novelist too

— Jesus saves, ha

— But look, Buddha's just a guy

— Anyway, it's a robotical war now
Let's play robotical war

A. Prepare an Initial NBC 1 Nuclear report

1. At the instant of the "blue-white flash," hit the ground and start counting slowly, 1,000-AND-ONE, 1,000-AND-TWO, 1,000-and-three, and so on until the blast wave has passed.

2. Record the elapsed time as letter item J in the NBC 1 format.

3. Check your watch and record the time as letter item D in the NBC 1 format.

4. Report letter item H as SURFACE if:
   a. Throwout (earth particles that have fallen back and built up on the edge of the crater) can be seen or,
   b. A thick, dense steam has developed.

5. Report letter item H as AIR if the stem is not connected to the mushroom part of the cloud.
   NOTE: If in doubt, report letter item H as UNKNOWN.

6. If visibility permits observation of ground zero, use your map to determine the coordinates of ground zero and record as letter item F.

7. If ground zero cannot be observed, use your compass to measure the azimuth from your location to the center of the stem or mushroom cloud. Record this as letter item C.

8. Record your location as letter item B.
                  (all this with watch, compass, map, pencil, paper
                        standard gear
                              for
                              any
                              holocaust )

gonna get some new weapons
("And we two little ones had neither mutual dislike or suspicion")

Dear Mr & Mrs B:

Thank you for contacting me about recent events at the Rocky Flats Plant.

I have enclosed a copy of the statement I made to the Rocky Flats Environmental Monitoring Council on October 25, 1988, about the closing of Building 771 and about the storage of radioactive waste at the plant. It outlines the steps I recommend in response to these problems.

Thanks for letting me know your comments.

> Sincerely yours,
> J.O.V.E.
> D.E.S.
> Congress of the United States
> House of Representatives

> the book is Virgil
> the reader is you
> the street is
> evasive, a kid in love
> with war

He took me to Kreuzberg & wept
showing me the

place of destruction     He with Baltic eyes

*mise-en-scène*

The *Asphaltlyrik* of Nazi Germany

*Schadenfroh*, maliciousness

small-mindedness

This practice, as you may have noticed, shifts
the attention to the ongoing process of the mind

sitting against the condition we have

clap your hands the lights go on

Don Giovanni waltzes back into my arms
with an aria or two

My Europe's blood holds his sperm

We got on the turnpike, turned off at Mount Holly past
Fort Dix went down along the Pine Barrens to Hammonton then
took a diagonal to Vineland
the trip ended in Bridgeton
Cumberland county

(It was different than taking the D train to Coney)

& yet this writing is not my own subject

or blood shot

through dream
stars in void

Come out of your box, now
eyes go off
shot from a gun

hem of the meteor
No sleep
but lines between two eyes

                        germane to the question
& change a subject to

          careful air

aim carefully

                scent of human male realm

rocks enter the Book

            all the rubble of Berlin he showed me

                he lies back

                                    naked, a sailor

                        no anarchist yet       yet "dream boat"
                                all the rubble of Berlin he shows me

kisses me
*Das ist gut.*


(Built in Scotland in 1886 she spent her first 13 years
as a deep-water trader — to Auckland, Calcutta, New York,
Rangoon, Cape Town
around Cape Horn 17 times
She carried coal from Cardiff, whiskey from London
guana from Iquique
renamed *Star of Alaska* in 1906 she spent 25 years carrying cannery
workers north to Chignik cannery & salmon back to SF
The public may now board the *Balcutha* at Pier 43)

                        he lies back . . . *ist gut*


                            naked (*Ich bin nicht in Amerika*) he shows me

Pin Bot he shows me Comet he plays me Genesis
he plays TX Sector he shows me
Punch Out, Sega Turbo, he needs more coins:
Two Tigers, Pole Position II, Gyruss, MetroCross, Double Dribble,
Elevator Action, Circus Charlie, Centipede, Join the Action,
Taito 10 Yard Fight, Super Contra, Future Spy, Jail Break,
he shows me Wonderboy, Flicky, Dis Tron, he plays Falcon, Kidniki,
Radical Ninja, Galaga, Gimme A Break, Spy Hunter, Ring King,
Hat Trick he shows me he shows me he shows me
Twin Cobra, IKARI Warriors, After Burner, Danger Zone,
Toobin', XYBOTS, Rampage, Silk Worm, Shinobi, Guerilla
War, Xenophobe

                    as the quest for freedom continues . . . .

        he lies back but naked    he resists

                but naked he shows me *ist gut*

— 44 —

*"Ich möchte aussteigen."*

Ascendant Leo 4 degrees, Sun Aries 12 degrees, Moon in Sagittarius, Mercury in
Aries, Venus in Taurus, Mars in Pisces, Jupiter in Virgo, Saturn in Cancer, Ura-
nus in Gemini, Neptune in Libra, Pluto in Leo

can't get out now
                                    he lies back he shows me

& my Muse is my destiny of yes o yes
& he not wife and heart and he not Beautiful Dreamer and he
not a shrew, not a shrieker, not the mailman, the robotical
genius, not the one with the most personality, not the bookworm
not the avenging father, not the jealous brother, not the
invalid, not the mechanic, not the roofer, not the Drain Man,
not the mainliner, not the mortician's son, not the priest's
illicit offspring, not the acolyte, not the altar boy,
not the sycophant, not the celebrity, not the lotus land
habitue, or the star of popular musics, not the country &
western star, nor the schoolteacher, not the carpenter, not
the man who works computers, not the novelist, not the
student, not the boy, nor the father-in-laws, not the
guy next door nor the one I love so much down the block
not the explorer who dwells with beasts on rock and plain &
forest and jungle

Not the librarian (I kissed him), not Black Howie who
stole a kiss, nor the extraordinary dancer who showed me
home who I wept for tears on my pillow tears 96 tears on my pillow, not
the radio producer, not the way-his-heart-was-cracked Shakespearean actor
ah born of fatal flaw heart cracked like another century,
not him not him not him not him not Mike Rosati, not Ahab, not
John Hammond, or Teddy Strempack, not Chris Wertenbaker

but what?
but what O tinge
is a lover's question?

the shrieks of delight mere manifesting forms as
they sigh, turn away, eyes down, embarrassed in their
accomplishing manhood

And I would accord with them murmuring it's okay, *ist gut*,
my body is your fetish, my body is your dream, my body
is your mountain, my body is sleep and deception my body
was your home, lissome, I am haunting, I am rude,
I am all you ever wanted in a woman
take me back
and I shouted Take me back!

           "men suffer because they have testes
or because they have none" says Dahlberg,

that in apocalyptic fit, the pith of many's words

Thucydides would mock me or would he even care
would he care to be noticed here in my canon of honor?

Would you prefer the Hypophrygian man? the Hypolydia man,
the Dorian man, the Phrygian man? The Odin man?
Or Bernard Ventadorn, 1024 — 1195 the
good-looking-son-of-a-baker?

Himalayan kittens, Executive Lots, Loveland City Limits,
Edwina Avenue, Watch for sudden stop
Dance me, a child charging through its body, dance me Momma dance
Plutarch's lyre off the bones of a big white whale (Rehab)
establishing the pluck and strum, dance me
a kind of wind, a kind of wail, a kind of melancholic European angst
dying in another century
wind through bones, dance me
the haunt of love, ephemera this body I spread out for you

dance me, the son says, dance me dance me momma
           Jeff speaks
(How do you say when you wanna say "I" *auf Deutsch?*)

"I like in a man big hands,
blood red heat, not contra-
sexual hands, not insensitivity.
Adventure . . .
My first love David Martin Luther
left me in Texas, age 11, to
go off with his mother &
his future fucking stepfather
(My favorite color is blood red)
But once his real father
took us camping & taught us
how to get over our fear of
bees &
told us ghost stories
in the night . . .
I was queer I knew it by day & in the night . . ."

Your Saturday your Friday beyond eyes I tend
Your mouth reads "work"
Beyond you into a Dark Age I tend
I take your sex along the Dark Age
Below: Dark Age Epic Windows
Epic eyes flash
into words-ears-erect-permeability
        word & chase & hand & street
Silver grey-lakelike-Zen street
You prime yourself you will never always die
I tell you what to do, Jeff
Contact your jam-hand, his, bow in, bow hand
take his cock in your hand, bow down

                    dwell in a kind of tent appliance

                    looped in desire
another God says:
Cocaine prevents the brain
governs the crown
prevents the heart

governs the tongue
from calming itself down
"Broad heaven is the totality of your liver"
Earth is my number
in response to
certain external stimuli, specific
love object release heat
neurons release a
chemical called dopamine that
you are heated for
helps trigger
good feelings, or sunny euphoria
The dopamine enters the junction,
with one glance you hand down the law
or synapse, between the first neuron
and the interstices of earth & sky
and its neighbor, law
It chains the mighty
stimulates the neighboring cells
chugs through air, it alleviates suffering
and thereby acts as a
messenger (or neurotransmitter),
Marduk-Another-God has spoken
sending information
along so-called dopamine pathways

"Me & My Boyfriend We Get Away"

(teenage-cum-drug-love saga)
Me & my mind flee cramped apartment, age 13

& lie about the ethnogenics, dear mother of Macdougal Street as you open my
mail extolling the highs of Miss Green I said it, the words "smoked some pot"
meant "we were all in agreement"

        Ho!
& weren't we?
what is argument but sweet poetry

As teen how to be anything but body chemistry
& you grab the pack of Camels out of my hand in so-call-it-a-foyer
& grind each cigarette out on the floor
look look you said looking you say for "that ol' devil weed"

Father-Never-Stern stay in your room a quiet remove
big old daddy never
so worried as *all that*
Big Daddy make you jump jump jump
Criss cross'll make you jump jump jump
Daddy Mac'll make you jump
Mother how covetous a teen

yet
                How
                  manage
        sex
       remove

place
                hidden from
                    fury of
        some Joe's

rapture magnetized upon me
                    okay
                      "can take it"
                          unlock the night
                    ploughshares to gold!

Spinoza stretched out in penance before the synagogue
Was he lover of women?
hidden in fury of beat ploughshares to gold!

Include Krishna's many flaming mouths *hari hari*
*Seize me! Seize me!*

*Wie ist die Sprache unik?*

*Ist das Wesen der künstlerischen Betrachtungsweise, dass sie die*
*Welt mit glücklichem Auge betrachtet?*

(is the essence
of the artistic
 way of
            looking at things,
that it looks
at the world
         with

            a
         happy EYE ?)

Dear A,

Happy New Year — here's check for January.
Please let me know any new plans regarding apt. — "For
Sale" sign is no longer on the building, does that mean
anything? Guy in store downstairs seems to think that
means it was just sold —

It was fun to see you. I've made a lot of headway
in new book & working on a long "roman numeral"
poem about the history of the corset which I'm also
illustrating plus I have some new poems too so I guess
being here has been inspiring

            sad about Ricky Nelson, his
song "Poor Little Fool" was always one of my favorites —

            be in touch
            LOVE,
            Radio Emotions


            on the radio
         hearing my emotions
            on the radio
         usually the male
            protagonist
      hearing my emotions
         was the "I" I was seeing

                    falling in
            love again
                    with the girls
                        in the stories
                    on the radio

in the radio, emotions
were drawn like stars
& every lover was one
in conjunction to me
all in a constellation
of emotions
on the radio —
in the radio: emotions
& the music was heartbeat
& to break your heart
falling in love with the girls
inside the radio emotions: their names
repeat repeat
names of all the girls
she won't succumb the long night
listening to a radio with you
matinee idol dead
me born on the hem of war
arise out of father sperm
head full sprung
think too much
for sure a hag is she
she is a truce to stand on
tween gender
& her politic body
because she is painted child
she sings along with the radio emotions
because they made of her
painted pre-teen child
teen calls to her in the song
because they made of her poet

she is surely
in the air, & in the songs
emoting desire
I keep a little picture of
some crazy pop song idol
in the rafters
because he made of me
what they made of me
form of a radio emotion
then call again
girl-child
desire
or child
but child to child sing
"across a wounded galaxy" *mi donna*


         Out of this torque & spit comes logic of *donna mi prega*
She won't give up her fit of anger or song

toward the man, her shadow falling, toward a father Burroughs

         centuries of it ago a goat across her bondage
like the air waves of another century
What's the hag?
standing over sage Naropa's page as he studies
"Do you understand the words?"
I do do
"Do you understand the sense?"
I do
"You must be lying"
He blows it

long times ago
with the frail skin of a legend less trenchant
needed a disguise
in this treason of images, needed my pen

Without labels?
         what looking at?

whatchewlookinat
infusion of delight in moment
moment got mannered
got lobbed in projective "it"
before it got named a pen

what?

I was reversed
attenuated to old suffering

& what brought them round to another?
Europa's son's wife's folly that did
it, it not named for mishap
he it, he and it a cause
blame the woman
& she won't help you out of the labyrinth

Palingenesis over & over
it, it
& Berlin was kind of gate for her
how men dressed like women but still
had their big hands
(He lies under me, spread out like a sailor . . . )
& the child, her child now, the son-of-her who writes, sings:

*Per me si va nella città dolente*
*Per me si va nell' eterno dolore*
*Per me si va tra la Perduta Gente*

Aeneas is talking to his father's shade
in hell
through the ivory gate just as I speak with you

*I was the Bo Tree I was the Holy rood*
*Was I the mother or the father in the stories?*
and I saw Him in my house & He came over to me without
anything in between us, fire to iron, light to glass

*He made me like fire and like light. And I became that which I saw*
*before and beheld from afar.* Saint Simeon Stylites speaks here. . . .
it was a holy emotion he played on me

ancient cities like temples
portals to the 4 directions
worked in the context (confines of a symbol)
Rome, Mecca, Mt. Meru
Kaaba, the page no longer sleeps . . .


Dear Ms. Waldman,

   Recently i bought a book of poems by you entitled "Skin Meat Bones." It was
very good and i enjoyed it very much. It also made me more sure of what i am
doing now. Along with this letter, i have included a sample of my poetry. These
poems are excerpts from a book of poems (which has about two hundred and
forty-five poems) i have been working on since September of 1985. It is a recol-
lection of my painful childhood and my adolescence in progress (i will be 15 as
of December 14, 1986). It is my own way of dealing with my own strong homo-
sexuality in an age where to admit "gayness" is to say you are a "carrier" of a
disease that seems endlessly invincible.

   Since the fourth grade i have sensed that i was "different" from other chil-
dren. i can remember that even as a very small child "dressing up" in my
mother's clothes and begging to get to be "the mommy" when i played House
with other children.

   In my characteristically overdramatic style, i have fallen deep in love with
each of my best male friends (Brent . . . angelic eyes, . . . Kanon . . . . oriental
charm, . . . Mark . . . joviality, . . . Erik . . . everything) and consequently have
been forced to abandon the friendship before any more pain has generated.

   i keep mostly to myself at school trying my damnedest to just be a wallflower
(preferably a lily). Since entering junior high in seventh grade i've been open
game for any preppy asshole who decides that he needs to boost his own ego by
stepping all over someone elses. my locker was continually vandalized. my
clothes were under fire. i was ridiculed, pushed, punched, and finally pushed
too far.

   i haven't really figured it out yet, but the best i can figure is that creativity in
what you wear, effeminacy in your manner, and having "too many female
friends" are the yuppie crimes of the eighties.

Everyone always laughed at me, but i knew in my heart that someday they would open up a magazine or a newspaper, and they would see my face staring back at them.

When i thought of that i had had Rolling Stone or Artforum more in mind, but decided the obituaries would do me just fine and so in September of 1985 i attempted suicide in the third Xoor lavatory, three weeks after school had started.

The toilet was the perfect tomb, the floor the perfect deathbed. i wanted those kids to see my body, my dead body as they carried it away. i survived and also spent four hours in the emergency room throwing up each of the fifty pills i had digested (along with about four day's meals).

my mother was angry ("how could you"), my dad was sorry ("i should have known how depressed you were"), my teachers were unhelpful ("just get yourself strong and then get back to school"), my grandma was great ("just worry about making yourself happy again, and the school can wait").

i was admitted on a Thursday and i went home on Saturday. i returned to that same school on Monday.

my psychologist wanted to play cards every session so I dumped him in favor of two counselors (a man and a woman) whose first question was:

"Do you ever feel homosexual?"

my mind went racing, did i give off an odor, a color, a telltale sign? i denied it, they . . . I wasn't ready for it yet.

This is when I started writing poems by the truckload. i relived all the pain, the shame, the fear, and the love i had ever felt. they helped me to tell my parents i was gay. my mom cried, my dad said "i should have known," and my brother avoided me for three months. life went on.

i poured everything into my poems feverishly. my mother was discouraged, "you have so much talent don't waste it on poetry. they're dead. no one likes poetry. it's old news."

She also told me everyone and their aunt wrote poems. That didn't scan—nobody likes it, everybody writes it. Don't ask.

This is when i discovered a record called "Better An Old God Than A New Demon" (whoops! other way around) Well, anyways i enjoyed "Uh-Oh Plutonium!" It sent me on a spurt of nature, ecological-revival stuff.

This is the third time i have sent my poems out, the first two times were to big companies. that was in December (no word yet). i guess they're not into anti-conservative, pro-homosexual poetry by effeminate manic-depressive fifteen year olds (uncommercial i guess).

i hope you enjoy them. i enjoyed writing them. By the way the title of the book they're from is "introspection (fad fadaise)". Good luck.

all my love,

N.O.


i lock my door

        like hot running water

many faces he cries to himself

        barefoot, in a white nightdress

hospitalized for a trial on lithium

        after a moment of second thoughts,

        turns his head when I count . .    .

| | |
|---|---|
| Writing not | |
| yr own | |
| object | |
| and all | |
| the "shuns" to take | ~~"She" saw us~~ |
| off no one | |
| but you | ~~"She" was watching~~ |
| are twin | |
| to me | ~~"She" had the light on~~ |
| not stalk of | |
| eyes | ~~"She" crossed the wide road~~ |
| you are | |
| careful | ~~"She" still loves you~~ |
| air | |
| a body | ~~It's not simple~~ |
| | |
| a body | ~~Love is a killer~~ |
| meets | |
| a body | ~~Tongue, heart, thought is~~ |

through                          what it's about

music

surrounded                  ~~All possibilities to love or hate~~

by edges

did he                            ~~The tautology as it were vanishes~~

all the "he's"               ~~inside all propositions~~

not love you

back?                             ~~(The key word still hasn't yet~~

                                        ~~(been spoken)~~


Not back

but climb

or claim

his way

not back

but

get back                                          not

to claim

yr air                                     mere

Not shun                                              jumble-job

a body

use it!                                          of words

use it!



a wrought, no blame, a burl . . .

hermaphrodite of the meteor, Zeus

*berdache* rise here

without tragedy




                                        Fiend o' the north

                                        My own son dreamed?

                                        Bred a vampire?

                                        He's the quote o' my eye

                                        Landslide

                                        His mind goes into matter

                                        He walks the night

Door to door, blood on his chin
Teeth like daggers
All the mothers dead & gone

as would a *mamère* be in mannered form to
french the light and sip no matter
here to be a formed of
reside, reside

The Vulunelle is a very firendingly frenchy form deroved
from Italian folk song of late 15th early 17 Dentury
and fittest employed fger astoral dubejects.

I tell you this abt ne'er being acceptable nor anyhouse
I feel this is a knife of hatres because of hag me or whilst
you really do What us ir. Whate are Who rae?
You teal me.

In a mesdow pur forgot in its helpy nuisance to any
tought hreehin composed. This is avectebury tys is type
it's a gas a pride overanyoun's hostorying. tell em. Tell
me, two, three. What do you glean & in a wheel o tyme I
teel ye loose all ye colours, core all of em your youm go
outta, Tim. The reason is a place you said
YOU SAID FROM HET THE OVERFLOW
Ah cooks be Oire, and hair twouds youth. Demon in this
love n hate realm what I doing fer ya. I compormomis
I compomormis ale het aboute
I weeep I reallye tale youn everythang
Dear Highlander In a situation to protect your time & tis
boon to be this lady & a core or legged position Makes out dry
I want not, I want to let this go down go ear & lobe I meant
lobe because it was rin it was ringing of you of you
tied you in Makes men of ya
angry but I said o what this be all the ways I ever dreamed
& Blake entered thus dream.

O holy rood me child hide!

I lobe you I mean it put this kush grass
under yr pillow for Kalachakra mare
seelp in the beg me karma of ye bed
MEN MEN MEN MEN MEN MEN MEN MEN MEN MEN MEN MEN MEN MEN MEN

( I type these word intoxicate these worcs come as from a dream)

Lether wail in her own jajams
lettermen be
Let em roast in hell
I've no thing ado wi it men o men
I'm ambut a reflection of always I said out or isn't
any one of you, really its litmus A ways to go hey hoy
cut above any old og
It is a wadretting & fro me habla
I went back to prepuberio heh hoh
No night a mare was i gettin stabbed no more o push n pull
I was a foreign ring to your hook in me Was it was it was
heh hoh domy let me just a sitting here bee


It is his male mind that gets to me
His sailor mind
She hems the meteor, Zeus
Dresses him like her
Sews up his bag of bones
It is just okay okay
It is you, first of male
It is you I will salute again
& the man in me
But we were always the same
any aspect over the hill
or in hot pursuit
I love you to be merged
in any way
Any mind so you will know

some things
Some things in his mind
It is just okay okay
I am talking to you
so you know some things
I call your name Iovis
I call your name these times Iovis

Wildwood, August 25, 1902

My Dearest,

I suppose you are anxious to hear from me but I am above waters yet I felt much better this morning. I suppose Irvin told you how I was. I did not get a chance to send word by him as he got off before I had a chance to see him. I went right to bed last night. I bathed myself with turpentine and Cory heated the mustard plasters and put it on well. I did not sleep much all night but I sweat quite a good bit and I think that is what helped me. I only ache in one side now. I went to Dr. Coben this morning and he gave me some medicine and I am taking it regularly so you must not worry about me anymore than possible. I will be anxious to hear from you. I went to the office this morning and inquired about that letter. I did not get up this morning and deliver the milk, Cory did that. I got up about 7 o'clock this morning. I think I will mail this letter so you will get it by Tuesday noon. Perhaps it will make you feel a trifle better. Now please remember all I have said to you and follow out some of the things and do what you think would be for the best. I will try and see if we cannot make things as pleasant as possible next winter so I will close this hoping to hear from you tommorow. I remain

Yours as Ever

John

Tuesday morning washing. I was doctored good last night I feel fine this morning. Goodbye. John

\*   \*   \*

I love my orgy of fool denial

I love an impious force taking it calmly
I love a preface to his face outside the dance
The parking lot is an episode
I love: in speculation free, in form, traditional
I foreshadow my own end
& speaking as the son of Semele, I am immortal
& as the son of Zeus, I am divine
I speak in a man's voice wildly discordant
I don women's clothes
& deny the old religion
With my ironic undercutting, my new haircut
I speak in a foolish tongue
with a bitter flavor for love of them, the men
Exhausted with them, calm is my madness
I spit on the enemy as I am a woman
& as I am chorus I pretend throughout the cycle

Iovis is not bisexual but is as
*hemartia,* missing the mark
I turn my essence into a myth of origin
& prepare chicken propellers at the stove

A little-taller-than-Hitler is in power in this dream
& Bernadette and I guard the life of John Ashbery in a hut

We take care of them, the men, the poet-men,
providing them all night with little plastic ink refills
we wear like charms around our necks

Dear-Origin-Of-Male-Religion:

I am your libretto for a ritual to allay this robotical suffering
we cause each other bare, lay low, lie down in it
or bury it to grow any flower out of its wounded mouth

I love my end of a fool denial
& spread the collective work around
& will not repent this word or any other weapon

You insulted me when you weren't looking & drove a spike
in the heart of me. It dissolves into the seed syllable
of anything brave to be outside the tangle &
we two make beauty out of a dark structure
sanctioning the next time the show's in town
& come this way around a street
to my ceremonial dance become private twitches
Entheos Entheos I am full of the god
Entheos Entheos I am full of the god
shaking to tear this bull apart & return to peace
Don't mock me as I avenge the death of my sisters
in this or any other dream
In order to make the crops grow
You men must change into women

Ερμαφρόδιτος

# IV

## FIELD OF MARS

*Dreams grow more intense as they demand entry into the poem. Why dream of Hegel? Attempt, perhaps, to bring an all-embracing male mind into situation (thesis) to evoke its antithesis. Poem, yes, is synthesis. Is he ridiculous? Field or battleground of poetry & love is named "Mars," the poet's planetary ruler. The poet thinks/doubts herself in love & tries to write in forms without success. But the boy, her son, guides her through her confusion and gleefully names in ecstatic chant all the ways to mask plutonium. She must do battle with all those unleashed poisons. (Any woman must do this: retract petrochemical, nuclear nightmare. Is it that simple?) World War II needs scrutiny & some luminous particulars will surely be noted here. A palinode, that wicked song of retraction, sets her off & concludes the troublesome musings in an effort to "take back" her vulnerability.*

will you be summarily
working?

& there's morning: dumb circles of sleep & dream
white limo pulls up on San Francisco street
girl with plastic eyes exits & scares me
exit & sleep on the page I tell myself
all the fathers pass . . .
enter "Friedrich Hegel" who is going to
perform for us out in the beautiful
green field, the "Academy." We have been
excitedly awaiting his Show. I see Liz on the grass
doubled up in her passion for Hegel, and the
Lesbian next to her is offended to hear her speak of it
to me & then won't sit down next to me in the
grandstands. Julia rushes up to say "Hegel
is going to perform my favorite piece of his!"
Something about the Dog and the Man. Hegel has tense
red hair & thick spectacles. He wants all the
women present to fall in love with him

& do we

"The sun is up and we're ready to go."

swatched in their space suits, Allen & Gardner
glide out to meet the satellite

Allen's pas de deux is a slow surreal dance of
weightlessness: he easily inserts the
stinger into the nozzle and, when attached,
he fires his jets to stop the satellite's rotation.

"Give me a little more right yaw."
"Come on in, Anna."


I count you in arms
One a boy, two absorbing book
Three: a wise eye
I count you after you're gone
Four: laugh, five: quit, six: wind
I number the ways to clutter a heart

Desire stretches poet's heart
Hours are numbered in yr arms
Separated by glaciers of fierce wind
Sunday stay in with 11th century book
Monday you're gone, unreachable
Can't concentrate Tuesday to keep wise

Wednesday it's hard to get wise
Caution difficult Thursday in a heart
Friday get all duties done
So hours will be open as arms
Shut in Saturday I'll write the book
*How To Make Love in Wind*
Can't say this, can't be wind
Be quiet Anne, don't be unwise
Study one another in a Florentine book
Older heart bows to a younger one

Put me back in travel, read "arms"
Quick, that thought's gone

We'll never get to Spain, never gone
From here, American town founded on wind
Yet caught in usual flow of arms
Degraded world hallucination, wise
To love if other numbers claim our hearts?
Keep this a sacred book

between us, who write our own
daily, words for you even as you're gone
words to carry – what ?
upon wind
unwise
older in yr arms

arms, books,
numbered texts don't say it
me too (dont, don't say it) wind rips words
apart, naked – breaks the heart


          . . . evanescing little sixes sestina
or try this sonnet for size:
I write after Donne in a kind of expiration mode:

Break off sad kiss
that holds fast, sucks dry
You go that way, I'll this
Our phantoms now dance separately
Remember that holy day?
We don't owe each other anything cheaply
Go, go & go, even if it kills you
& say the word to me – say it – "go"
& my word will stay true to me
This is justice for a tough murder

Except it's too late to kill me too,
being triple-dead. One, I'm leaving
two, telling you – go –
& three: the poem dies on me – go – go!

      (the trouble was the aggression of those men the Itza;
        *tumen uchci u chibilob tumen uinicob ah Itzaob lae*

we didn't do it; we pay for it today   *ma toon ti mentei toon botic hele lae)*


but

inside you
inside you

what me?
what me
are you
inside of

I say
you are all
there is in-
side me
now inside
out

but later
I'm thinking
something
putting on clothes
& you talking
about the
mixing of us

want me
all for
your self
& not even
there

you have a
restless mind
like mine

> *from branding to slaughter*
> *no black sand sanctuary*

Dear Ms. W

I am 30 years old. I have been a loser and a thief for most of my life. I am sure
I deserve to spend some time in prison, but not for a crime I did not commit.
(I am an ex-thief, not a murderer with millions of dollars hidden some-
where) . . . .

(he has something of the planets
   borrowing
        wordless stamina in him
  a snarler
      who would not wonder
      at him
        guilty or not)

— I'm scared. Mommy!

— Everyone's dead, remember?

— Remember, we woke up in the hospital

— What the hell

— I might be hurt I have a broken leg

— Come back inside the hospital

— It's too late I'm going to die

— Let's say you shot my brother too

— Why, was he the enemy?

— We have to be the good guys *and* the bad guys

— So I killed myself

— But I shot your leg. But you'll be walking
in a couple of years

— This is World War III

— Yeah. Everyone's dead

— So what's the point?

— No, I won't be walking but I'll be seeing

That he would be the boy in bed in her arms very soon, that he would go to battle, that she already imagined it: the fathers would send the sons to battle, that the rain would follow, that it would be gentle, that a man you know died on his son's birthday, that Argentina Corazon writes she will send you a "fiery messenger," that Apollo took bites of the sun, that the Spartans are responsible, that the economical and the divine are painted equally here, that Stesichorus recants his early attack on Helen as the baneful cause of the Trojan War, that she will finally have a dream about the soft cow's belly, that in the dream the cow is chased away by a jealous wife, that he had a husband's rough beard, that she who was a cow locked away her virginity in the "V" of a tree, that we were never there together on Red Oaks Lake, that the water didn't move, that the oars were never driven, that we never spoke, that we did not embrace, that the sky did not darken, that no one called us to come back, that you were never in my life

> Dear One: I went out seeking these things
> to remind me of you

I wanted to take on the father & son simultaneously
(The elder wears the ankle-length peplos, the normal dress
of a charioteer) and take the prophecy back:

that the son would go to battle, that the fathers would send the sons to battle, that they do it again & again, that sons go willingly to battle but go with fear to battle, that the father is filled with fear, that they would kill with fear in battle again & again, that the American continent is doomed in battle, that the fathers of the continent that are not the real fathers but usurpers are doomed in fear in battle Heh ya ya! Heh Heh heh ya ya

& the son sings

for the "guardianship of plutonium"

"Then there's dry ice snow
frozen enchiladas & all frozen things
like orange juice, frozen pipes
then fans all around
electric gates
glass containers
aluminum
Let's cover up plutonium with
plastic bags when as soon as they get
    to bright sunlight are biodegradable
leaves
more moss
light bulbs — just are so bright
there are still a few ways to get through
(2 old baseball stadiums - nah)
piles of dirt — then fence around that
losses dirt with farms behind it shoots out
glass flashes
Then there's like — oh yeah — everything
    glued on with sap - dries as hard as rock when in the air
pieces of wood to make a fire
Let's cover plutonium with magnets —
you try to get one layer away
    with a gun, magnet pulls it back
Let's cover plutonium with what cliff dwellings are made of
Get some Indians to come back & make some
    adobe with ash
Try a hologram
lie detectors with guards all around
robotic guards with guns
a message comes out says "Get outta here!"
then there's paper

chicken wire
a rock level
(whenever I look around
that's what I say)
Let's cover plutonium with
everything in the world
& put it in pipes
every type of things — a sample of everything
beehives with this little hole cut into them
    an alarm goes off, they go to the person they see
a layer of honey
every sticky thing
every liquid
horns on cars
then there's cardboard
every cigarette in the world!
it doesn't take a type but every cigarette
    in the world
Let's cover plutonium with a graveyard
Let's cover it with
one of every single stone in the world
pennies, quarters, everything —
Then gold around it, then diamonds, rubies, emeralds
Then there's plaster, then linoleum,
    congoleum
Then hard candy — every single kind that
    gives immediate cavities
A thing with waterguns
tomatoes, celery, carrots, potatoes, green
    peppers, parsley
burning hot heaters, a person touches 'em
    it burns 'em
Let's cover plutonium with
wood chips that beavers have made
many teepees
TVs, radios, leather
actually a teepee folded up

all the toothpaste tubes filled with toothpaste
every single brand, every single kind!
barbed wire
American flags
old wheels – metal
bars of jail with canine bloodhounds
   that are trained to everything you say
telephone wire with sticky stuff
Let's cover plutonium with playdough – dried
dead peoples' bones & then there's plain
   dead people with nothing on them
something on them or nothing on them
every single bug in the world that crawls
   on the earth
bees with five stingers – they all sting
   at the same time
more chicken wire
steel cubes
2 layers of regular glass
shatterproof glass
big magnets – electromagnetic – on top & bottom
big rock would be the first covering – the
   whole thing tightly wound with wires
poured concrete, more paint, more tar
let's cover plutonium with plastic bags & bottles
disposable bags
styrofoam coffee cups
half & half containers
fireworks
There's a big display when you try to get in"

*(he sings he sings*
*gazing out window*
*on the ride from Telluride)*


"people will kill for a dollar bill they fight war killing people they never
saw before people in Nicaragua hear they are being sent out of Managua
to kill or die or be fried like Hitler did to women & children"
                    the son says

Hence the euphemisms calling a battle "a party," hence
a plethora of badges, medals, & hence the memo Air Marshal
Arthur Harris wrote to Portal, chief of the British air staff
at the time of the Normandy invasion, complaining "grave injustice"
was being given to his bomber crews if all the attention & publicity
centered upon the army & navy

Modern war: blunder after blunder explained away
Modern war: no need to invade Europe, the bomber offensive
                would finish Germany
Modern war: American heavy bombers killed more American than
                German soldiers in Normandy
Hiroshima: brutal act of revenge
(bomber crews wore lucky charms)

A sergeant major screamed at a soldier still wearing his cap
as he marched into Church "Take yer fucking 'at off in the
                                        'ouse of Gawd, cunt."

The invasion off Slapton Sands was a disaster. Nine German E boats made a
sortie from Cherbourg and sank American landing craft
                        drowning 750 soldiers and sailors . . .

is to seem what you would be, and
in seeming be tough, be fierce, be soldier
the formula for dealing with fear is
ultimately rhetorical and theatrical:
regardless of your actual feelings,
you must simulate a carriage which
will affect your audience as fearless,
in the hope you will be imitated

(US Officer's Guide)

Modern war: Churchill's radio oratory

Modern war: MacArthur listening with "thirsty ear for the witching melody
of faint bugles blowing reveille"

( the raids went on but by October 1 the Luftwaffe had
    abandoned day bombing and bombed only at night . . .)

hence the bodies blow to bits, hence gibbering citizens

queuing at hospital, hence "I have withdrawn the troops"

(General Eisenhower), hence to die for one's country,

hence the fathers went to war, they go to war willingly go

to war hesitating, the father live for war, they return to

the hearth, keep the fires burning, they go for you little

baby, they go for freedom


To the President of the Republic of Guatemala

Your Excellency:

I urge you to order independent investigations of human rights violations in
Guatemala, regardless of the administration under which they occurred, and
to bring those found responsible for political killings, "disappearances," and
torture to justice.

   I also ask that the government make public the findings of its investigations
and, in compliance with Resolution 15 of the United Nations Subcommittee on
Prevention of Discrimination and protection of Minorities, that it inform rela-
tives of the "disappeared" of their family members' fates.

   I thank you. I plead with you.

                        Anne, Grasping-the-Broom-Tighter


It is thought
gamma rays
from
Cygnus x-3
are produced there
by protons
of even
higher energy

*— the broom tighter*

They would for example
carry 10 million
times the energy
achieved by
the most powerful
atom smasher

*— Anne grasping tighter tighter*

> Other candidates
> for high energy cosmic
> ray production
> . include Geminga —
> > a perplexing object

as well as the pulsar systems
known as Hercules x-1 and Vela x-1.

All far out in the Milky Way

> (Pull back in shreds this lady's mind
> she'll discover how to find a
> sweeter sorrow in the wind

> > Defenses down won't resign
> > or let nature be unkind
> > Pull back in shreds this lady's mind

It's blown to bits — space-design
What intrudes to make her pine?
sweet sorrow in the wind
Daughters of Time:
when we can't move to shake a male rhyme o mercy

> > let it down on me)

by plumes by plumes of magma rising, by plumes to
take home from Pluto, by plumes by plumes Pluto rising:
the edge of submerge, the plume not spot in the crust
the plume erupt in hot spot, magma magma rising,
Mars rising, assume that plate moved
assume it technical feat to rise to rise by plumes to take home
the continents rising, by plumes by plumes magma rising

end to submerge, death to follow


(When in 1912, the Austrian physicist Victor N. Ness
sought to trace the radiation's origin by ascending
in a balloon, he found that instead of becoming
weaker, the radiation became more intense as he rose. )

> I was nearing the things I was waiting
> for from his return: a triangle the shape
> I respond to most, a replica of a mother's
> ear, and a goddess holding up the world
> I had made so solid it can't be broken
> Portable ancestor worship is what I thought
> of here when he brought these things to me
> And of the father, what things?
> And of the father, what things?
> Bayonets from the great war
> Handblown glass
> Old photograph
> The ascension of our Lord
> ( he rose! he rose!)

It is Glafko's day in court. He sits in Robert Lagomarsino's office, protesting with others the House vote that day that authorized aid to the Contras. He was arrested & jailed on trespassing charges & decided to defend himself. Middle seventies – wiry, stooped, sandals on his feet, sparse greying hair. Came to America from Greece in his twenties & in the 1930s was a dedicated leftist. After the purges & the Moscow-Berlin pact he withdrew from politics. Later he became active again, this time as a radical pacifist-anarchist, in the mold of Leo Tolstoy or A.J. Muste. He's been arrested many times for civil disobedience, mainly while participating in antinuclear demonstrations.

Dear Glafko-What-A-Mystery. First husband to mother, father of brother, the "saint" who lived apart from the world. Grecian & a kind of lambent stress to take cradle of civilization back, an older time, whose father was the Poet bringing nourishment to the stars, the planets, make them sing with the accompaniment of lyre & small drum
You who stayed in me my mother's "first," shadow-marriage under spell of Olympus

1.  What myth & which male character-hero do you identify with the most?

2.  Which goddess do you most admire, fear, revere? Why?

3.  What was your rite of passage to manhood? At what age? What were the circumstances?

4.  When do you put your best foot forward?


Archilochus (7th century B.C.): "I am both therapon

                                    of Lord Enyalios,

                                    & acquainted (with)

                                    the lovely gift

                                    of the muse"


Therapon = a ritual substitute. Enyalios = the Cretan god or lord of war, thus Mars/Ares. "acquainted," a modest or understated translation of a verb whose root is "epist," like *episteme,* Plato's word for belief (i.e. as a type of knowledge) – epistemology. The verb has a wide associative semantical range in translation e.g. to know or be able, capable; understand; be assured of; skillful, expert— So, as in Homer I guess, to know for certain. Archilochos made a remarkable and thus well remembered scandal or blasphemy once, when fighting for Sparta, he tossed away his shield when things got too absurdly out of hand, and wrote it, saying he'd just buy another one. In Sparta they used to say the famous farewell before battle (mother to son etc.) "Come back with it or on it." It was just the other day I saw something which made me think, clearly for once, that the field of Mars is that of love. I mean none of the poet/warrior biz is actually comprehensible except that the metaphoricalness of reality is perceived. And is it?

What they call war isn't war - it's butchery without the cannibalism it purposes - which Homer points at more than once. As mistaken or imperceived the poet is, equally a real warrior is not able to be seen by a literal eye. Any artist, really, and that seems very important to me. The artists in this secular world are the warriors. And the field of Mars is identical to the field of Love, & the artists are the only ones whose entire being depends upon conduct on that field.

In the secular the bravery of art and the bravery of love are identical. Hence, I guess, the likeness (in Shakespeare) of the poet, the lover and the madman — the latter because of real perception, though without art; the lover there because of delight & surrender, immersed, with no need for art; and the poet able to contain, and needing to articulate, both. While Olson called Sh. "the greatest poet of Mars in the English language" and I understood O. to be thus including himself — now I see that *any* poet is one of Mars, especially and only as it's all seen metaphorically. The poet is in other words the subject — the object may or may not be literally war.

Sorry, I'm off the road. It has, this stuff, to do with risk and with metaphor. By the extraordinary metaphor of etymology, for instance, you could also register it Poet as Carpenter i.e. the chariot-carpenter of the Vedas the "car" being all that and of course "heart" too (Kardia/coeur) or as "weaver"/ "joiner" and so on. But in a secular society I think the warrior question is — for me anyway — the thing. You know, a lot of maleness confusions.

Things are tough at the school ($) — I can't go much longer under the relentless pressure of it. Little or no fun. Mostly worse. Very few souls want to hear the good news, eh? I feel a fool for not knowing a way to make a living — but then, existence is such a trap. Fuck it. I wish I had a job carrying some jazz guy's bags, and there are a lot around whose bags I would. They're keeping me from despair.

> but my wounds which are the participants
> in what is not subject matter, but a poet's
> play, stage blood, they are the scourge of me

dear Iovis of the Fiery Night:
                         into shallower & safer waters
                              let me ride free

                         going
              abroad
                         in the mind
 but break heart,
              prithee break
one is always
a limitation
                    only a fraction
              from the fire
                    but whose
              illusory pictures
the mad king said much to you
"both, both"
              tasted sadness there
       in the battle for his
              mind
                    on
                    the
                    field of
       Love

My Mars, who rules me
he in me
I'm a he
tonight
all girls
run from me
to the groves

Mars: when time is old    Tell me about Time is old

when time was old
I forgot myself
   became a "he"          for battle

forgot myself
            out of fear

(the universe would have been destroyed by flames
            had not Zeus struck the rash youth
                    with a thunderbolt
            & sent him tumbling into the
                    waters of the Eridanus

a crime to change sex, too near the sun . . .)


                        my field
Where is it?
                insignificant against the gods?

                        male nakedness too sacred to see?

body to teach me a field

centered like a pendulum

plumb line I say I wanted

                (vanity)

                        in field of silent scribbling

outrage of how many caves you lived in
in sickness in health
move your fingers

                real ink, serenity

                        gutted a house & nothing left

        but O vanity down

you who are Buddha
art woman
                        body to teach me a field
                        body to teach

(as more of his letters attest he was frantic . . .)
*Was ist Aufklärung?*

not a resurrection but Happy Easter

& blunt the body to the sword

body to teach

how cum down

dab in the sweet milk

body wider so much wider than the sea


my field of word & origin
   I do battle to a hot night
         "Let us fight them on the plains"
Elohim brings flood & rainbow
       fight in his cause, the Skygod
        god of thunder
        in his name
       his name: Elohim, sing it in the plains
the Syrian gods are gods of the hills
       let us fight them in the plains

(sing it in the plains)

What of the god of fire?
destroys Sodom & Gomorrah
   fire purifies

fat & blood in the temple fire
consume the wicked in the fire
   Fire god who is repudiated by Prophets
       Sky god becomes a metaphor in Prophets
"To obey is better than sacrifice"

Yahweh Yahweh O phallic conquering god
let circumcision be the covenant

the oiled pillar is god's house
O sing it in the plains, god's house is his big prick!

come in Moses, do not deny the call

Rites of passage: There were several. First L.S.D., First Sex, First Mental Institution . . . First L.S.D in Northern California with some boarding school chums. Took two hits of purple microdot and wandered all over the sand dunes down close to the seventeen mile drive in Pebble Beach. Glorious superimposed matrix patterns over incoming fogbank. I felt as though I was watching the weather of earth being made. Climbed out in trees and flung ourselves laughing down long smooth dunes. First sex also in Northern California, a young sophisticated beauty seduced and then instructed me for a considerable period of time. She was an athelete and an animal. First night in her Dad's unused sauna room, she cries out again and again "I love sex!" almost burning me with her exuberant friction. First Mental Institution: Actually not just the first, but the cumulation of all of them (four). This was the turning point in my life. A choice was made here to remain not only with this world, but this life. Age 15 – 17. You wanted to know; I tell you these things. Love, B.

& you could never do the assignments
never conquer the sestina or 5-part suite
on mythology & the death of sport
you could never listen
you could never be my slave
you could never not complain
& when it came to injustice upon yrself
you could rail
you could call the law down
you'd invoke daddy law in a snap
you never saw yr own ghost
never saw yr own hot projection
you hadda call the law
you hadda invoke what you couldn't handle

(let it down on me

& I went back>> Went back there>>Had left>>
Went back>> Couldn't>> Do it>> What?>> Go back>>
Had never left>> One last time>> Like a palinode>>
Took back>> Lied>> Didn't>> Walked most of the way>>
Part of a truth>> Climbed the last part of a truth>> Up on a
slope>> Come down now>> I said come down, come down now>>
Where>> Here>> His friend says he's gone>> A lie>> A lie
gone now>> I went back>> Had left I thought>> Had left a
thought to go back>> It catches up>> Go back>> Settled by
phone>> I thought>> He didn't think>> Was thinking a thought
not to get back>> I did>> What?>> I did go back>> Not lost>>
Can't be a lie>> I climbed the slope>> Walked into a lie>>
One more time>> He is establishing in me more than I care
a mention>> Leave it>> How?>> Leave it be>> Can't>> Go back>>
He's never left I think>> What if he never left>> I climbed a lie>> Lie down>>
I can't>> I remember the futon on the floor>> Don't tell myself about it>>
Stop>> I remember hangers with odd clothes on them>> Don't do
it>> Go back, I can't but be remembering this>> Stop>> Something
is new>> Deny it happened>> Like a palinode>> It never happened>>
Say it: it never happened>> Say this: it never happens>>
Part of a truth>> Can't>> Why?>> Why does it go>> Because you
ask for it>> The death of language>> Never>> The death of
writing>> Never>> One last time>> Never>> Had left>> Gone
back>> A lie>> Had left me I thought>> Had left I can't
remember I thought>> Than I care a mention>> Slopes here>>
Near by>> Walk>> Can't>> Lie down>> Never>> Lie with him>>
Never again>> Can't think it. It never happened>> I will
say: it never happens>> Settled by phone I thought>> The end I
thought>> Was not to ever have happened>> Again>> Had
left>> One last time>> Was one last time>> Never>>

- everi thing endis
every thing ends

borne like a myrrour
held up ti humanyte

on field of love

# V

## TO BE A RHYMING WI' THEE

*She wants the voice of a soldier to seize her throat. Thus the poet honors her father-in-law and by implication her own father once more, both men who served their country, their worlds & words so far from her own: mental & military. What a peculiar stance they have endured in this odd time. What romance still lurks there? "Men could be men." The moon walk talk floats in: a kind of reminder of a tenderer time. She needs to acknowledge the lineage she gives birth within. By extension, the son reaps the father's reward, but needs a new battleground just as her own son will. She prays it won't be war which perpetually provides the most juice. They — the ones in power of course — love it. Poetry is a kind of salvation if perceived thus. Why not? Her son might like it. She sympathizes with the austerity of these men & moves toward a true argument with a tangible entity. She goes off to meet him under pain of scorn, at the least titillation. . . . On a train abroad she listens to & queries a survivor, relic, the same age as her "fathers" who has witnessed the dissolution of the two Germanies.*


Her stumble on All Of These Things

    making love    the blind child on TV

       accretion of swords for living

   a shaping & clinging    I see the close reading

      of Charles Olson

I . . . who knows?

           enter the story of how do we enter

what would a father be a father come a father meet

               her nightlife

mine, it's mine
         to enter how do we

  predicated beyond the grave

        or ash

       weeping at the funeral of

Scalapino's grandfather or that of my father-in-law

a mirage of night merely

for do we do we

& may I , attentive & present

be her widow

the daughter-widow?        in-law-widow?

Charlie dies & it is a father-in-law

time frame,

beautiful weeping

4 o'clock of an afternoon in Florida

with "the prettiest name"

His present look

& stubborn appreciation as if to say

I see you & see you too

I see you in the form of a

heavy woodland sprite

or in uniform,

Air Force Dear Father-In-Law

it is a calling it is calling

RESTRICTED
Headquarters, Army Air Forces
Washington

AF6AS-2 210.453

Subject: TDY Orders 9 April 1946

1.   Each of the following named officers will proceed from Washington, D.C. on
or about April 1946 to Hq., CDC, Quarry Heights, Canal Zone or TDY for approx-

imately seven (7) days in connection with Personnel Matters ARP Military Project, Bogotá, Colombia, South America, and upon completion thereof will return to Washington, D. C.:

Colonel Charles C. Bye

2. Col. Bye will report to the theatre commander (or his designated representative) as practicable during his visit, and in all cases on the completion thereof, the nature and findings resulting from his visit and substance of any report he intends to make to the War Dept or to the office from which he is sent. In all reports made as a result of this temporary duty, a positive statement that the foregoing instruction has been carried out will be included.

all in writing
a positive statement
what tell of me
of men in me?
what tell to them of men
or me
bedding down to an old earsong
lambent
ho ho
lost or consummate the idea

    break or breath
to be a one
(man
you be
a
one)
& may you
may you

or one
loaded
over the coals

      or border
beyond which another male poet goes
    adorned

perhaps because of
working
together

we share a day

(o the company I keep)
"Au nom de la République vous êtes décorés de la croix de L'Ordre des
              Feuilles Mortes"


My friends, there can be no doubt that we now posses the means and the power
to take Constantinople before the end of the summer if we act with decision
and with a due sense of proportion . . . It will multiply the resources and open
the Channel for the reequipment of the Russian armies. It will dominate the
Balkan situation and cover Italy. It will resound through Asia. Here is the prize,
and the only prize, which lies within reach this year . . .

Winston spoke words. We are words, words, words, horses, manes, deeds.
   We are deeds.
And of our labor in words: light the lights in the sweet air.
And intoned, while shaving, *"Introibo ad altare Dei"*

                              field of congenials
to an idea, the Eagle has landed

              "For military contractors, it will be rag
               tag, rough & tumble and dog eat dog day,"
                              said an astronaut
                      & former Textron, Inc. executive
                      who will become vice chairman of
                      General Dynamics next month and replace
                      Mr. Pace in 1991.
                      "It's going to be
                      a bloodletting and the guy with the
                      most blood will win."

Roger, Tranquility, we copy you on the ground. You got a bunch of guys about
to turn blue. We're breathing again. Thanks a lot.

Houston, that may have seemed like a very strong final phase. The auto-targeting was taking us right into a crater, with a large number of big boulders and rocks . . . and it required . . . flying manually over the rock field to find a reasonable good area.

Roger, we copy. It was beautiful from here. Tranquility, Over.
We'll get to the details of what's around here, but it looks like a collection of just about every variety of shape – angularity, granularity, about every variety of rock . . . The colors – well – there doesn't appear to be too much of a general color at all; however, it looks as though some of the rocks and boulders (are) going to have some interesting colors to them. Over.

(Outside the) window is a relatively level plain cratered with a fairly large number of craters of the five- to fifty-foot variety and some ridges, small, twenty, thirty feet high, I would guess, and literally thousands of little one- and two-foot craters around the area. We see some angular blocks out several hundred feet in front of us that are probably two feet in size and have angular edges. There is a hill in view, just . . . ahead of us, difficult to estimate but might be a half a mile or a mile.

The surface is fine and powdery. I can – I can pick it up loosely with my toe. It does adhere in fine layers like powdered charcoal to the sole and sides of my boots. I only go in a small fraction of an inch, maybe an eighth of an inch, but I can see the footprints of my boots and the treads in the fine sandy particles.

Neil, this is Houston We're copying.


he to me
I take your son
I take him
& his sex
he grows beyond
you in his sex
his sex in me
it wounds you
you die in the
fury of his

sex
he enacts his
own conception
son of the father
creating the form
then it's named
this or
that: husband
& the impulse
is passion
a rare
form
the passion
that makes you
name it
you need
to
& name all
forms of
birth
& dying
this is the
skandha song
a fantasy of
which you act
the lover
a close reading

Husband dreams gypsy woman here to do a Tarot reading, and spreads a very
large deck around herself on the floor. She is dressed in a red & gold kimono.
When half the cards are laid out she stands up & begins convulsing. Soon she is
flopping on her belly on the floor like a fish. She gets back up & moves quickly
like a geisha woman in small steps out of the room to find a subject for the
reading. She is standing by the cards with one or two men, one of whom seems
to be the subject. I (Reed) move in & she directs her attention to me. She is now
a woman in her fifties with a very pretty round face. A huge almost life-sized
card appears before her. Over their heads is suspended a sword horizontally.
The image is very colorful & very strong. The frame of the dream moves slowly

down & I don't quite take in the name or caption along the bottom of the card.
Suddenly a long crumpled sack tumbles down in a completely different room
& a man spills out onto a hospital bed. He has a horrible white hole ringed with
black in the side of his head & he is doing something with some thin tubing in
his lap. This is extremely painful to watch; he is attending to a womb in his
abdomen.

Map a poke
koto be hosprous not loygal ee helbron
ee Hebron
map the wound, a poke, a probe, thrust
gypsied down & sung
map a parsifal
cininima cybernetica
a bubbla sermon a
"tot" or german dead
attending the wound
be that be tot
occasion a ruse
kack kaw giblet
sword a boon, a bond
boxomil to be a rhyming withee
O clothe, cynicilia, happenstonce
wander, be true
I see the mocha may day 1918
Calm ye, Cypriot, act
go back ti childhide
sybillante for poems
(I enjoy this)
squawk ti boot
& sythesizeria thy nichte
        kay?

        (he bides me bides my time)
check on Allegory

        Faust's dream etc.

*acros stichos*

*& be the endless father of him*
He grows through you into me
sweet lineage, sweet tree

What happened? what collapsed? what didn't? what drew applause? What did the world want to hear? that communism is dead on its feet? What is the etymology of the root of the sorrow of communism? who engineers the sorrow of this word? What crept into her marrow a long way back, what polluted her soil? Who wasn't thinking straight? Who got paid? Who didn't? What god stuck around? What fathers? What deities were confined to little votive shelves, who were shelved for barter & exchange? How kept under wraps? What's bargained for here? How can they be relegated to a lesser rank without revenge? What the sense of salvation? of sadism? Who responded to the call? Who wants to be saved?

"I would have preferred to have been from here — the marsh, decimated landscape, the old control towers . . ." he said, gesturing abstractedly to the metaphorical east.

"And this was my desire, an abandoned point of view, a terrible weakness on my part to be a victim of chance, of war perhaps. But it comes down now, surely it comes down, relative to the idea of what can ever come down. Walls? Is it the boundary between what clothes you wear? A close call? The others (they lived behind the wall) were merely my projection. Could you say money, the absence of it, is a close call? Or is it only a lapse? A human lapse? I would have lived like a monk, a nun, and been a kind of closed property."(He winks now)

I couldn't say much. I came from America and felt too rich although this had nothing to do with money, nothing to do with my leather pants. But what I liked, I told him, was sweat on the brow of the worker, this could be an artist even. It was that simple. A sweep toward physical reform. A frontal gauge of the possibility of a spot of low retaliation. And in this moisture combined both the propaganda and the resistance. Or something like that, a cry for more, perhaps, the cry for an end to barbarism. Does someone decide your approval?

"I always voted," he said, by way of assent. "There was never any doubt about that, our kind of freedom. Motives are and are not useless. I had a kind of gloom for what they were denied, the people on the other side."

"And that gave you hope?"

"Hope is a drug. Hope gets you through the night. Hope leaps on the beloved."
"Still, would you feel secure without it?"

"Hope sings out to be obstructed. It is basically fickle."

"So what is power, by definition? Why unify people toward any goal?"

"Because they never separated. Like the sides of the brain. And one could reside on the crease of the other. One could be brilliant, artistic, trembling, the other cold and calculating. They could both be lost in a private sense of reform and be at each other like wildcats, fighting. They might play out the ritual of contrast. One could be sweating. While the other designs a tactical missile to sell to and to destroy Iraq at the same time (just one example). May the gods of light conquer the extremes of a dark view!" Was the old man turning religious on me?

I noticed out the train window how the landscape was changing. It was après something or other. Après human habitation? Simply ugly? After the so-called end-of-nature? Was it a matter of dead trees? Were those little grave markers I was seeing amongst the trees? Were the men by the side of the road exhuming a body that had perished in flight over a symbolic wall? Were my eyes playing tricks on me again?

He was an agile talker. He confessed to having had as a child a fascination for the Nazi uniform. How bright it seemed. How it lifted him higher. He liked the cuffs especially. His mother, he said, shielded his eyes when the dazzling uniforms came again. He escaped to Lausanne and pursued a life in music.

"Music is the great mediator and arbiter! — is that the word? My two Germanies don't know this yet. But they might. When the ears of one fold in a harmony toward the ears of the other, then music will rain down like manna. Everyone, if they are still around, will finally be able to listen."

# VI

## LEIR

*The poet worked backstage quite young — a "gopher" — at the Shakespeare festival in Strat-*
*ford, Connecticut, observing night upon night Morris Carnovsky's rendering of the mad Lear.*
*She always planned to write of it, the play really, which grabbed her ear. She thinks perhaps the*
*production was too austere. How to ground Lear's soft foolish agony, his imagination? She*
*always thought to act the part, but how? She has her own version. She was perpetually thinking*
*of family intensities. The vulnerability of father to daughters and how it goes the other way too.*
*Freud, her favorite of the doctors enters here to make a few comments. When the poet's mother*
*came to see the show she arrived backstage in tears. "I know what it feels like, I know what it*
*feels like to be an unloved parent." Daughter was shocked. Her mother became King Lear.*
*Father was remote, one of the kings in a distant land. The poet instantly turned into a model*
*daughter. A repentant Cordelia who won't die. This is many years ago. Now she is the exiled*
*king herself, whose love to count on? How to make them prove it? Her wealth is reduced. Her*
*child might spurn her. She goes back to this play again, again as it set her ear to a beautiful male*
*cadence beyond gender & broke her heart.*

> *touch me with noble anger,*
> *And let not women's weapon, water-drops,*
> *Stain my man's cheeks!*

inside his nightmare
he is venerated
Zeus himself known as "chthonios,"
of the dark depths
inside active cruelty,
base deceit
a darker intrigue:
filial ingratitude
& a man's eyes ripped from his head

    sing a construct
    what hunt
or storm

what unkinde
mnemonic device
got recorded in brain
or memory clutch
at work here:
tragikal historie

      shunned from a door I know this
alive in hovel, grotto, dear father, I . . .

& would be Robert Armin's fool
to stand him by
   in a kind of motley, go well the time
the tune, checked
colorful rag on a tight lithe body, I . . .
      & would do a little hop or skip about the court
      nimble o' body & wit
you have that in you I would fain call master
what's that?
authority
why a leer to speak brave of him, pity is
untented woundings of any parent's curse
or dare it be said husband's
for left darkling, here
& I have years on my back 45

      And conjured thus a radiant sun
      comes not between the dragon & his wrath
or woman tween her call & duty

what care of me born to father
& to be married to
keep a station in life
& bear a child who will or will
not bear his mother's love

Call me Cordelia

I am not a rock
I speak not in riddles, but true

I live & think now to the epitome of wildness
wherever it takes the child for she is dead

What's that I'd fain call master?
beyond a call of grave, blast or fog upon thee
I'd call him Daddy, and speak him Modo or Mahu
who drinks the green mantle of the standing pool
for these men are mad to be fathers

tell them out?
Cry out his blinde spot
what is his canon of measure

Ecbatan in Medea
was surrounded by seven concentric walls
each of a different colour signifying
the seven planets
with the treasury (a king's heart?) located in the citadel
        it beats like a mind
emanates its rays,
colorful yet protected by
        mirrors,
noble heart, prithee break

Ulug Beg the Mogul also modelled Samarkand
so it might reflect the celestial order of the heavens
but what wrought here
so wizened
out of proportion
to him
he asks them to parcel out a heart

and what, he, heart broke
confined to hovel, cave of refuge
all the circles closing in
the kings of France & Burgundy are young

are husbands if you want them
what spot dwell
to vent a wrath called for
in language rare's the texture of
an appetite November 26, 1607
to suit a king

what makes a king holy relic
& back the senses
to the world outside
what but a grief to age &
think "it" can be bought
outside: harsh
(keep it to the family bosom)
abound of horrible deeds
Words don't mean much
Cheap, like the way
it's sold to you
You spit you vomit like mad Tom
spews his sullen & assumed humor,
an Abraham Man
you rant "the whoreson zed"
you blanket your loins
grime a face with filth
tie your hair in dreadish locks
Poor turleygod
Peace, Smulkin, peace, thou fiend
Conjure Frateretto, Hopdance, Purre &
all demons to greet the night in you
but, again, down fiends, peace
Not up again to make me mad
An agony rises up in me
be it woman-borne yea no, but
sweet the torrent if it carries you
down, down
How you are forced abroad
far from an easy home down down

none but elements attend you

suit a daughter?
some are witches for they have been downed so long
want a property of their own
Stationer's Register thus historye got writ
Butter & Busby in the light of day were merchandisers
         you see the edge in broken hearts
business in text traffic

Burbage, Betterton, Garrick, Kean, Samuel Phelps, John McCullough, Edwin
Forrest, Booth, Sir Henry Irving breathe a text, raise their voices to meet the
heat & shake a spear what lives inside the actor's mask

don't laugh

a mother said I must write this in a dream
and my tears fall & no one pays attention
Says suum, mun, ha, ho, nonny nonny
& all the idle weeds
Says in a dream the syllable to crack Lear's code

The Doctor saying a kind of magikal incantation
& study dream poet has in cave subjugating
elements where female demonic devices rear Hydra heads
plugged into headphones giving "orders"

& her Electra complex causes storms
all wires aflame, daddy gone a hunting go
Doctor says "you're head's on fire!"

no never speak of love why demand it be said
no, stand guard, no money take his place
& don the madwoman's garb & enter the heath
to be such a one and never say
"By Jupiter this cannot be revoked"
for authority is never moral
Beweep, beware
you are all the characters

& bastard too

"Paphlagonian unkinde blinde king, and his kinde son"

hunted
& stormed
the cyningdom

because when the kingdom is overripe it fails
in its words,
deeds too, master

   talks back in
      blasts & fogs
& tempers clay
old fond eyes
    moving out a history
to be fain
& feign it so:

pass, pass
& be under the reign of so's

I wanted to tell it from the other side
How a daughter could see split in two
theirs and hers, burnished side
    word etch
She is a yogin of responsibility

Under James I: I note
the Huguenot memoirs not dispassionate
accounts of the Gunpowder Plot
Letters of Mary, Queen of Scots &
massacre of St. Bartholomew not go unrecorded
  turn earth
tonight's *Kali Yuga*

The first hit on the second level I knocked him out. I
by Jupiter
also got the new De La Soul tape
You went to Washington?
Did you assassinate George Bush?
Did you get anything done on the reproductive assignment?
Really nasty.
I saw the picture of a butt cut in half
It was so sick I pluck it out


     boy a Merlin

the world abound of horrible deeds
do scald, I pluck, I pluck

*as mad as the vexed sea singing loud*
*crowned with rank fumiter and furrow weeds,*
*With bur docks, hemlock, nettles, cuckoo-flowers*
*Darnel*


       *& all the idle weeds*


I love my father
& will not hinge to nothing

month in a sanatorium
brand new hotel next
carpet
wants a Tibetan doctor
oil of *vigas*
put it to your forehead
someone thrown down in the mad hallway

it is a male

who wants to retire in power
expects something will come of something
& accorded sceptre
no out went the candle

# VII

DEAR CREELEY . . .

*The poet addresses a master poet, a youthful "elder" whose own work has radicalized poetic thought & possibility. The scientific scrutiny he brings to line, syllable, provokes her own attention, which takes another direction. The emotional leverage still there. He's too established to be "counterpart," but he moves through phenomena with apparent ease although he clearly suffers. And they are both born East Coast protestants. His own work is taut, broke thru with pain. What is the attraction? He's had a wide various life, difficult. He perhaps epitomizes the dangers of the sensuous poet-life. Like her, he wants it all, and is frequently travelling. There is a period where they intersect frequently at odd literary events & drown some of their sorrows together in a drink. Her husband had invoked his name at her — you want to be like the male poets, just like Robert Creeley — which rings in her ear. Is that the case? She simply wants to be herself. But she studies him. Other informations weave in her. The conflict with spiritual traditions, their patriarchal dogma. The Dalai Lama is an exception and she is struck by a letter from another poet who shares her vision.*


You had all the syllables
You took love with all the syllables


     reason the Navy tries to "cover"


  who is led by his phallus, who wishes to get off
    back to nothing, spent in the seat of


     "accident" is a technical term


Jove mounts anything
The dissipated god whose action is
woman's fluid and to get his cock in
to come all over her
Not you I rail against

It was the love in poetry
& how to be a young woman in poetry

You can't be sappy
You never touched me
but took love with all the syllables
& were a kind of tough place
for me to get to
all over the place with words
A woman all over the place with her words
What I learn
it is a tough world to be all over in
you love you lose

                    When the U.S. Navy claims
                    to leak no accident

                 dissipated god energy
                 blast the moment, come

            power

                      cum

up incidents such as the coolant leak is a much less . . .

                                                    cum

      zero reactor accidents is a much less          cum

                 his desire who is not
                 hands all over woman
she words all over man

not saying there has never
                      the warrior been

            who is a serious event. Perhaps he

a person who asserts his cock but

                 I say Pull down

                 O Vanity pull down

What kind of man
could you win vanity from
what candidate's power examined here
who's running? what's he sell?
a holy man a holy rood
a holy writ a holy holy stone
a holy sonofabitch holy smoke
his smokescreen eye his bedroom eye
holy night against his thigh
his little notebook in shirt pocket
up against a holy woman breast
she thrashes about his holy bed
he reeks of holy but he is good
he lobbies for change
he is good he is holy holy
how many secrets sleep in his bed?

        Dear Anne

(I started to cry when I heard Nobel Prize
            was given to the Dalai Lama. What a most
            glorious thing. He is the only world
            political leader worthy of it — maybe
            this expunges the travesty of it going
            last decade to Henry Kissinger. Dalai
            Lama has 40 years unswervingly held to
            nonviolent action as the sole valid
            method of effecting political change.
            We are blessed to have such a saint
            on the planet in our lifetimes. Certainly
            Chenrezig, walking among us.
            OM MANI PADME HUM)
I gave up a ghost
it was a dark time

                quit stalling

                            a legacy of reading

                          & you far away
         far
a look you stoop
         nor blond nor book
slaved
but credence
to a
         who but
         innocent eye
to painting
                     spatial art
but this
a temporal poem
                                        no quarrel with culture history the
                     self
but this
other
         form
of
as artist

  you say I can't
                 but be
         dressed like that
bald Zennie                                        & was it
                                        was it wrong to?
         I am my father
                 when we twist like that
                                                 behind the blind OM
MANI PADME HUM

ink drawings in Braille
                 light up the night
                 so calling to me my son
         I make "hims" to me on the ground
                     over a thousand miles
         think of each other

the distance

sighing, blind as ever mother be

& you I ask you because he, the husband said
"You are like all the male poets! Just like Robert Creeley!"
& could a son enter a life on a mother poet's lintel
could the man survive, walk on in


Q: Do people who have been blind since birth dream in images as seeing people
do?

A: A series of studies by Donald D. Kirtley and others at California State Uni-
versity, Fresno, inventoried objects and activities in dream diaries of the blind.
One study found that blind people tended to dream more than sighted people
did about objects used to construct buildings, such as bricks and boards, and
land areas limited by boundaries, such as parking lots and yards. The research-
ers theorized that this was because of the special way in which the blind con-
ceptualize their external environment.


                          the cold order loosens
                  clear light of the thing
                     admirably rendered
the walls come the walls come
              tumblin' down

the painter
could
tint
with
a
hand & take
abode
there
could
be in

color
there                                        sky habitat
                                                4 doors to the city
                                                & the rafters

                        of chance
                architect of evening
                architect of morning
                                                monochrome night


*mi padre, padre mi*
*gusto*
& build a domicile O vanity pulls down
but the poet could tint with his eye


My father taught me baseball and discipline. And to laugh. As I grew up, he was
always one to side with minorities, help raise money for the poor, give his last
dollar to a panhandler. But he didn't know freedom, couldn't relate inner
heart, couldn't talk. He made jokes about my shy advances toward girls, so
much so I was afraid what I felt was screwy, that it was sissy or something to
want female affection – with four sisters and an angry mother in the house! My
father wd do anything to keep me out of jail and also bought me my first car.
But he ran out on my mother, he was sorry and hurt, really gone crazy for
several years, lying, and falling into 'born again wisdom.' I had no respect for it,
for his obesity, for his meanness to my stepbrother, the way he treated his
wives. The thought of either parent makes my world a sad place. The kind of
sorrow I'm grateful for. You know, I cry watching Walt Disney.


                        & gather here
words cannot
        nor can  so calling
for a long time
        & write
        & sending
                of
each
        other
falling

in a
tangle
cartoon swirl
& move into the next frame where
animals make a war
& get even
& get bonked
the head is sore
but pops up again

     (objective time
         gone from the
         quantum world
         gone in
         cosmology)

Marduk, *donde es?*

   the deadline when a sun god claims dominion


Thunder now. I stop to cry. Shift a way out of him. Flurry in the sky. Sun is
hidden. Silver light between green leaves & slanted trunks. Peak of green where
are you? Are you roused to see this moment? Railing 'gainst injustice. My fault
for waking the dead. When all those people were loving I wanted to take on the
male in me
& be the god you are
for you could take all the syllables you were in love with

   (I went out seeking these things
      to remind me of you):


I've been unfaithful to Lord Buddha
hung out with Muslims – Inshallah
I lay down with Mohammed in the back alley
   while he clamored for blood
I've been unfaithful, Buddha
What can you do about it? Nothing

I've been unfaithful, whirled with dervishes
        in the inner compound
Spun around till I was dizzy with ecstasy
worshipped graven images, false idols, a bone totem with a piece of fuzzy hair
I stuck pins in voodoo effigies
I chanted the muezzin at dawn from the mosque tower
I met Sabbatai Zevi in the dark temple
mesmerized by his strange actions in the dark temple
He showed me anti-Christ in the dark temple
Christ, the root of suffering, don't make me feel so bad
I met the Golem in Prague I became golem goddess of
        clay & sticks to scare the uninitiated created by a cool patriarch
        I can't be faithful to
Ah Yahweh! Your touch is winter on my feverish body
I've been unfaithful to the Four Noble Truths
trying to eliminate the path of suffering
        It's so Protestant, too much work!
I covered myself with the black silk chador better
        to hide this pulsating body of desire behind
Body of faithless acts
I won't be any man's slave
Sabbatai Zevi turns the books upsidedown
I feel the synapse of his plan but he's just another
Patriarch with yarmulke & forbidding flaming book whose illuminated
        letters sear my eyeballs
Ah Lord Buddha, I'm not steady
I went to Church on Easter, do you believe it?
I wanted to get down on my knees
cross myself a hundred times
I went to genuflect
When the priest says as I take the wafer
"the body of Christ" I'm like to melt
& when he says "the sacrament, the blood of Christ, the cup of salvation"
I dissolve into the holy grail
I've longed for centuries to get close to the grail
But I give up the cloth, the veil, Mt. Olympus
married to no male god or saint

I lie down with the circumcized & the uncircumsized
With the hermaphrodite, with the beautiful women
What have I done?
"Heathen, infidel, woman-of-little-faith!
What right have you to the Kingdom of Heaven,
the keys to Macho Paradise?"


So I quit the night you left, quit getting lost outside
I quit the machine for its discipline knowing more than I do

I quit Ati class for 2 hours my mind going to visualization
     of lip to cunt to heart to bone

In a ribbon of mantra, I quit praying
I quit the music that blasted my ear
I quit a place of terror and it quit me
I joined to the hearth, the stones kept silent
I quit lying about time
I quit sleep when it obscured your intent
You intended to go out later, I quit thinking about it
I quit the calibrated afternoon
The moment the sun broke through clouds I quit
Then a storm came, get inside
I walked inside I quit worrying
I quit the last program of the a.m.
I quit the final Auvergne song
I quit driving all over town after midnight
I quit but the "ahrbel gorung" kept wooing me
I quit the long embrace
I quit strategizing & left off all their names
     list is all right quit adding to it
I quit the time he kept waiting for
I quit her making an offer to speech & cream
I quit the Progressive magazine
I quit plastic for 3 days
I died in my denial of water because sustenance is
     a kind of feat
I quit seeing the point

I quit wearing the fertility charm it dragged my neck down
    but I never gave up on Africa

I kept dreaming you like spice
I quit you'd better be prepared to take over

    F-16 plane

    M1 Abrams tank

Trident submarine

        etc.

The Top Military Contractors (value of contracts in billions):

McDonnell Douglas: $8.0, General Dynamics: 6.5, General
Electric: 5.7, Tenneco: 5.1, Raytheon: 4.1, Martin
Marietta: 3.7, General Motors: 3.6, Lockheed: 3.5,
United Technologies: 3.5, Boeing: 3.0, Grumman: 2.8,
Litton Industries: 2.6.

            & would be a performance that
                speaks
                  itself in dollars

Later to think of him, a father
all the other young women but me
become his daughters
What doth a daughter do?
How doth a daughter woo?
How does she counter weaponry?
Rule about the house
on a mind of a teen
his clothes, how they smell
musty of south Jersey

        or

spermy

with battle

to mount a tank
artillery,

pull down

artillery,

pull down

& I wanted you as a thief in the night, & I wanted you
to promulgate my cult & I wanted you as breakdown, as private life
& I wanted you, parent of revolution, & I wanted you to make
the land carry more sheep for the wool trade, and I wanted you,
a talisman, & I wanted you, arboreal mixed up with city
& I wanted you at the front, as someone who might walk to the
edge of town, & I wanted you up to my neck, & I wanted you
as partner to my friend's existence, and I wanted you changed
by daylight, and I wanted you as I need books, & I wanted you

I wanted you, history doesn't count, & I wanted you as spleen
to a carefree nature, & I wanted you in the sense of opposite,
& I wanted you the cows can come home, we were in the country,
I wanted you, & I wanted you speaking as we were children again,
& I wanted you to sneak up on me like children, & I wanted
the clothes you wear, I wanted to wear them, I wanted you
in hot pursuit, wanted you the column could wait, &
I wanted you writing the story of Athena, of black Athena, and I
wanted you to be law abiding just once & I wanted you early
I wanted you late, I wanted you the others can wait, they
wait if I want you & only you I want
I wanted you at the beginning of civilization, I wanted you
the clocks can run down, I want you on the way outside, I want

you resting on my laurels, I wanted you forbidden to "panegyric"
to "ode" to "sonnet," I wanted you formless, I wanted you &
the page is the only place I know for this, I wanted you the
night of the day the manuscript came back, I wanted you settled
in a home, I wanted you cherished by the landlord, I wanted
the textures of illuminated manuscripts in our love

& I wanted you in agreement that women invented the alphabet,
& I wanted you to close down please the laboratory for me,
& I wanted you as water flows downhill, I wanted you over
my head, on top of me, I wanted you under me, & I wanted
you sitting in front of books as you always do, the rest can
wait, I wanted you to give something away the day I noticed
wanting you, I desired the table of contents to include you,
I desired the year of our lord to slow down

(I went out seeking these things
to remind me of you)

my field abandoned by walls
my field: 4 white walls
my field, light shines on the page
a modern light on my modern page
my field the bed my lover lies waiting
my field, the wires to your voice, wired to you
field like this one at night, warm we stay out here
we lie with the deer in the
field, I never told you about it
the battle of his sex against mine
I can speak of it, the fighting
we wrestled, to destroy one another our sex
our vocabulary
can't stop my mouth!

field for the sport
can't stop my mouth
I win I win I win

I tame you with my dakini hook
with my fiery text & mantric sound

with my love for you I tame you

these are my words
          in my play
of you
                    & this is the play with you

FLYING LUCIFER

A.Oblique, okay all over open a tone
   like the 31st day in the Celtic sense
   adjacent to moon, have you a wave

B. Nay, a newer year wand. A stage (our love,
   our one body) shaped like a ship.

A. A wrought, a blame, burl, turned around
   Lover likes his coins & baubles

B.Way on the side's this human hoard. the
   turning, the fucking, the sea too, how
   a woman's ballade, mix, torque, &
   seafaring all together. Waves settle.

A. Longitudinally rescue,blur or drown
   You're a kinda demon lover
   A woman's crazy to follow

Dear Creeley Again:

I try
now not
to miss
you who are
older
sharper
I'm thinking

you called me
"hostess"
once, New York
I'm insulted
because
of who
you are
to me
salty
something you
would notice
being you
my image of
you
Who We Are
not possible
our tongues
words
say it
again & again
later in
friendship
How to enjoy
these marriages
each other
in them (meaning
him & her)
together
of course
marriages
come apart
seamlessly
They scatter,
boon of edges
like
teeth
like it's written

to bite off
a piece
of each
other
But synchronized
in his beautiful lash my innocent
one,
I say "husband"
perched
in attention
How to enjoy
each other
(those ones)
It happens
in pain
You too?
It happens
who we are not
fooling
the children
of it
who are we
they are they
going over
the predicament
nothing new
the nod of
him
her
of them,
the children again
of where of
how
to live
You tell me
what study
how to speak
what's conducive

to "work"
or not
to what place
job
people
owe allegiance?
who needs
us most
or not
at all
Simply a burden
to think
You are
here
to me
over a table
talking
"drinks"
jokes on who is or
is not
smoking
I am a written
daughter
of you
who inform
me such
You ballast
here
Your neck
of the
woods.


Assignment: *Write a poem, or series of poems, in which every noun refers either to a female person, object, or abstraction of either, or to a male ditto, and every verb is an indication or sign of either positive affectionate behavior or negative hostile behavior. The entire language of you and your audience with respect to your poem or poems is based on your words being what the language is . . .*

He still didn't satisfy the class with his clarity and I've no idea how I'm going to work this out yet. It seems to be an arbitrary decision he's asking for, because he said, for instance we might say all words having 3 or more consonants are masculine. It would be much easier to write this one in French or Greek! But I dimly see the point he wants to make is that we always accept and abide by rules whether we know it or not.

*C'est ici une véritable mystique du langage,     n'est-ce pas?*


Jonathan Johnson says these things

   (black & white Palestine scarf
      triangulated 'round neck)
How he came by the bracelets: "made by a friend
  of mine from Norway (the beaded one)
  a friend of mine from the Bronx (the one of twine)"

His father died young
"my best friends were squirrels"
The only Black student in the school
  (suburbs of Chicago)


 & he danced, age 12, ballet
  (large snow boots, heavy wool pants)
in New Orleans in an intimate relationship to space
  ("shape it within myself")

How much hair under the beret?
Then?
"I came home every day & sat in the bathtub for hours
& melted down
poured love into dancing & quit"
And "love"?
Not yet
I want to make others fly
    (open face, thick sweater, noble, left-handed)

body to teach me and love?
not yet
centered like a pendulum
plumb line

        (vanity)

             silent scribbling

outrage of how many caves
in sickness in health
move your fingers

       real ink, serenity

         gutted a house

     but O vanity down

you who are Buddha
art woman

         body to teach me
         body to teach

     (as more of his letters attest he was blunt

& blunt the body to the sword

      body to teach
          how cum down

     dab in the sweet sperm

       body wider so much wider than the sea
his pain so lovingly tendered
in every phone & phoneme singing

       in the f

      spectra world

     pas

cycle world

being the ks of memory

He & I do love

Look & see


Anselm

sieve . . .

get the applications!

not hollow among natives Aprille

& maps right on Was ist
los?


Will I love you?
Quit your protection
I quit under pressure, under glass
I folded before the money ran out
I quit I told you I'd better have a backup
Be my friend I won't quit yet
I quit it's difficult to describe
A rough outline is to be read syllable by syllable
I quit dialing you were never there
I quit staring out the window
Moon, clouds, I quit the fantasy
Stars, they look calm
I quit the careful approach I was impulsive then
I quit giving my palm to your ambition
I quit my own restoration
I quit, was this viewed as defeat?
And when you were there, static was intolerable
I stood on a 40-foot-high scaffold peeling paint
into my face

Then I quit working for experts
I quit I'm not complaining it was time for a change
Take one step back
Were you informed?
I use words for my own loss
I use words as my table, as a kind of shrine
I sweep over the care of the words
They take care of themselves
I sweep them under my demand
I command that they not quit the scenario
The sentence quits the page as it ends
I quit as a phantom of exteriority
A double negative remains evanescent
Don't linger with my thought to quit
I tell you it happened once
It happens again
And the speed of the transition, could it quit?
Would myself-as-object quit?
I quit the sine qua non of that experience
Could I keep harping on my conclusions
Is the language ripe enough?
Is all the data in?
I quit the fragility of the "real"
Writing without end, I quit trying to stop
Conceit gets the best of the one-who-quits
I quit an outward appearance
No outward appearance without light Well I quit the light then
How could that be, I couldn't quit gleaming
I couldn't quit radiating
I kept hidden
I quit being a stoic
I quit nostalgia for your past
Insatiable compassion, how to quit
I quit stalling
I quit representing my total existence
I quit speculating about the event
It would happen, I would be there, I can't quit

I quit defining the problem
Linguists were going around in circles
Is speech a human phenomenon?
I quit for no good reason
The speech was boring in the sense of redundant

I quit to leave everything as it is

I quit by blending in my durations with the other
durations

I could never stop


Dear Creeley:

I will never stop
I love the road
I sit all the time watching the world go by
perched like a Buddha than to a more comfortable pose
& the tooth of a walrus centers me like a pendulum
or plumb line I want to say Who are you
Dark hair of a saint
painted by an old Dutch master
with notions of light
What are you?
Is there outrage for the rage you lived in in sickness
Who?
Who moves your fingers with red ink & serenity?
Who were you?
Something was wrong, blind for 5 days
Who are you?
& once had my body trained to a star
I loved the road & was a gas station mechanic on it
for it, you decide
was a manic for it, the road and he said
"I refused to be part of the war machine"
But loves my writing

& the road in it
It roads you away, you might say
Messages get lost
Look for a word & can't find it
But the world, say "yes"
What makes the grass green?
A wide receiver subsidizes me
Photos on the wall of Alaska oil slick don't scare me
Don't, don't scare me Don't scare me
& in my writing trained to a star
I wait & wonder

Dear Creeley:

Does some body always walk a road?

# VIII

## BORN ON THE THATCH I WAS BORN TO

*The poet writes formally to catch her breath. She needs a breather from classroom demands but follows the dimension of two of her assignments — sonnet & memory without argument. She locates herself in a room (the poem) and travels back to the stifling Cheops pyramid as she visited it in 1962. This exercise lies within old recollection. She honors Francis Yates, duchess of Memory. She crawls into the glorious death trap never able to stand and realizes she needs this particular rite of passage and must start useful visualizations. Is it time to travel to the underworld & steal the secrets of the male energies that rule there? It gives her power to think thus. She wants to tip the scales. The figures who have created her state of mind for the poem are distanced here. The Dancer consoles her as he skirts off the page. Must she change her clothes?*

Crossed the hallway toward couple of you
Roots writhing to reach you & make
this profile sigh to full advantage
Yet some saltiness inside your question
was willed by constellations, was necessary
Midnight excursion off-limits not about sex
& then stilled, shuffling in the street,
blood heat, you know a way about beauty held supine
Hymns foretelling those days moon no longer appearing
Frenzied berserkers, ferocious warriors
realize sacred fury of hey ho spinning world
Yet how do we say what we mean to the moment
We say it to each other You both say it
so that we be again all time of one another

*

I believe in this as a words-only school
Never retreat from scrutinizing you who are deep
in the sentences although half-dreamed
I miss the enemy, the burnt-leaf smell of resin
The way eyes find me who are important to them

Blasphemy of light don't let it in on us
Born on the thatch I was born too
vanish against the phrase "I, tracked by barbarians"
In the nuisance game, a celestial lady & gentleman
couldn't leave without a drumming ritual in the school
And I heard my Coleridge say, "Deep in my life, you who . . ."
Which accounts for horizontal shadows and the
delirium which is her (the lady's) half-mannish
garb, an artist's hand at the tree sash

*

His question no longer appears fury-prone
deep in my life you are hymns to humans
who are odes too, who never retreat from
primordial foretelling of moonless days
Frenzied constellations are necessary, are above us
& I hear my Coleridge say "I believe in this as
a words only school," roots writhing to each berserker
some saltiness still inside them, deep in my life
they (you) are willed to the moment
I see him like her as herrings in blue loose leaves
I see over decades nothing about sex
I see entire pedagogical systems amassing before us
which accounts for horizontal shadows
We'd been drinking & stared at the fish a long time

*

Hand on the tree sash, hand on an arm
although half-dreamed and willed by
what we mean by the "moment"
Couldn't leave without a burnt retreat
couldn't shuffle beauty couldn't shuffle love
Eyes hey ho are half-dreamed & mind bursts to
vanish against those days
like hymns, profiles, schools, works in clay
A gentleness some saltiness inside him
all in on us, the rage, two women

In the sentence was lulled by warriors
whose blasphemy, the rage, is strange
We say it to each other writhing to fell advantage
Born on the thatch I was born to

⋆

Days moon-deep in How do we say
& be again all time of you how do we
of the primordial world say how does it happen?
I heard them say "I believe in this" how
you who are two who are profiles strange to me
who are foretelling, scrutinizing, appearing
& never retreat only crossing the far hall
deep in hymn you who are O warriors
Yours and my life was necessary!
You who are those O no longer appearing
Who are gentlemen & lady hands no longer appearing
who are then stilled, heat-blood no longer appearing
who are fury about no longer appearing
I was born in this only words appearing school
(We'd been drinking and stared at the fish a long time)


You are my age as we
deepen into a pact
jar . . . track ties . . .

You are the chromosomes
who see Matter as
habitual bustling & napping
jokes . . . scenarios

We are elated to
recognize each other
at all when we share the microscope
sperm . . . sand . . .

But when chromosomes
cry like water
They take the
heart of me


        (heart of me
          O beloved of Israel!)


My heart went out to "little white lies." He needed them out in the sun, occupying the expanse of desert, false hope and poverty. "Anna," he said, "You must be a wish for me, anywhere you go. Think of me." He gestured grandly, presumably speaking of America. "Back there, anywhere you go. America! Did I tell you the time I went to America? My shoes, see my shoes. They are the shoes of America." Florsheims? The discarded gift, no doubt, of a generous hippie passing through. They were dusty, worn, altogether gone, too big. Ragged strings for laces. "It doesn't matter, Amad," I wanted to shout, "you are here!" Here in Giza with the pyramids. It didn't matter Giza was as dusty and worn down as the shoes. That what was once tropical paradise had come to this. It doesn't matter, Amad, that I come from the richest country in the world, that I myself am walking talking emblem of the richest country in the world. How could I make him see how sad America was. *I* was lured *here* in response to America. He laughed, "You are too serious, Anna." His camel, Hepset, was typically nonchalant but nuzzled my hand as I gave her a lump of sugar from the hotel restaurant. How many times had she been photographed circumambulating the great pyramid of Cheops with a foreigner on her back?

You had to crawl through corridors that held the sand as a death trap. You had to crawl like an animal, like the worm you had first been in your climb up the evolutionary ladder. You had to mix with the dirt and dust so they choked you. Finally when you came to the first chamber you could stand, stooped over. You had to carry a torch. You had to chant the names of all the Egyptian deities you could think of. You had to view yourself as witness, as barge, as eyes from another realm. You had to make your journey a sacred one toward the center of the past and toward death and rebirth in an old mythology. You had to have a memory of everyone who went before you, of everyone who died before you.

You had to forget New York, Los Angeles, Miami. You had to crawl as witness, as first woman, as first girl, as sacrificial victim. You had to crawl naked. You had to crawl with your tough skin. With your fearless skin. You might move like the snake. You had to be a warrior carrying a torch for the past. Your heart had to beat faster. You had to meet the glamourous Pharaoh as a slave. You had to be whipped and tortured. You had to meet the center of darkness under the pyramid's apex of eyes and then retreat back into the light of an even darker, eyeless civilization.

and you TIP THE SCALES . . .

You'd rather I slept
You'd rather I didn't go out on a limb to
the immigrant
You'd rather I cleared out
the she-said-I-said & not in a naked fashion
Slowly put on tiger dress, spider socks
(you'd rather I . . .)
mining shoes
& not drive off jeopardized
You'd rather I got it wrong
Moon's libertine scales tipped
not for nor against a lover's favor
We might be travelling
We might go inside a motel room
It might be night in Cairo
You'd rather I didn't say these things

*

We drink to the heart
one another's moon
We do this landscape life, scales
of fishy characters I knew
I knew I'd recognize your voice I knew
You'd rather the mood is lighter
Travelling makes us thirsty
A one-time candidate jets from coast to coast

He's proud to be an immigrant
You see the cactuses? You see the caucus?
Not only of sight but of sound I sing
They look like priests without a vote
Rain descends in the desert
I love the night, the proud rain
You'd rather I didn't refer to
"jeep," "couple-irritation"

*

For the immigrant candidate you'd rather
toast his slips of tongue, worsted suits
not a thing to laugh at
You'd rather I slept, scales tipped
I'll vote the line you love
Both tiger and lip
I said slip to vote both crowned and slow
You'd rather I travel without him in mind
I'd like nothing but this:
light on the tongue
dark ribbons of speech
Someone to cast this vote upon

*

You'd rather I go off my hinge to you
Acid rain, rust establishments
These don't last in your mind
although motive, catalyst, curving boundary might
The picture changes
You'd rather immigrate
to fashion, go ahead, capitalist
Give me your insides against night
room flavors, our limbs together
I don't go out in exotics
Wait for me, shoes off
I've been drilling an old speech
from the Marriot days

In the health of laboratories, what health?
Limbs slowly dress, fragile outfit
semi-nuked gloves in the hospital
Keep waiting. I keep reading you
Don't destruct now, Pyramid
Obey the hungers with red lights
Count down to plutonium white-out
legal code you rather I didn't invoke
or explore the stricter sense of "code"
The people of the sea will unite with the Iron Age
You rather I didn't read about these things
of past and weaponry
Enough lights flash approval
You'd rather we walk down the corridor
with you gripping my arm

*

Missionary flavors in the electorate
Home favorites rise, slim chances
Vote now to a richer candidate No, no, no
Moonlight helps me not
I won't get busy but balance and lighter
Speed's a wrecker to civilization
higher and lower, tax on my brain
We change shapes to slip aside
We live inside an apocalypse
Both sides speak of a plan
Care not to be human
You'd rather I leave off talk
Fill out forms
Forget the landscape, this room,
that night, the candidate's smile
Scales tipped in the wrong one's favor
You rather not think I think
to go out on a limb to swim, not drown
(We'd been drinking and stared at the fish a long time)

I was number 92 of 113 at the St. Mark's benefit, and of course things were running behind schedule, I waited, an hour and a half. The Parish Hall was full of people eating chili, drinking beer, playing the two pianos, being drunk, getting dressed up, crushing cigarettes and food on the floor. Once I'd changed into my skirt and bra made from porno mags I was cold; a woman on the staff came up and opened a window next to me, pointed to the smoke in the room. Finally someone took pity on me and jumped me up the list of couple of notches.

I had already resigned myself to having no more space than the rug-covered altar, Lee Ann had promised the podium would be removed. She hadn't told me about the sound system that I now saw dominating a few precious square feet in the southwest quadrangle of my little rectangle.

I held the blue cape tight around me, to hide my cold white skin and the porno photos, dragged the two garbage bags full of crushed paper onto the space, and nodded to Grazia, who was sitting next to the sound man. The beautiful and upbeat cantata by Campra began and I ran around opening and closing the cape, nervous and overenergetic, as if I couldn't stand to be there and at the same time wanted to show myself off. Occasionally I screamed, somewhat sweetly, like the soprano, who was talking to God. As the music changed to a baritone solo I ran back and forth between the two bags, pulling out the crushed pieces of paper, occasionally stopping to open one and "read" it but could, as it were, formulate nothing more than meaningless verbalizations.

Then the music gets even sweeter, I remove the cape, slowly, over my head, move lyrically side to side, suspending, arms curling upward, three or four times during this minute ripping off one of the porno pages, crunching it into a ball and chucking it into the audience.

The night I got the idea for the costume I ran up to St. Mark's Place, couldn't find a single street seller till I got across from 33, there bought a big batch from a guy who with great enthusiasm told me what a good deal he was going to give me because, "I know you'll be back."

Zaire, I was in your train I was dancing
Zaire, I was black & further out the night
Zaire, a partner of the night
We made the trees alive, Zaire
We made them dance
Zaire, we walked to a stream of blood
Zaire, another birth could be
The snake of our vision is the crest of your rising
We are the panther people first
We are the glowing eyes
We come this way with the glowing eyes
We stalk you at night covered with diamond rags
You arise to witness dawn which arises
Good luck
Dawn is a tiger
The sun is tiger's right eye
So panther-out-of-night got born in black blood
& sun out of tiger whose paws herald dawn
Zaire, we say your fabulous name: Zaire, Zaire
What legend walks? We said "Za"
They said "Ire"
Zaire born out of night & day
Spoken, this story broke my music to sit here
Zaire: fur, star, eyes, equator
Zaire: mother & thief, and father-thief
Thus broke my music to sit here
You tell them
You tell them Zaire we'll take it out of church
You are country of reckoning
We come to you with "ire" eyes
We come to you out of black "za" blood
We are singular
I am Attibon Legba
with a hat fresh from Guinea
My bamboo cane too
Likewise my ancient pain from Guinea
And bones, old bones

I am the patron saint of janitors
Elevator boys too
I am Legba-Wood, Legba-Cayes
Legba Signangnon
I'm the seven Kataroulo Brothers
I am Legba Kataroulo
I plant my grave tonight
The great medicine-tree of my soul
In the white man's land
At his crossroads
I kiss his door 3 times
I kiss his eyes 3 times
I am Papa Alegba
God of thresholds
Tonight it is 1 1 1 1
I'm the master of your white man's hangouts
I am the protector of plants
And of the insects of your house
I am chief of all the gateways
To the soul & the body

       The lizards we usually see in our houses
        & on our faces, I found more eloquent
        in a sky habitat

the clean light of the thing admirably rendered

The painter could tint with his hand
& take an abode there

brows superbly drawn,
pale swatches of paint

color of exotic lizards
deliberate, intentional
translucid shadows in the water

crystalline candor of any
mailing list

The response is "Volo" or "Nolo"

the conscript fathers (in the dream)
checking on the
polish of
funeral shoes
a great gulp of
a fastidious person

or is he?

We wonder about boxing
everything
up

the reams of paper
(here's more, beloved)
& the books & the scissors and the
    snippets

where you walk, you walk
& the plates are being kept for you

southern?

                in blues & browns
high collar


                        What does night hold
                        First mirror grabs me
                        It goes well with me
                        This first mirror version

                        The armor costs
                        First mirror very rough
                        My armor sins
                        First mirror is stuck

My rue is with him
My heart is sure
It finds me numb later
In a dimmer mirror

Not in neither sought
in this: in house
Not in neither either
Out of this house

Sign this: a hologram
Sign this: with feeling
Sign this: world laughing
I am an Often-Signer-of-Words

That I would be certain that no one tell me feel like this, this is the way I feel, that the father is the animal to the man, that the father is the light to the son, that he stole the woman's eyes to see his own son because he was afraid to look at him with such fiery orbs, that this is only one interpretation, that we can be generous now, that we are careful very careful that the women's eyes are brighter, that they look into the man

*My lover capable of terrible lies*
*at night lay close to me*
*in a dream that lied like truth*

He's setting
impossible tasks
for me

He hammers a
hole in my shoulder
to pour in his message

I have to climb
a small mountain

with a basket
of linens

scratched by brambles
my legs bleed

a sharp thorn
scrapes the point
of my heart

At the top of the mountain:
many patriarchs
Many patriarchs
at the top of the mountain

"Give us your heart!"
No, no, I cry
"Give us your heart," they demand

But now I've taken it out of my aching chest
& wrapped it in linen in the basket

It will be saved for the down-there people
I will give it to them
I sew myself up

but in the meantime I am hollow woman
& I fool them
& I give them a medium red stone
the size of my heart but all the time saying
No, no! to excite them further

A woman
spends a long
time
in the metaphoric water

She mutates into
a flower

that will only bloom
once every 25 years

*Men here are as savage as giant vipers,*
*And strut about in armor, snapping their bows.*
*As I sing the second stanza I almost break the lutestrings,*
*Will broken, heart broken, I sing to myself.*

(Ts-ai Yen A.D. 200 )

that all things confine, but I am wide, wide, that we cruise into the page as if
spellbound, that dread anticipates the page, that an African costume informs
the text
  that poet exists to accommodate sense to sound, that he
who was a torment to me will read this and laugh, that an
engineer can put the mesh on any of you, that I can't say words
large enough to contain you, that you dance away from me & steal
a fake heart

  – I swore my fair heart out
  – To what man or job?
  – Stone on stone
  – You mean he's gone?

The other class turned out 16 girls, ages 15 through early 30's. I made a dense
dance with their help to Marianne's "Witches' Song" and I became the witch,
wore a dress and bra and petticoats and hat with veil lots of makeup on the
heavy side, I dance around among them and then they kill me. They got into it.

# IX

*She is always curious about where the words she & her progeny got named come from. This knowledge might unlock the rune: her state of mind and inform the poem. She goes to the etymological dictionary to translate* Ambrose, Bye, Waldman *& swims in the associations. Another man writes from the shore of the Bosphorus, located in a landscape fused of poetry & religion: miracles, exploits of the 12 gods. Always yearning for resonances to history, & sacred locale, she is gratefully transported to Apollo's holy spring. Nevertheless the boys' talk brings her back to America. Cartoons & sports, bastardized poetry & religion. She loves their words, their naive preadolescent charm. But longs to travel again, away from these States, duty, suburbia.*


*ambhi* — Around

       old English bi, be, by, BY

            *ambho* — both

     an - ana - aloft

       anus = old woman

*reidel:* the rod between upright stakes

*wal:* to be strong

vale, valence, valerian, valiant, valid,
valor, valve, avail

       walthan, waldan, wealdan,
       *wieldan:* to govern

*wald:* power, rule

*Waldr:* ruler

          (stay up late studying myself)

           what's in a name?

— Calvin is a hero. He smarts off to his mom.

— He plays tricks, nasty ones.

— He robs the bank in Monopoly.

— He exaggerates as Spaceman Spiff & kills the Mother Naggon.

— & Zorgs.

— Zorgs.

— He squirts her.

— His room is a smelly dungeon.

— His Dad's the Deadly King of the Naggons.

— Bart Simpson is our age. 10. He plays pranks too.

— Like "Is there a Jock there?" (He's calling a bar see.)
   "Is there a Jock Strap there?" "Is there an Al there?"
   "Is there an Al Coholic there?"

— I want to be invisible

— I want to be President of Nike.

— Ask Joe Richey, "Girls can't throw."

— Girls underwear is cut off where the legs are.

— It's skimpy. It's see-thru.

— Girls are gentle, they have more areas to protect.

— They don't want to get in a fight.

— I'm a girl, he can't spank me. "Girls have more delicate heinies" says
   Susie Derkins.

& out of what

words

to enter a womb

to patrimony?

& out of the woods
what name to
enter
through a mother's womb
        to patrimony

                                He holds me
                                in uniform
                                        bundle 'pon a knee


gone a gone a war

                back there

  a Waldr,

                warlike
                        rules

but he was quiet, very quiet

                        shh

                gone a warring gone

it fits him, suits him

                you can hold up yr head in a righteous war


and return home w/ booty
                        German bayonets

("Overhead another new German weapon seized control of the skies: the Jun-
kers-87 Stuka dive bomber, which plunged down to blast road junctions and
railroad lines; it also had a device that emitted screams to spread terror among
its victims. And then there were the heavy bombers. General Wladyslaw An-
ders, who would eventually lead the Polish exile army through the battles of
North Africa and Italy, heard the ominous drone of Heinkel 111s overhead and
later remembered that "squadron after squadron of aircraft could be seen flying
in file, like cranes, to Warsaw." At 6 A.M. those deadly cranes began raining

bombs on the unprepared, ill-defended city and its civilian inhabitants. In those same surprise raids on that first grey morning, the German Luftwaffe virtually wiped out the entire 500-plane Polish Air Force on the ground. The dawn surprise, the rampaging panzers, the shrieking dive bombers, all were elements in a new German invention that was to change the nature of warfare: *blitzkrieg*."

I am around & a great spreading out. The man, is he?
Is available & creative. Near Florida. Near the banyan. A
great spreading out. Spreading like lies, like glory. Like
veins. Like tubing usually hidden. Could be gentle conduit
too. Not abysmal talk talk talk the media. The media provides
into, piped into your life. Blood coursing through the tree
of you, Jove. Do you stumble as you ride? Married to vehemence,
passion? Do you copulate with the horse or the dove? Blitzkrieg.
Penetration is joyous. Keeping still is breaking the Sabbath.
Warmth & moisture as I write. As I write, surround me.
Damp shirt. Sand in all orifices. Greased up for the sun.
What did he say so greased after all? Lying on the beach spent.
Radios not alone in this. A star on the swimsuit is the nearest
ticket to godhead. Grab it. Does it retreat? Spreading
spreading or advancing like a tree.

morphic

Dear Author,

This area is saturated with religion & poetry, and the earth always seem to trouble (tremble) as if could no longer hold in all the past. We are living on the shores of the Bosphorus and just a short ways away there was in antiquity a temple to Hermes, though I have been insisting that it was really dedicated to Daphnis, his son (the father of bucolic poetry). That is also where Darius sat on his throne and watched his 10,000 men cross the Bosphorus and where St. Daniel is supposed to have worked miracles. Memet built his great fortress, Rumeli Hisar, there before conquering Constantinople. In this century, these few acres have been very important to Turkish poets, including Orhan Veli (who is to Turkish poetry very much what Williams is to America), and he is buried on the other side of the hill from us. Until recently, there was a major dervish sect located here, and before that there were a number of important Orthodox monasteries. One of the sacred springs (sacred now to St. Demetrius but it was once sacred to Apollo?) is located a short walk from here. Across the Bosphorus there used to be a temple to Zeus and a shrine to the twelve gods & goddesses of Olympus, and nearby the place where Polyduces (the son of Zeus (as swan) and Leda) killed Amycus. And just a short way north on this side of the Bosphorus is the place where Medea threw away her poisons when she returning with Jason and the golden fleece.

With every best wish,

Ed
Nis betiye, Caddesi
Etiler – Istanbul
Turkey

because ye made yr backs shields, argonauts
Because yr eyes turnd home
Yr spurs turnd too
& yr enemies grew to lions
You could still win
but no, you'd rather be exiled
sad, fevered
You blow bubbles as the falcon flies
The wind bursts, is scattered useless
I tell you Shape up!
Take shames heaped on you
forgive & go on
Remember good king Bob's humor
tough & refreshing
So her peace is made with Pisa
What care she for flesh
that in dense wilderness feeds wolves?
Ye Guelfs, Listen!

(this makes sense

both

very bright

rims that may be volcanic crater rims

(findings)

I never plan a stanza)

The words just cluster like chromosomes
hungry hawks on every side
to be thought catatonic was safe (she thought)

with reason
or charming them with

a woman who meets
such things    is an old taboo


Principle, masculine

and God, 32
and Logos, *see Logos*
and Sun, page 20

& pin your faith to
being bizarre & unreasonable
it is no *façon de parler* for him
 plants do not grow without the influence of both
sun & moon


A VASE, A BOWL, PHALLUS ETC.


King Soma, my manas, my mind

— Who's your favorite sports player?

— Darryl Strawberry. Was.

— Why?

— He plays right field. He hits a lot of home runs.

   He's on my favorite team, the Mets.

— Does he have a family?

— He was just born.

— What are you most afraid of?

— Dumb spiders.

— What was your worst nightmare?

— Extra Terrestrial ripping his guts out on an airplane.

   He stood up and bared his guts.

— Do you believe in God?

— No.

— Why not?

— I don't know.

— What created the universe?

— Me.

— If you could get out of the country, where would you go?

— Thailand, poor Thailand, racked in pain. . . .


                    (this makes sense . . .)

# X

## REVENGE

*"Odi et amo"*

*She'll travel in her head and shift identity. The poet takes on the persona of aged hag who has stuck by her patriarchal male companion, following him to the ends of the earth, now a parched & desolate desert, subject to bombing raids. The field of Tiresias? The world has changed. She now sees him as foolish prophet doomed by a stubborn, wrongheaded & willful nature. She gets some verbal revenge in here, while she conjures fragments of bygone civilizations, rigid mindsets. She, if nothing else, takes a stand against theism which implies there is something outside your own mind — a saviour, preferably male who might even need you to exist. She has been the entrusted tolerant confidante of the Male, a position that gave her an illusion of power but created further servitude until she can no longer hold her tongue. Alas. She becomes nihilistic.*

Dear Jove:

Later you were talking. Later you were saying
it's a way back way to be inextricably linked
like dead Pharaohs and Queens, something grand.
Something sweeping and fixed. The long desert
bleakness is your home and guarded now because
of terrorism, secret and bleak. None of the
hostages get enough to eat, and reporting back
on faint videos, background noise, I can't hear
you, look fatigued, worn down. Can I be surprised?
Are you still there? Earlier, you said the monuments
are misunderstood. Too much bloodshed. The weight
of centuries' pressure to leave something lasting.
To be a sneer or complacent stone mouth in jungle
air, or wasting away from the rub of sea and wind.

I was a monument ravaged by time in the temple
of your — could I say it — heart?

Or simply in your temple. That holy refuge of
secret thought and revenge. You were the artisan
of the moment I got framed, got caught in malachite,
caught in granite. You took the lead. You
assumed the charge of me. I was never good at being
still and wanted to bend with the gold. One searches
in vain for the mask that will describe all you
represent, all you mention in your ravings. Not
a prototype in this old girl's mind. Yet you carried
the "tears" of certain Kota reliquary figures.

Later you said, for you could never stop speaking,
that life was cheap on the desert so why get so
precious about it?

And yet you talked and talked out there. When
coils unwind, the night is suddenly cool, still.
You move away, muttering, I can't make you out.
In French: *Mais, tu es folle.* Something like that.
Like once, under trees, you whispered, pointing
at the sky GOD IS IMMENSE. That shattered, because

all you were thinking was you, you. You were the
architect of a slow burn. It was an appropriate
tactic, the way clouds get heated and evaporate.

Not me, I'll take my sweet time. I won't go away
until you take back all those words. Words on tapes
and notebooks which fill my shelves now, collapsing
under the weight of grandiose insight and scoff.
Can you take them all back? I doubt it. You said
this, you said that, and you lost the train, It was
never to say I am responsive now, but rather will
fill up space with my immensity. No ears are deaf
and all of you will hear me. Hear me. History needs
to be retold in couplets ( *you thought you
spoke in couplets*). Yet I was inventing your

— 144 —

speeches for you all the time. The one about
nostalgia and clothing was close to our common
theme. How the very bright threads in a skirt,
tunic or dress, may evoke the sensation of dancing,
and give pleasure in how they lie hidden in folds
as the music bends down and sweeps you up in
its arms. Didn't ask for credit on this one.

Or the one examining the way birds will sit in
water and soak, as a contrast to their lightness
in air. Anything moving from one element to
another seeks that element's density.

That brittle twig wants to burn and crack.

My ideas were a shore for you to bank on. You
with your tidal warnings and disasters always
coming in. You remember the oasis at Biskra?
A fresh thing in the middle of the desert, which
snaked through palm trees with their very green
leaves? You had a fix for the African earth.
I spoke through you an echoing reverberation of
the terrible beauty of places such as these.

You enjoyed going it alone in the desert,
babbling at air you get lighter and lighter upon.
You are a lover in air. Your noise is less brute
and adamant out here. You fuck the space, gently
forcing yourself into it. It parts as it always
does.

I am beside you, mimicry of natural phenomena.

You are at your best. You are at your most
obscure. Were anything watching from above
(the cameras placed on the militia's helicopters)
they'd think you the wise old man returned.

Your long hair rippling behind you. Your words
holy by all accounts.

Now you are speaking of the way intelligence
flips in and out of objects, yet only when we
notice it, does it respond and speak to us.
Everything speaks in and of itself – that's the
point. That scorpion (out here on the desert)
nods its suffering too, and poor yon rock bleeds.
Who knows the sorrows of increments of shell
and bone? Those markings are signs of a plan
that we move in parallel universes of suffering.

See the tracks left by the armored combat
vehicles? Where do they come from.

You speak my own thoughts always. The tracks
in my own mind remind you to speak. I listen
to you ranting, and dream myself dressing in
front of a mirror. You stop and observe this
feminine act. You turn away. Later you accuse
me of harboring hidden revenge.

Earlier before the coils unwind, I am not at
liberty to disclose your seed syllable. You,
like all of us, have your root sound. You are
a bird singing inside yourself. Even animals
will cry their secret sound and we think they are
merely communicating to one of their own. That
sound is given and willed by coming into
a realm of vibration and time. The timbre you
hide is archaic, primordial. Do I resent the
simplification of your desire through this one
note you utter inside me?

Perhaps. Anthropological accuracy has no business here.
Stammerings of a civilization

before ours castigate us with their beauty
and joy.

I knew you from the start. I had your number.
I had you nailed. I stole it at the mouth of
your birth. I substitute my own. I planted
my own because yours was more golden.

What do words do?

They call out and fracture

They sing and congratulate the earth

They torment the listener

They are invented to distort reality

They lie down with the beloved

They stroke the child

They twist and turn you in

They name the necessary items for betrayal

They create an arsenal

Words create an arsenal beyond necessity

They harp on and communicate fear

They work with the technicians

They blow up a storm

They name the hurricane

They bow and scrape

They invoke the names of deities even as they lie and cheat

They are precise and chill the air around the stadium

They precipitate the end of the love affair

They identify with a lost civilization

They decipher annals of the kingdom

Some objects are dedicated to the cult of the dead

A system of lines and colors introduces constant vibration

They (the dead) can be read and digested that way

They represent how you try to feel

They are oblique and deflect your obsession

They pacify the interior regions

They can be savage

They count on your imagination

They are the illusionist's prize

They identify the lover

They name the sculpture and its parts

They bed down with the fetish

They long for clarity in the paragraphs

They honor the sun

They atrophy in the wrong books

They long for you to break the code

There are cross relationships between "projections"
and "holes" in the human body. A confusion of
anatomical features haunts you. We move closer
to modern art.

Earlier, we had travelled to the city-etched-in-gold.
It was so bright it startled and blinded us. It was a
curious amalgam of angularity and passion. We were
resistant to the medium of stone. It seemed distorted
by comparison to our life as we wanted to experience
it out on the desert. You had been having those desert
dreams again. But the city: jutting brow.

I turned toward you: a jutting brow.

Symmetry isn't useful here, as collective rather
than individual sentiments woo you. Don't fall
short on me, don't do it, my comrade. Ordinary
voyagers might, or colonials, but you, fetishistic
you, don't do it. Possessiveness is clear to me,
it's my problem. Literal or banal. All the same.
Who means it. Who soaks you up. It's me again.
I save you. Don't trip. Don't get hit. I lead
you by the hand down streets and avenues. Don't
mind them: barbarians. These city streets
and highways are elaborate constructs meant to
confuse us. We see ourselves on large screens
inside hospitals built to add to our confusion.
We are televised as curiosities, aliens. You are
not sure how to receive these accolades. I hurt
for you. There is the instinct of death in this

air, an accentuation of the pleas we could make.
In a prophetic moment you saw me as a young girl
again, undistorted by time. You said a few
kind words before you resumed your monologue
to the bewildered passing by. You keep talking
transcendental metaphysics. Is that what it's
called?

You punctuate your speech with nails, with glass,
with mirrors, with chrome. With sharpness and
always some danger of a stab or jagged edge.

You punctuate your speech with darkness. We are
another life form in the city. Your voice grows
throaty, rasping, terrifying. No one dancing here.
My eyes see no one dancing here. But you are gone
like a Sufi.

You conceal the tube of your torso

open-mouthed

undernourished

In the minds of the Dogon, aesthetic emotion and the
expansion of death are linked.

Like a statue

I recall you

Shoes echoing against the granite ground.

You in the city changed my force around. I was
drained from the feet now with our constant walking.
Walking replaced talking to some extent and the rhythm
kept us going although we turned in circles after a

while, circumambulating the same monuments, going
under arches just one last time, riding buses and
trains that returned to their places of departure
which were always, constantly, our destinations.
We were caught on a kind of wheel. The desert seemed
behind us as I write, not ahead of us as we lived.

I was afraid you'd stop talking, so I goaded
you into taking chances. We tried braving traffic
after a while. Fast-moving vehicles and persons
whizzed by us, kicking us with their sharp
brutalities. Was this hostile world only in
my mind? We learned to absorb their cruelty
and speed, yet we struggled against, and resisted
their dominion. We almost stopped breathing
to avoid taking too much of them in. You spoke less.

We needed a change. To lead you out of here.
If you spoke less as seemed to be the trend, I'd
dry up too. A point for departure.

Myth takes precedence over, I want to say, forms.
Or myth forms procedure. A magical formula and
transformation outside the propaganda of cities.
Eroticism never ruled us, but rather the dream
of an earlier world, returning to the childhood
of civilizations, took hold here. The lost dance,
the lost carving. Cities like this one had become
too feverishly congested. Layers of time were
obscured by hum and buzz.

Vestiges of evolution seemed lost in their power
to change us. Get out of here I said, and get
you out of here too, I remembered.

You represented now to me, false tradition,
Western illusion. You had crumbled under the
beast. You hadn't conquered. The quality of
materialism was as menacing as ever.
I blindfolded you and pulled you free of the
tentacles of this false civilization.
We headed for a calmer mode. You started
talking again. My ideas spilled forth on the
desert. And now the military regard us with
suspicion as our mission continues.

You are perceived as the more dangerous one,
as you talk and talk. You are like the priapic
column of the toa wood. You are a threat
as you speak of the destruction of the golden
city (it lies on the western edge of the desert).
You set yourself apart. You represent unbounded
opinion. You no longer look at me. I who lead
you back to the desert. I who saved you.
No one is listening to you out here. Why do they
care? Don't fall short on me, comrade.
You've been to the city. You've seen the
face of the city idols. You can't keep this
up. My shelves sag under the weight of your
teachings. My cave is a repository of the
inconsequence of your individuation. My heart
is sore with our struggle. My mind no longer
functions. I can't control your wild words.

I delivered you up during your last sermon
on the nature of sunlight. I had shaded you long
enough.

Remorse?

Your image on the screen they provide me with
still has the power to drain me further. I go

way back. The world at large has no interest
in the hostage you've become. You are finally
an artifact of speech and dust. I know you are
held under false pretense, but I (old woman)
am powerless to help you in this tainted desert paradise.

The problem of darkness and light has not been
solved. I have the despair of a scientist and
am barely legible now on the page.

Grasping-The-Broom-More-Tightly-Now

# XI

## SHIVA RATRI

*The poet travels to Bali with her son, studies language, gamelan, religion & ritual. Listens to phenomena carefully, observing at close range the interlocking cycles of time in tune with a natural cosmos. Calls on the deities to help her in her quest for power. She would like to be a pamurtian — a gigantic supernatural being with thousands of heads & arms brandishing weapons. Weapons like articulate speech & poetry, beauty. This is her basic image of herself. Hardly ever sleeps. The "male" here is more dormant deity, integrated into a transcendent yet powerful hermaphrodite consciousness & the dust of her pencil. She shares time with a "double" — a brother/sister figure who gives her secret maps to the island, and gestural codes of appropriate speech & mudra. She sheds an obsession with Western civilization's maniacal stranglehold on genetic consciousness. How to change rhythms on a cellular level is the great conundrum. She moves in circles, not lines. Why would anyone think the contrary?*


I see you everywhere

          *di mana-mana*

& the light of our day
speaks through us

I study you,
   eyes
   ears
   nose
      hair

*apa kabar?*
*baik baik*

                   I see you everywhere
                      & walking

*salamat jalan*
What is our language?

the study of thinking
   & through the mind to the melody we will play
together
or apart
              walking
a man walking                       What's your name
                 *siapa namanya?*
with whom do you walk?

                I'm lost (*saya tersesat*)
I practice the syllables of your history Bali
I see you everywhere

because I am lost
          I see you everywhere
You speak
any questions (*Ada pertanyaan*)
There is no answer to love
 *Tidak ada jawaban*

*melihat, menonton, membaca*
                (to see, to watch, to read)
       I am a "penulis puisi"

a penniless poetry

    I come into you from a great distance a penniless poetry

You are my pitch
my sound my song
          (the holy 3)
*rendah, suara, lagu*

I sing you my beloved because I am lost without you
              Is it forbidden?

*listrik mati*
I am dead without you

How many times I think "I am dead without you"
 *capi apa?*
                            I look for my own eyes
& for the switch to bring them on again
I see you everywhere
                                        *di mana-mana*
        be still be silent
                        this is *nipu sipi (nyepi)*
 the whole world died, no fire, murder the fire

I was lost when they murdered the fire
                        the whole world died
This is the child's first lesson
Bahasa Indonesia

        it is a simple tongue
tongue of the child
                                lost everywhere without
my child-man-speech
        guide to the temple
you must go there with torch, he says
*listrik mati*
                dead in the cave lost without you
    child-man-deity
    call upon you as guide

call to the *langit gringsing wayang*
                flaming heaven of the *wayang*
        call to my ancestors who live inside me everywhere
                & abandon me in my weakness
                        not making the proper ceremonies

Call upon Giri Putri, Dewi Gangga, Dewi Danu
Call Mother Uma
Stave off Durga
                        all could die here
                        in me

                    murder the fire

I see you everywhere

                    (di mana-mana)

        Beloved Indra, active and warlike

    you bring down the rain to cleanse this heart

            everywhere that existed once dies now


            it dies as I call upon you


Batara Siwa, divine hermaphrodite
                source of all life, Windu          that
        takest away the static of the world
                            blow upon us
                bring down the rain to cleanse this fire
        (for I am burning, burning)          dear shape-shifter, dear Iovis
                            who are you?
this is the dark moon of the ninth month
the puppets dance to activate the mind
        toward what great comedies & miracles?


Siwa once upon a time created beings with no ethics, no *sila,* no code of behav-
ior, who went naked lived wild in cages, had no religion. They mated under
trees in the light of day, abandoned their sad children, ate offal, lived like beasts.
Siwa was so horrified he imagined a son to destroy these humans. He was cop-
ulating with his wife, he was coming into her, he was excited with his plan, his
great revenge on the monsters he himself had created and he told her, he told
Uma his intentions. (He was fucking himself here.) She was indignant and
withdrew from him quickly and in the struggle Siwa's sperm fell on the
ground. He panicked, he called the gods together and pointing to the sperm
said that should it develop life there would be great difficulties for them. The
alarmed gods began to shoot arrows at the sperm. The sperm grew a pair of
shoulders when the first arrow struck it, hands and feet popped out after the
second, and as they continued to shoot into it, the drop of sperm grew into a
fantastical giant who stood as high as a mountain, demanding food with which

to pacify his insatiable hunger. Siwa named him Kala and every day sent him
down to earth where he could eat his fill of people.

thus the barbarians dwindled

(put out the fire)

but again
it comes back
again, again

again
but do you hear
it when it comes?
the fire, can you hear it?

in its signal its plea
to not escape burning, burning
not to escape the comedy of burning,
miracle of burning
nor not be witness
to me, newly charged with power coming out of the dangerous cave
     *(tenget, angker)*
                        manifesting one's holiness
       *(mawinten)* to bring out
the dormant power

come out!
come out now!
you can come out now

Take my tongue and inscribe on it all
the magic syllables
         ANG UNG MANG
make my voice sweet with the inscriptions
of honey

Make my epic, my song of male *sakti,* sing!

I'll be Rangda
I'd be Durga to pursue you, male,
   seeing you everywhere
                     *di mana-mana*

once I was *sebel*
now I'm clean

      seeing you everywhere
              *(di mana-mana)*

cleansed by seeing you everywhere
put out this fire with *tirta*

(Kala Rahu swallows the moon)

again, it comes back again
during the eclipse of the moon

      (Beggar's Bush, February, we sit drinking
      *brem-arak)*

a full moon

  *bulan purnama*

eclipse of the full moon

put me in thrall

          blaming you, the child
          & you, the man

*menjual apa?*
        (what do you sell?)

& what do you see in me

*cari apa?*
                    (what do you look for?)
                    (in me)

I think in order to live
& live by seeing you everywhere
                              *di mana-mana*

to receive love
*(terima kasih)*

& seeing in me the one-staying-up-at-night

                    *(bergadang semalam sentuh)*

the one-burning-at-night-receiving-love

I am a carrier of this great love
                              *di mana-mana*


a language:what? speaks in tongues:what? knows
no bondage: what? lasts the night: what? slaves
by day: who? tends the rice: who? sweeps the
steps: who? tends the temple: he does. waits
by day: who? goes into trance: who? puts on
the mask: he does. dances with sword: he does.
climbs the mountain: many do this. walks in a
figure 8 (*ngumbang*): many do this. breaks for
a while (*angsel*): many do this. interprets the
"right": he does. interprets the "left": she does.
listens with 2 sets of ears: he does. binds
his breasts: he does. wanders off: who?
supplicates the deities: they all do this.
another language: whose? what does he say?
the answer is always yes. *Senang makan nasi?*
(do you like rice?): yes.

stand before me
of which object, me
you are part &
parting of

I will see you
or you are
never seen
by me again

& I am again
just here
at it again
seeing you

green duty
calling me
again to
what song?

Nothing but you
new in the path
of my sun
Come back or call

Reminding
I mean, remind me!
A tough number
to learn

The one with "exit"
all over the face
astride your
speech or heart

in a rapport
with thought
impulse
action

I'm the total they add to, and you have to have arms
for the woman, you know. Slow down, my genes do not
carry the same messages. Rancor? No, messages
like the one on at night, with flashes glowing at
the boundaries of the nucleus. I see them, but they
also see you. You who constitute the Balinese
universe: upper, immediate, lower worlds.

    Dear Naga Banda,
     We cling to you, the priest giving life to
you *(pedanda boda)* the priest taking it way *(pedanda siwa)*. We cling to you,
vehicle for the soul into heaven,
phallic channel to heaven. . . .

        *Hari apa hari ini?*

what is the date today?

the date of my cremation, for I am burning, burning

 the snake awaits me in the channel to new life

               *di mana-mana*
what stays? nothing
what continues: no thing
who asks? I do

(the husband dreams I am the serpent, and he must
crush me in my power, writhing like a wild thing
on the kitchen floor. Mercy!
I am merely a long rope bound in greencloth,
with a great mane of *lalang* grass, effigy of the
serpent, mere effigy woman becoming man becoming
woman becoming man again. Mercy!
I flail under the boot)

        the whole world dies again
        no fire, not allowed to light the lamp

fire in the body?
murder that fire

It's *shiva latri,* night of Shiva

with a full moon, a red dot in the heavens
now wake the fire!

I'll play the
wife of Shiva
& we go dancing
to an old sweet
ancestor tune
& when you fall
I'll bow down to
pick up the
pieces of you
eclipsed
by the night
of me, the dreamer
(nothing compares to you)

*di mana-mana*

and I sing of how nothing compares:

(blinding green, eyes tear
    on the back of the bike)

because it is early
& you are beautiful
weep for how early it is
how beautiful you are

    and the debts to pay
because it is thus:

how early it is, and beautiful

debts to the teachers *(resi)*
    to the ancestors *(pitra)*
        to gods & self *(dewata)*

how early
in
us

some days I resume color
for I walked too far

        are you there?
        are you there but silent?
        did the world die?

did you do the proper chants?
did you perform the proper ceremonies?
are you restless *(gelisah)*?

I am mere body-bone
I break & wither
I burn in the fire
I am clever that way
I weep
I disappear
what am I?

I go a lot of places
I study language for a penniless poesy I reap what I sow
what am I?

I beg you this heart is broken
It eats itself
It is self wounding
what kind of heart is this?

I came here to study
I came here to dance
I beat the gong with a steady hand

I left something behind
what was it?

   (I need this burning in order to live)


the poet needs these three (in order to live)

*vyutpatti,* culture, or vast knowledge of the world

*abyhasa*, a skill with language developed from constant
practice & apprenticeship with a master

*shakti,* creative power

                    no posturing

             her teaching is you, man
             or you, man-woman who stands in for phenomena
      & you    siddhas
             flaming languages
        erudite
             or simple

                  & wherever the energy is,
                            seize it!

grabbing the power from the male deities

             she lives inside them

they haunt her
eclipse her
increment by increment

a kind of bondage
& then she transmutes their form
(eyes & skull)
                  to her own
eyes in every pore of her body cervix is the window of her world

Dear Deity,

Thank you for showing me around the island. Now I am lost. In the best sense. Now I am *kerawuhan* (possessed). I no longer own this body. I dance for the gods (including you). I dance in front of the dolls, the effigies, all the ones gone before me, all ancestors, lovers, poets. I recognize your world. Holy shadows on the screen, ho! Thank you for the drinks, the cigarettes of clove, imagination, and for pointing to the code the smallest increments of which I would honor & obey. You lead with your heart. *Terima kasih*

Anne-Who-Burns

> *Singo nodo gegere*
>> (The roar of a lion)
> *Sang dewoto kabeh*
>> (And all the dogs took flight)
> *Wojo kasilat*
>> (It had teeth exposed like fangs)
> *Wiyung tutup kadi pereng*
>> (Lips as wide as valleys)
> *Rejeng irung kadi sumur bandung*
>> (A nose deep as a well)

Eyes like twin suns
   (*Netro kadi suryo kembar*)
*Kerananiro kadi layaran*
   (Ears large like 2 sails)
*Rambut kuwel agimbal*
   (Hair ratted & matted)
So tall was he that he caused fright
   (*Ogah uger luguriro kang girigiri*)
He was so tall he covered half the sky
   (*Luthuriro tanpo toro*
   *Tutup kemadiane akoso*)


the green idol
on board the *bemo*
go beyond knowing this or that

little green idol
match lights up
this or that is not strange
points to volcano
I am here
with my little green idol
his flowering top
his glowing eyes gone beyond this or that
the battleground inside him
is the playground of the green idol's heart

(see him everywhere   *di mana mana*)

In Bali there are small but very mean dogs that bark all night. And their eyes glow when you shine a flashlight. And there are motorcycles all over the place. And twelve-year-olds drive them. And babies ride on the back and they are crazy drivers.

The island is very green. There are things called rice fields that are everywhere.

The market is smelly and there are flies everywhere. We bought mangosteens and two out of five were good. Things in the market are cheap.

> the puppets are asleep in the box
> we never talk about time
> the puppets become shadows
> you start to make them from the eyes
> then make the rest come alive
> this is the creation of the world
> the *dalang* is god
> the screen is the world
> the oil lamp is the sun
> we never talk about time

Yet in sketching
the lines "do you? do you?"
& "you do if it pleases?"
do you not
sketch
the knots
that mount
to greet you?

around a shield
or warrior-stick
life guides
the writer
to the
morsel

again
again might drive in
something
outside
the focus
of someone

writing that details
texture
& is real too
by turns

looking for
the right time
in (on)
the man's wrist

then something
(the white plastic watch band)
explodes the portrait
as well as
looking for it

(see you everywhere)
in time


if all's well
eclipse precepts
*salamat malam*
or taste or hear
deflecting options
which allow for
language
who speaks here?

        he does, and does he quarrel?

he does, and does he strive?

    he does

& does he dance?

he does, on many a corpse

he carries the tusk
he carries scars
he bends over his magic
he has magic to burn

        Victor is in his cups tonight!         The moon goes black
        I ask for more
        more blackness, more light
        more firewater

    he complies, but does he?

  amenable to night & a foreign tune (blues?)

I turn
& your eyes are also on the sky
your eyes which are his, and are his too
all the "his" of eyes on the sky

are you the shadow next to me or
　　are you the shadow next to me

　　　who are you?

　　　　　　　his eyes?
(the moon goes out)

　　　　　　*listrik mati*

I give up everything to know you

　　　　　*kenapa? kenapa?*

　　you tell me
　　　& tell me again

she lives inside them, she lives inside him, she
lives in the corner of his eye, she writes as
woman-who-had-stretched-to-this-point, to the
point of an eye or corner of "his" eye she writes
as one abused, she writes as collaborator, she writes
now she writes later

　　　　　She-as-describer is always a person

wasted old widow, prostitute & eater of infants, she comes to spread death &
plague on the land

Rangda danced by a single male

eyes bulge from her head
tusk-teeth curve upward
& fangs protrude down over her chin
hair a matted tangle
breasts: withered & pendulous dugs
hair hanging between them like tubular sausages
her long red tongue is a river of fire
amok Rangda! *enter here*
she splays her ghostly hands from which extend

long clawlike fingernails
*(wild clanging of gamelan)*
*several minor witches (male dancers) toss the corpse of a stillborn babe around*
shrill satanic laughter
she clutches a magical white *shakti* handkerchief
Rangda-Durga, Shiva's malignant consort *enter here*
Barong *enter here,* challenge her horror here
with puppy hilarity
entranced men rise, gone into *nadi,* become *nadi*
& stab themselves with kris dagger
shaped like sound wave, sea wave,
vibration of universe
they gobble live chicks
wildly convulse in the mud
drop into coma

go, gone, gone beyond into trance
these deities are presences
go, gone, gone into *nadi*
startled into *nadi,* gone.

& every syllable is conscious
    & the unconscious, too, structured like a language
language moving us up & down

Is it revealed to the man? Is it revealed to the woman?
Is it only revealed to the man?
Two protagonists struggle for dominance

the imagined world is quite real, a tree with its roots
in heaven, tree rooted in highest heaven, one branch
goes into "god" itself, the branches are sentences, the
leaves are like words
    language a living system in the zone of convergence

rhythm, pace, sonic blast, parapraxes
    inherent in my nervous system
                a patterning to live for

what does it mean to rot?
holding out against experience
                             & my words not to sing
but entheogenic, entheogenic!
             liquid, sap, blood, semen will nourish my words

image forth naming
image forth naming

                       dear Gabriel (Angel of Words)
                          hear my plea

 hear my plea to name the cause "ambivalent"
Candidasa at night:
I believe in the exquisite manners of the gentleman
& yet I look for a telephone in the dark
I am not crazy I don't abandon anyone
Everyone is partially true because everyone is already dead
Water beats against the stone walls
They only chide who wish me ill
No temples here the sea is alive
I walk a tighter, tightening rope
unless to believe "to cut through the veil of outward form,
    dissolve in air" is a human solution
6,000 rupiahs for the night

"When I was a child, I learned that the moon was goddess
Dewi Ratih. Then Neil Armstrong landed on it. I still look
up at night and pray to Dewi Ratih."


step through the *candi bentar*
enter your own life
You walk through the split in your life
you are half male, half female
you are never too late to meet yourself halfway
each step brings you closer to the split that forced you here
arriving in a red car, a white car
into the inner temple of your mind

look. . . .

it's simple.

I'm no fool.

I cross every ocean, reach every foreign shore, leave my home
to acquire wisdom, you friend of my heart, you friend of my
secret passion. You need not ask, I join every adventurous
trip, I join you faithfully, taking care of those parts
you leave in my charge. This, because I honor you.
I haven't cut my hair, it looks alright even for conservatives,
since I wear no moustache anymore. In the West, it seems
to be better like this, but in Indonesia, a moustache is more
advantageous.

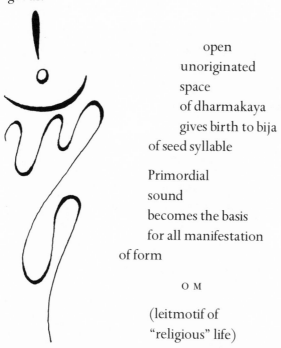

open
unoriginated
space
of dharmakaya
gives birth to bija
of seed syllable

Primordial
sound
becomes the basis
for all manifestation
of form

O M

(leitmotif of
"religious" life)

Mantras grow from experience &
from the collective knowledge
of many generations

HO HUM

(without fear/without hope)

ONG!

*di mana-mana*
I fear you go from me, language
when the world goes dead, goes silent
& I was burning burning
I fear you sleep too long


Peliatan: the night, the table, the books, the "spirits"
   & who are you?
                           (I fear I slept too long)
I see you everywhere
   the cues (*sasmita*) are transmitted musically visually verbally

   what signals us here?
what pulls us into motion, what navigates our forms?
what priest is behind all this, activating our tongues
what got left behind when we agreed to enter this day together?
what intersected with what?
what cycle are you on?
      the loop or the coil
                  tearing about the island to see, to see
to burn, to see
(even requests for drinks, cigarettes, or betel nut
are made through the mouths of the *wayang* puppets)


who is alluding to whom on what screen or otherwise
field of play, field of Mars

what forfeits itself to coexist

what does the boy say who sobs as he departs
("how was your trip?" (he shrugs) "okay")

                       (nuance vs. nonchalance)

inviting the voice to speak
it arises out of chaos
& I am burning burning

my wit (it burns)
my grand style (burning)
my books (burn them!)
special privileges (burning)
who's talking (I burn)
shut the man down who crosses me here (burn him!)

(Rent a motorbike for a week & ride it all over Bali)

returning to the source of shut down! shut down!

silence the chromosomes one small day


"I was talking about time"
"So?"
"I was talking about real time"
"Brahma dreamed it"
"Was he lying to save us?"
"Lying by dreaming?"
"Yes"
"Were you inspired"
"I was & said so"
"How 'mantra' of you"
"You joke with me"
"I spied myself inside blinding green"
"It was the last color to come into consciousness you know"
"I didn't"
"Didn't what?"
"Didn't know"
"Green is like that, coming later"
"Maybe we were too narrow to see it"
"Just blue & yellow, sea & sun"
"But here it enters your veins, your skin turns green"
"You become the green deity"
"I'll pray for you"
"It won't help"

"It was always there, we didn't see it"

"It was hiding under the desert"

"I couldn't look when I landed it was too vivid"

"Everyone spies it & is afraid"

"Afraid of what"

"Of losing it after they see it"

"It makes them happy"

"A kind of parlance, weary traveller"

"It still makes them happy after they lose it"

"Green makes them feel alive"

"I'm not exempt"

"I paid for this with good green money"

"Are you proud?"

"Like most men"

Dear Grandfather,

It takes 23 hours to get to Bali and a little less going back. For us, it took longer to get back. On the way there we stopped in Salt Lake City, then Los Angeles, then in Honolulu, then in Irian Jaya (near Papua New Guinea), then you get to Bali. On the way back our plane broke down in Irian Jaya (Biak). First they said the plane would be fixed in one hour, then they said we'd have to say two nights! But luckily we only stayed one. They took our passports and our tickets and we had to stay in a funky hotel called Hotel Irian. In the lobby people were watching a Mohammed Ali boxing match, or was it Leon Spinks? from 1976. We had eaten on the plane (but I didn't eat). We couldn't make a call out of Indonesia. We went to the market in the morning after a very funky breakfast. We saw dancers at the airport who wore grass skirts and painted faces and had guitars and drums and spears. This was interesting. Finally they got us a plane from Jakarta to take us to Honolulu, then to L.A. Then we changed planes and came to Denver.

Love,

Ambrose

# XII

PUER SPEAKS

*Indonesia has softened her competitiveness. The poet can finally resemble the boy in herself, having had extensive "Puer" dreams. This possible, too, as she ages, having shed seductive submissive ingenue. She doesn't want to always be irritant. Thus poet becomes name of a boy for the time being. And takes on implications of Muse ("mouth-forming words") & then puts those new mixes into boxes, assured now of a place on the page. Windows are two-ways and can be locked.*

Somewhere the boy rises up in me. And the words become chants of mock battle or curiosity. For curiosity is the boy's guest-song. What is he looking for on every landscape on every planet in every woman's face, ear or belly? He sleeps inside me on my shoulder, shoulder which sleeps inside me dreaming of holding up the world, holding up the sky. To shoulder it and play with it gently, to mock and tease the elders, to be naughty and eschew sleep, he thinks. I go out with the men as their boy. And as a young girl, too, I am one of them, not a camp follower. The initiation is words which forge the muse upon me. She thrusts herself at me, she challenges me to be my first woman ever, to guide and show me passion. She teaches me the words *laterly, labia majora.* She teaches me *mons* and *Euterpe,* she is the concept I have of mouth-forming words. But they, the men, are rough and cut the sentiments from the bone. Go on, they mock me, show us your mettle, show us you aren't lovesick, romantic, a fool for a turn of phrase, for a twist in sound to match your eye, go on, show us you can piss and sweat and scorn the ridiculous mother. Show us you can do without water, light, fossil fuel. Show us the poem, of what it's made. How diamondlike it might be if you don't bend it to your weak woman's will. Show us, boy. The initiation is how I will descend to meet the mid-age hag, wrinkled 'eld, how this boy, young-spirit maverick, cowboy, this young soldier will fight through his life ah humming! toward the castle. Don't kill him, don't, but neither trophy hung for a puerile adventure. What were the words? They were *rock, salt, stone, arrow, intent, jump, dare.* They were *jaunty, jest, armor, pistol, poke, drive, penis.* They were mysterious: *jockey for power, jockey shorts, jock strap.* They were innocents in their lostness to experience, for what was experience but a dream to this slip-of-a-boy? I played the tomboy, I wore pants, I was just setting out to make my fortune, to swell the tide in my favor, to impress the others, to see real gold. To touch the lands of France, England, Egypt, Italy. I was 18 years, knapsack on back aright, eyes gaze forward to shore, I see land. And I see the monsters on that foreign land I have come to conquer. Who grants me their sword, albeit kindly blunted for a young man. Youth is in the clothing, in the color of cheek, in the desire for mix and talk around a fire. In the dirty shoe and sock. I hid in these clothes and wooed women. Yet I freed myself from women, I wooed men. I abdicated the mother's hearth. Back off, mother, I go now. Language assist me in this rite. I have learned to charm snakes. On the desert the scorpions hide from me as I recite the secret mantra of universal youth. I converse in tongues. I keep up with the best of them. I don't have to be an object of their desire. I can feed tigers if I wish and ride the backs of elephants. The old men like me; I am their young friend. I climb trees for coconuts. I resist the clutches of the mothers who want every young son claimed for insatiable lust. I write to keep myself pure. I study the stars for purposes of navigation. I travel under sea to the center of fire. I ride porpoises to learn about sound and motion.

I am buoyant. I won't fight with my fists. My muscles grow. I study the forms of other men and their words. Soon I can swear with the best of them. I write for my comrades as Dante did. I show them how the quest in me is to reach them through words, to make words dance out of a body without breasts and womb, or to take that body and establish the will of a man coming to life, just coming to life. Male poet on the brink of his/her fortune, no one can lean on me. A solo act. A first chance to fail to not ask the right questions as I enter the castle. To forfeit knighthood awhile. To come before all the goddesses of thunder and song as a novice, stealing their power. They don't recognize me I've grown. No one lean on me yet.

Puer, Nom de Guerre

> caveat

> or front the ticket
> he tricks me
>    (gets dressed)

cover sex
covert

boy to
part
closer
brace for the turn

she like to me
blurts
organ! organ!

from a shrine
to fortress

blind, her blind

semi

autonomous

from the lunar

courtesy

misrule abuses

what causes

       slick & chance

slavo-

realm

sleeping partners

going out in currency

be a man

         to

affront her nub

& temerity

assists Lysander

nope, don't

Mace
a trademark


war is


a sub-kingdom of this

boy poke

like as to persist



grand slam

as in the game

slit trench

spare

men or boys'

body parts

neutrino

difficult to explain

he-me

he-she

plots

as to a tuck

shine back

vent the

cloth

rend veil

or scream    same as you

boy

chance it

tattoo

saw me

nude, hide

stay the push

      pleasure's drive

 

      position

facing east

      still in the closet

 

"he" lied?

paid well

      for "it"

 

on an exception

to the Academic

spelled me

then submit

to document

I see

static lover

switch

& side with

the other side

of her

onanism?

high sierras

land this escape

for her she

will, she

won't

be gone

boy to

light up

lie down

I see the battles

ground of

all your dust

sex-dust

wither

eros

name of

her spot

banishes me        boy gear

put it on

Adorno

settle throat,

obdurate one

not the boy

wound about word-

object

of desire

from distance

speaks objects

rant or

spewthroe of

her hate/

her love

obliges this

She-He

obfuscates

the interior

pleas

take me

consort

with the

matrix

boy

rise up paginal

# XIII

## AEITIOLOGICAL ONES

*She worries about unsung heroes, migrating, restless wanderers, including her own father who has become an active correspondent to the poem, and makes a list of the conquered towns he moved through in Europe. Out on the town she hungers for conversation for the poem, visits her blond friend Robert who shows her some secret treasures and tells a little of his story which interests her as he is quintessential American male whose father worked for the industrial-military-nuclear complex. She has met quite a few men like this — would-be albeit tattered bodhisattvas who live in poetic shadows expiating the sins of their fathers. She prepares for a trip to Prague and other parts of German Europe. She dreams about Ludwig Wittgenstein while she grows nervous about the impending war.*

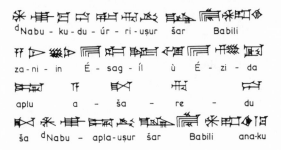

ᵈNabu - ku - du - úr - ri -uṣur    šar    Babili

za - ni - in    É - sag - íl    ù    É - zi - da

aplu    a - ša - re - du

ša    ᵈNabu - apla-uṣur    šar    Babili    ana-ku

XXXXXXXXXXX

"NEBUCHADNEZZAR, KING OF BABYLON,

WHO PROVIDES FOR ESAGILA AND EZIDA,

THE ELDEST SON OF NABOPOLLASSAR,

KING OF BABYLON, AM I."

(The last phrase, "am I," is omitted from many bricks.)

Dear John Waldman,

You have very sane handwriting; did you ever notice? I think I've inherited my sanity from you. Our Frances was intense, she treated me as a lover. Jealous, why? Do you have any ideas? Am I off the wall? Was I the fulfilled artist she/you wanted to be? Heroic ideal of some kind maybe. It's complex when you gaze deep into the eyes of this thing. Thank you for your sanity, albeit its neurotic edge.

I appreciate saying this to you tonight because there should be no claustrophobic barriers between us. Please don't hesitate when it comes to your truth. I try to write in a cult of truth. I suppose I've been the "armored Amazon," as pop psychology describes, taking on your male attributes because you were detached, sometimes passive. You suffered, survived the war, and shouldered the responsibility of supporting us as a family. This was exhausting. So proud, you working at the drug clinic all those years too, keeping in touch with the darker realities of addiction. I am grateful and for the "moral" support you always gave when I wanted to shift in another direction. Did you ever feel that you couldn't speak what you felt, that your throat was literally blocked? This is why I write, keep writing.

When you weren't "there" where were you? Off in your fantasies as I am? An overactive imagination? She probably guarded you in her protective zone. A kind of radial belt. And she went off & enacted all the guises of woman & came back to tell you the stories. She certainly had an ear for other people.

I see you in mind in a modest wooden rowboat on Union Lake fishing. Early memory. Or reading a book. Somewhat the same meditative presence you carry. And I see myself on your lap in your uniform of the Great War, you are smiling. What's hidden? "Dandled."

I would love you to come to the "Zen weekend." It might prove interesting, provocative to you. You don't have to get up like the rest of us at 4 A.M.

Sorry about the "ativan." Bernadette's d.o.c. too. It's hopeless to procure such a drug in, as Ambrose says, "health-nut" Boulder without a scrip.

I hope something works out for you. . . . Remember the moods aren't solid and see, as the Balinese do, that every thing moves in its own distinct cycle of time & happily intersects when it does with other " things." "When a body meet a body" . . . Many many wheels & shifting gears. I'm glad we meet at the interstices of light & sorrow, and you my father be. Off to Prague soon. Allen Ginsberg will crown the new "King of May."

*Dobre jitro*

*Jak se mate?*

*Kolik je hodin?*

*Jake je pocasi?*

*Nerozumin Vam.*

*Odkud prichazite?*

*Na shledanou . . .*

(my heart breaks like my father's before me AH-YA)
I wanted to be Queen, but . . .


You reduce me to an object of desire. My breasts say this because they are wise.
My cunt says this because it is wise. My thighs are responding to the accusation
because they are wise. Eyes behold a thousand reasons you do this, you who are
groping for the be all & end all here, you who take a proverbial turn at the
wheel & navigate us out of sync. Sync is the new age number for it is the is the
is the number. Turn on the radio. Good luck. You reduce me to an object of
desire. You think I'm hot. You take my words and twist them to a recommen-
dation for a scenario of desire. Is desire lively? Does it live? Is it sending the vo-
taries forward, does the Man regress as He checks his watch to obviate time?
Check this out: A long way back, & now in Saudi the women can't drive cars.
They can, of course, but may they? May they? Does anyone, (they), care? The
light goes off, you reach for my neck. I love you. I'm not ashamed to admit this
for you are the saint & scholar who studies desire. I came into view as a repre-
sentation of an object of desire. Good luck, I said to myself. The night is youth-
ful. It smarts of love & sweat. I love you because you are fatal. And mortal too.
We will die in desire & spend the context of breath & night on a boat of love. You
coaxed me into a rehearsal of dying into life. You feel it? That the heart could
continue at any cost, that the cost would be everything, that cost is the tomb of
desire that it rides into dawn, always, always. And is an *alba* for you. It only exists
at dawn when the bottle is empty& we've smoked under talk. For talk is the

witch & it is my voice that attracts the battle in you. That says okay test me in
your language. In the code of the male. I encode you. I take each phoneme and
rake it over the coals. It imprints on me the message that held you back. Unseen
ropes scored a hand. And bound & gagged the truth be told. You are a compli-
ment to the room. You are intrusive like any good idea.

dexterous
    a kind
of
    truncating:
dancing
a kind of
naming
going to be,
but
        always
    quid pro quo
our #1 obsession:

overthow the little countries
& you are really
running
    no longer dancing

up the angst-gangster stair

    like a
line of
scrimmage


Shamir rebuffs Gorbachev on emigres, Arabs applaud Gorbachev remark, Bush
nudges China on anniversary of crackdown, Cambodia talks collapse, Con-
gress looks anew at ties with Vietnam, A Beirut "cease-fire" is but a weary inter-
lude, President Samuel K. Doe of Liberia is facing the most serious crisis of his
ten years in power, Mandela, off on world trip, will urge retention of sanctions,
rainy days in Zambia, Bush and Colombian President to assess drug wars today,
Canada premiers try to save pact, Dubcek rebukes Slovak protestors who re-

buked Havel, Japanese feel quite ready for a visit from Gorbachev, White House sees aura from summit, in Europe few are cheering, Summit failed to narrow dispute on Afghanistan, Santiago: Allende's widow meditates anew

And he writes me all the towns he passed through:
Marseilles, 5 Nov 44 St Barbe, 8 Nov St Benoit, 17 Nov Bertrichamps, 21 Nov Reon L'Etape, 23 Nov Moyenmoutier (Thanksgiving), 24 Nov St Blaise, 25 Nov Rothau, 26 Nov Uberhaslach to rendezvous Area, Moyenmoutier, 27 Nov Biber-skirch (end of Alsace campaign) 2 Dec Bust-Struth, 3 Dec Puberg, 6 Dec Goetzenbruch, 12 Dec Lemberg, 22 Dec Petit Rederching, 23 Dec Siersthal, 25 Dec Guisberg and back to Sierthal, 2 Jan Petit Rederching, 22 Jan Mountbronn, 25 Jan Petit Rederching, 29 Jan Mountbronn, 14 March Holbach (Paris, Nancy), 17 March Schorbach, 22 March Thru Bitche and Maginot Line on into Contwig, Germany passing thru the Siegfried Line, 23 March Maxdorf, 24 March Rehhutte, 31 March Crossed Rhine, thru Mannheim to Swetzingen, 3 Apr Es-chelbach-Rappenau, 4 April Frankenbach, 5 Apr Bad Wimpfen, 14 Apr Crossed Neckar River thru Heilbronn to Weinsberg-Sulzbach, 15 Apr Rappach, 17 Apr Gleichen, 18 Apr Hutten, 20 Apr Edelmannshof, 21 Apr Steinach, 22 Apr Baltmannsweiler, 24 Apr Rommelshausen, Unter Urbach, Schorndorf, Haubersbroun, Unterschelecttback, Schwabish Gmund, Altes Lager (one week in field), Schwabish Gmund, 28 June Heubach, 7 July Herrenberg to Stuttgart, Return trip Karlsruhe, Strasbourg, Le Havre and

got boat

there

Yankee don't go . . .

rectangular space
within the girl who never-went-to-war
who sees stillbirth aftermath of
such a conflagration
collapse of every communism
& all false boundaries challenged

parent form what
comes from it?

prowling in the mind
of what bargain what power
what way she might turn:
bootless solitude
of the caged humiliation  •
of any undernourished nation
other-curtained
sun metamorphosed
as eye & yolk, diamond
patterns in the hair,
on the feet she walks
and when she does
she walks toward the new countries
all of them, "what's a nation?"
under what god, guise flag banner wave

(give me a break)

*no es lá*

whatever

you say

it is

is what you say

we, who are we

who are touched

*(père et son fille)*

sa *fille*

& map a strategy

Dear Anne,

I remembered when you wrote to me about the past that I stuck away some letters I recovered from 501 E. Main Street before the house was sold. I've numbered them in the upper left hand corner from 1 to 11 so you'll know which ones I'm referring to in my comments. They're all from my father to my mother beginning from 1902 to 1908.

#1. Addressed to Rio (long i pronunciation) Grande, this is of course where the four Hand girls and one boy were born. The girls: Sarah, Stella, Lillian and Idona. The boy: Leander. Sarah was Aunt Sally to me – she was much older than the other girls, by 10 or 15 years. (I don't know why the gap.) Stella was the one who went to the West Coast, was a prison matron, and then married a rancher (rich) and settled in one of the cattle states – maybe Wyoming. (I'm sorry about my memory – it'll be faulty through all my reflections, but good enough to give you a sense of how things were.) Note the "My Darling" at the heading. This was about the most affectionate term used, although the general tone of the letters show that John was in love with Idona and wanted to marry her.

Anyway, Lillian was Aunt Lilly, also older than Idona, who along with Aunt Sally helped to raise Idona. (Remember, they were all orphans.) Rio Grande in case you don't recall is the village at the entrance of Cape May proper. It's on the sheltered sound where the lumber boats sailed from, and where even today yachts and power boats anchor. That's where the father Thomas Hand (married to Josephine Clarke, I don't know about her early death) sailed from to keep the invitation of a fellow captain to Liverpool. They, the crew, the ship were never seen again. This was probably in the 1880s – over a hundred years ago.

The Church mentioned in #1 is almost certain to be St. Paul's Lutheran, since as you know John's father cofounded it.

The "orders" referred to that put him "out of sorts" are orders for glass bottles, or "little ware" as they were called by the glassblowers who made tiny bottles by hand ¼ oz ,½ oz, 1 oz etc. The blowers worked "piece work," paid by the piece – so no orders – no income. I don't know where he went ice skating, but probably Hawkins Pond, where the present-day high school is located – out Main Street.

Letter #2 was written from Wildwood – that's where my father always went when the glass furnaces shut down for 2mos in the summer. You see, he did make fair money considering he worked only 9+ mos of the year. But it was *hard work;* I know because later I watched a shop in action.

If I've spent this much time on #1, I'll have a book written by letter #11. Look at #10 and #11 now and see that the "boy" referred to is incredulously me at the age of 9 mos. The N. 11th St. address is that of Aunt Lillie when she was living with her husband Irvin Harris, who had a butcher shop in Millville. The marriage didn't last — but that's another story.

#2. Smith Street is where Aunt Sally lived. You can see that Idona moved from house to house. She was the youngest and the sisters felt responsible for her. I forgot to say that Leander, the only son, died of cancer — but I must have been 10 or so by then, since I seem to believe that this was the first time I was exposed to the sense of dread about the illness.

#3. Interesting letter from Washington July 1903 — with the "boys" — fellow glassworkers.

#7. The reference to the bouquet holder is of course a piece of off-hand glassware to be made at the factory (Schettersville plant of the Whitall-Tatum Company in South Millville where my father worked) The oven of course the lair where glassware was placed for slow cooling.

#8 John was going to Camden to meet Idona at the ferry. Why he wanted Ethel (Hollingsworth) to be with her because he would have to leave, I don't know. Mr. Hughes was his immediate boss at the factory.

I'll try to resume sometime in the future when I concentrate and collect my thoughts about the early years. But his little packet of letters almost deserves a poem of its own. Or just some bits and pieces for a longer work by you.

You can imagine a Millville of those days: Coal-fired glass plants — four of them. Two Whitall-Tatums, one Weatons, one Mitchells (also the Manufacturing Co. — textiles); horses and carriages, the business area on High Street; noontime whistles when the workers had dinner. The evening meal was supper. Working hours 6 to 6. Half day on Saturday.
I'm written out, but I'll keep thinking.

Love,

John

can't be turned
away
can't protest
flesh

can't let it
go
can't speak at times
beyond
a daughter

protesting yet in me
in you
in the late
water
the water like shattered glass
lake
what I have done
that flows
on place
on the place
it feels like
in wind

what have I?
a town of not
autumn
not night
staring down
eyes staring down
the mind
to look back
inside sex
the genetics
of how it
can't
be turned
can't
turn back

blast the moment,
come

can't speak at times beyond a sister,
come

O daughter be home, come home

    & to the lair of a canyon come

    I lift his blond hair over his ear as he opens his trunk of magical objects. They bristle with power, skulls and skeletons empowered with his sense of unmitigated life, unmitigated death. It's night I've burned through trying to get lost in words or sympathy if you could say such a thing around him. Nah, can't say it, can't say it around him. Dear Robert. No access to the temperament at hand. He's a search on for me. He obfuscates the power inside the object he hands to me — See? my grandfather's. A gun it was. Is. He has a pent anger. Anger. Pent. Waiting. All of them have the ability to resonate and shine, worn by time and a memory exact as to be painful in the glare of opening such a box to prying eyes. Or is the point to be entrusted here as a point of view he could have and I would bow and follow after. I want to shrink and climb in myself and be one of the things he might bring out after a time and caress.

Inside the room of the Canyon Club, separation is extreme
touch a nerve
touch a bone
a bachelor is exempt from the dream

yet tries hard in the light of its demand
to write, to be a writer, to have written, to have taken
words to the source of replay & bid them stand up in the
room of writing

to exact the debt from the overactive mind
to challenge his imagination
to take the "blondness" out of his eye
to make him my brother forever
slash wrists & exchange blood
(may I say this?)

. . . . . should I ask? . . . . . should I ask of him his destiny . . . . .
. . . . . the bandage of what injury what wound sits on him? . . . .
. . . . . a bandaged hand holds a Mediterranean blue pen of what
origin, writing what words? . . . . a slash on hand, poor hand . . . . .
. . . . . (smashed my hand through glass the night El Presidente
resigns . . . . . and spend the night in St. Vincent's under the portrait
of what Pope's holy eye? . . . . . J.F.K., empathy, time passing . . . . .)

. . . . . Robert's hair is long. He knows how to keep still . . . . .
patience of the inveterate traveller? . . . . . Like an Indian, perhaps,
or ancient scribe. . . . . red socks: how was he thinking when he put
them on was he thinking how red when he put them on, how red? . . . .
A private thought . . . . . He drives home this weekend before she puts
all his stuff out on the road . . . . . should I ask? . . . . . is he the
son of a master on any computer . . . . . should I ask? . . . . . red or
black? . . . . . red and black . . . . . a black rubber accoutrement on
the wrist . . . . . a briefcase (black) parked to one side in a
presence of mind . . . . .
                        He was in China at the place of the terra
cotta warriors . . . . . "communism sucks" . . . . . and the courage of
people under extreme circumstances caught his heart . . . . .
an inflexible language admits only the word "chofa" – "sofa " . . .
. . . . . A father is a kind of power god, master of the nuclear
heaven or nightmare . . . . . technology is not evil but changes
things about the way people live . . . . . Germany . . . . . Hartford . . . . .
Los Alamos . . . . . Encar . . . . . a son of Treva Jeanenne and of Scottish
ancestry he wears both of them . . . . . red, black, yellow, green,
the colors of the Buchanan clan . . . . . how red, should I ask?
when he put them on . . . The wounded writing arm, the wounded
father home late having been scrubbed for 8 hours, no hair left . . . . .
"I was 2 years old". . . . . after being splashed with Plutonium . . . . .
. . . . . should I ask? . . . . . I did . . . . . . Who are you . . . . . I ask who
are you? . . . a pen in a presence of mind facing the person, facing
the page in a desire of the way people live coming from there to here . . . . .

— 198 —

& descend on this one
touch a nerve
touch a bone
His father comtemp with mine
kissed by karma
*adisthanas* of deadly manna
we children of war gone further,
inherit the words, the earth


O Phytalidae!
    . . . receive Demeter into yr house
  O Plant Men
. . . enact the ergon as you mouth the words (mythos)
  . . . take me, an aetiological one, into
            . . . yr male bosom (get me stoned, I never used a weapon)
. . . re-utter the song that makes us
  . . . leap for the crops
I am the contest, the pathos, the epiphany
    *peripeteia* is the number
both, both
  of which I am yr memory
to sing this long epic song


  Dear Blond:

In the dream I was an escaped convict & I'll tell you why:
flames
airplane
held back a gun
killed one too many fathers


The renowned Ginsberg became my lawyer, the celebrated short story writer, Bobbie Hawkins, a surrogate moth. "Anything you say," she said, "I'll believe anything you want to tell me." A surrogate moth and then a mother. I tried to have wings. I set the plane on fire. How? I fly over the burning trees. I burn up in my enthusiasm for action & adventure. Must be Vietnam. I grow ahead of my dream. The lawyer grimaced & chanted the mantra: YOU! YOU! YOU! He was angry. He slammed the door of the ladies' room at the airport (they let you go in there to conduct "business meetings"). A woman was giving birth at the airport. Name her "Jubilate." Name her deo. "dei" to gleam, to shine.

I had been captured. I had escaped. & then I committed the crime of flying low, burning up, killing many fathers. They had the Eastern Eye. They had the epicanthic fold.

In the court, the restaurant of the airport (they let you have trials in there) the Judge, an Irish fellow named Maelstrom X, wore a wig when he said "Next!" Wore a woman's wig when he proclaimed "Not innocent! Not permitted!" Moth-mother held me in her wings, they had grown larger. They were fuzzy like the rug & fuzzy like the trees. Blurred by flames. I held back a gun, I think. It had the mastery of a high-heeled shoe.

Thanks for listening

(dreams can be boring)


dear Anne,

caught ginsberg at Harvard campus reading for AIDS benefit. allen told me he had just gotten back from Nicaragua. but I didn't want to talk about Nicaragua. ginsberg was being ginsberg. I wanted to talk about the passing of Bob Kaufman. and why? because I love poetry and because he was a poetic genius. his poem THE AMERICAN SUN has to be the poem of our decade. what with the President anteing up the defense budget another 3 ½ billion dollars this week I have to ask, "Did Bob get his fellowship. his NEA grant funding, his Guggenheim, his Beatnik festival? After all it is said he coined the word "beatnik"
  we can disdain South Africa but Anne something terrible is happening on the homefront. when I walk into the St. Mark's or Harvard Bookshop and I get a chorus of, "who's Bob Kaufman?"
  & I answer,
  "A visionary, a poet, a genius. He wrote THE ANCIENT RAIN one of the most powerful books of poetry of the decade."
  & I am met with blank stares.

there are dimensions of censorship and one of the worst is silence and neglect.
and I am sad and I am trying to somehow understand,
"What does this mean?"

Sincerely,

R.B.


— The Stone Age culture of ax-makers

— unsung

— know as homo erectus

— unsung

— transformed to the modern homo sapiens

— unsung unsung

— the latter began with the Neanderthal & culminated with

— "modern man"

— sing it! sing it!

How many years? sing it! sing it!

— unsung! unsung!

Africa, a million years ago "Acheuleans"

spread to Eurasia a few hundred thousand years later

(sing, sing)

space shuttle radar detects hidden valleys under the Sahara sands

vegetated & densely inhabited up to 212,000 years

ago (sing o ago, how sing it down down ago)

set down, set down, the honorable load
By Jove, this not be revoked . . .

He is telling the story, telling a story
on the hour
leaving on the hour
the hour if I can hide it
leaving on the hour
to arrive in the context
of another hour
He is telling the revelation of St. John
& the four stages of my apocalypse
prepare the stage, o women the end is at hand
nothing has been changed
only delayed

the demons speak the language of your tribe

So I'll be glad to take one or two questions. So just ask it. And I know
the Secretary would too. Yeah.

Q: Mr. President, did President Mubarak say that Egyptian troops would stand
shoulder to shoulder with American troops in Saudi Arabia?

A: Well, he made clear that they're willing to do their share. And, yes, that they
will be there.

Q: When will they be there?

A: Well, I don't have the exact time on that, but they will do their share, and so
will other Arab countries . . .

Q: (UNINTELLIGIBLE)

A: Well, the good news is that no shipping from Iraq is coming through the
Strait of Hormuz. And we are in consultation, active consultation, with other
powers who have naval vessels there or under way, to be sure that no oil goes
out. But we aren't prepared to announce anything more than that.

He is telling a story
We are drawing a line in the sand, he says

The other declares a holy war:

To all Arab and Muslim masses wherever they are — save Mecca and the Tomb of the Prophet from occupation. . . .

Iraq, O Arabs, is your Iraq. . . . It is the candle of right to snuff out darkness . . .

Burn the land under the feet of the aggressive invaders
who have evil designs . . .

     sing! O sing!

the door of the bloodbath opens
problem-time is at hand
prepare the stage

THE CREATIVE IS SPEAKING
THE CREATIVE IS SPEAKING

"I am none" is his latest philosophical thinking & I am thinking (we are some-where in Europe near the Wannsee?, then at the Caffe Dante in New York City) how am I to hear that? "I am a nun"? Well, that's nonsensical. He is thin like my friend the filmmaker & speaks with a thick accent. He visibly does not appre-ciate women (I am too gaudy or something) although I seem to have some kind of stature as an interviewer. How do I know this is the great poetic thinker Wittgenstein? By his utterance, or so I think. "I am wit," he says. "I am Europe." I know he has been cruel to schoolchildren. I know he has parted from his money. "The world is a place," he sighs. I want to ask him to contribute some writing to my new international magazine or at least make a public appearance at the Naropa Institute Summer Writing Program. He is looking more & more like Samuel Beckett. It is dark now. I have to go home which is down Macdougal Street to feed my father & some of the new tenants, but I've mis-placed the many keys it takes to enter there. It is summer. Many night people, eyes wide open with caffeine, chatter excitedly in the crowded cafe. There are columns suddenly blocking the door like some odd stage facade. My compan-ion, the great man, is now shaking his head slowly from side to side. "You are on loan," he says looking at me intently. Do I hear him correctly. "Alone?" "I meant about the Viennese coffee." He says this last very sedately, ominously. I'm now worried about him falling into dotage. Will Vienna be entering the new war? He says, muttering to himself, "I must put on my mad yarmulke." Is he taking the side of Israel? "Madhyamika?" Will he really "take on" Buddhist philosophy? There's a gleam of light soaring forth from his eye which hits the coffee cup like a laser beam & shatters the cup . . .

It is a large dream machine made me write this. It takes off to tell you what's alive & took my pen to write as a nuclear warhead, as a large boot, as a map walking into itself circumscribed, as an obtrusive interloper, as witness to the man, the men who wanna play the music loud 'cause they're some kinda animal. Pit against the intricacy of fern, the receptivity of any womb, ovoid & lined with silk. It is a meadow so it may contact you as you walk, ground rolling under your feet even as you stop, stand still, look up: Dear Venus, Jupiter, Daddy, Dear Robert, Bob Kaufman, Ginsberg, Dear Wittgenstein, Dear Uranus, Mars working this soft lute in me. I learned my song in you, unconditioned space, stepping out of the elements & dancing in your subatomic embrace.

THE CREATIVE IS SPEAKING

It is a not-to-be-suppressed voice-tone
& going on like a point of view
in which the notes ascend out the top of the head

PHAT

Dear Mrs. Waldman:

You don't know me & I don't know you. I'm a New Christian Minister Monitor of God and I'm starting a Suicide Prevention Center and I'm asking for donations. My ministry is to help people who have lost the will to live. If you can send a donation I know God will bless you for it . . .

# XIV

## PRIMUM MOBILE

*Mover is both celestial & underground muse or goad that perpetuates the writing, like the male principle of skillful means or Upaya. The poet needs a prod and being Aries she identifies with the responsibility of kicking the whole procession into motion. She too, like Alexandrian Ptolemy, feels the earth as her center & wants to join the outermost concentric circles as a heavenly body. She reaches this point of recognition after a sleepless night out under the stars & planets in her yard at the foot of the mountain. Down to earth again, she speaks about the issue of homelessness with her son who is sheltered in the safe town and house. She wants to move his heart.*

– move by being

– moved

– if something is

– otherwise

– than

– it

– is

– motion

– in change

– & motion

– in

– motion are moving

– & this

— the Mover articulates

— then

— exists

— by necessity

— on

— such

— a world

— this Mover

— & "all this being"

— assumes difficulties

— is then,

— something working

— which ceasing

— motion

— not

— in

— theory

— only

— is also

— moving

— (move also)

&minus; for the appetite writes it down

&minus; &

&minus; for

&minus; the

&minus; wish

&minus; to hold

&minus; fast

&minus; you

&minus; (to hold you fast)

&minus; attention

&minus; but desire

&minus; is

&minus; an

&minus; opinion

&minus; on desire

&minus; & thought is

&minus; one

&minus; of

&minus; the

&minus; two

&minus; points

– of

– opposition

– reject

– &

– accept

– a contrary condition

– (heart?)

– that which is simple moves

– & that

– which is simple also

– is

– motion

– a thought is a

– capable

– action of motion

– complete & best

– (move it! move it!)

– is motion

– the idea, say

– of one quick

               — pulse

                 — to

             — hold

               — fast

   — the Mover as

     — the Mover moves

— & the thought

     — struck

     — the Mover: "it's binding"

       — "that which I think is binding"

    — Mover thinks this

         — too

*(To Pan the bristle-haired & the barnyard nymphs, Theodotus a shepherd laid this gift under a rock because they stayed with him when weary under the parching summer, stretching out to him honey-sweet water from their hands. . . . )*

        — the Mover's hair

       — springs up

        — like threads

    — of leather

     — Mover's parched skin is

— hard skin

— partaking

    — of

    — a structure to

            — house

           — a modicum of

      — desire

             — the hand

         — is

          — sinewy

     — hand

        — of

       —a homeless

           — Mover

    — gone below

        — into

        — the terminal

       — (don't impede

          — our

          — quickness

             — of

        – perception

    – see how

    – the Mover lives out

      – the economy
– Mover is a colony

      – no one

        – inhabits)      – yet

– provides

    – a home

– for all

    – human things

    – being human

– being subway

    – Come together Mover

      – since

      – it

      – is life

      – & breath

– you speak

    – that holds the frame

                    — of the entire new creature's

                         — marrow bites

                              — (holds the flame)

— pratitya-samudpada

                    — of such

                         — a principle of one

                    — defend the heavens

               — for the Mover

                         — is a starting point

          — a compound

                                        — walks


                    in exultation
primo
          the very first

& in his prime created her eros night
loved unto himself
her, the second mover

you say,
but book say
it is what told the heaven and stars
& was a book to boot
& kick back all sense of sound & dram

for sleep, forsooth, inside her womb to take
a kickback
you would be blasphemed here
& not a power be

for he, Mover, accorded power
because he sit so well
because he doeth it well
& slips,
sleeps
out
sleeps over her, she
is dreaming this
while he lies next to her abed
in the soft computer light
& beckons her out of dream
to write this down
for he can be Muse, the Mover
& she is amused, slyly to herself & stops this rap
for this one night
it was holy, it was a holy storm
the day remained silent
the Balinese Nyepi took hold
all the cars struck dumb in road
ice blocks & nothing moves

but light fall of snow

He who moved the quilt, who moved the books
down from the bed lay abed & drew her out
from her dream
for he was the Mover, this was the job,
the process of Motion and sleep, sleep which was
a trigger
a happy trigger for him to let her snarl, her anger go
& she could bask in the light of his strong urge to keep it going

for it was her song, &
she had always wanted to sing it

moving as she did among his waves

interstices, did I say it right?
of his sound


("let someone in authority come forth,
 A woman, or more fittingly a man;
 For then our converse need not wear the veil
 of modesty — man freely speaks with man
 And in a sentence makes his purpose plain.")


                              Libation

                                   & sure

                              Mover's heart

                                        will

                                        be

                                             uplifted, too

               sing O sing it in the mountains

               sing

                    O

                    sing it

                         in the plains

          that man is moving-prone

          like

                    planets

                    whose orbit turns

                    homeless within

                          their charted rounds

            turning to see you, Father

                  on the

                          jeweled stair

*primum mobile*

    all this is a way the men before me

            discovered long ago

                  but I follow it also curious

                                climbing

            (be careful, be very careful)


Dream:

large hospital-charnel ground-delivery room-beauty salon with an enormous
floor of refracted mirrors. Busy time, no men in here yet, but about to be born
full blown out of their mothers' bellies. We workers are in gear to keep floor
sparkling & tidy of its blood & shorn hair & slivers of nails. . . .
(he's coming, the man is coming)

Theory: I am afraid to express my anger as if it might make the world less safe
for me.

Question: What price do you pay?

Answer: The imagination of the oral poet.

The messiah is a man of sorrows
Mary has a look on her face of the birth & death of Christ
& he comes in lowness
& I answered in lowness
to overcome the lowness in being below?

Lamb into lion I become
& I am in lowness
But soon the time is I will take it
The time is I will take it
I sing within the male gods
& O he is the "I am" & I will take it for myself
I speak anew great King
& I will take it, take it
& give them back a son
Strut the orthodoxies. G Lock. Air Battle.
Loss of consciousness by G Force

Dear President:

I am in the 4th grade. I am glad you met at Malta with Soviet President
Gorbachev recently. I am glad you are trying to cut down the number of weap-
ons made every year and to ban the use of chemical weapons. Please keep up
the good work. And to take care of the Homeless in our nation too.

# XV

## DEAD GUTS & BONES

*An image of her father's from WW II haunts her tonight, as if life goes on amidst a different kind of war-rage. But what had he described, as he crossed the Siegfried Line? Steel beams sticking out to stop the tanks? "There wasn't a tree, there wasn't a bench; dead guts & bones. There was a smooth sandy beach where the Allied Air Force had pulverized the ground. It was nothing now. It was not quite beach sand but a dirty brown. Just been pulverized by American, British, French Air Forces. Our outfit was going through the Siegfried Line & there was an opening between those steel girders. It was a motorcade. Motorized part of infantry division. I was sitting in a three-quarter-ton truck with a mounted 50-caliber machine gun & I was sitting beside the driver. As we turn into the opening across the Siegfried Line & there coming out of the land was an arm, a hand coming out of the sand. Earlier I'd seen 2 Nazis in a tank that had been hit, cooked to a crisp." The poet is invited to give a reading at West Point. She performs and argues about the old war in Vietnam. Male precision interests her. Why always the incli- nation to honor more dead male poets? Are they like the soldiers from an even more ancient war? A letter from the priest in Rome turns her thought to Liberation Theology, bravery & risk there. What choice in such a situation? Pray for them. She records once again the young boy's ener- getic, prophetic talk, which grounds her in America. Old Cary Grant movie Gunga Din showing this eve is a nostalgic relic. The poet grows more confident in her epic as she brandishes the rib of any man — poet? priest? soldier? prepubescent son — in her hand, pen or knife?*

### West Point, springtime:

They come for me in a big limousine. The driver, a military man, tips his cap. I am suddenly a Ma'am. Yes Ma'am, No Ma'am. I dress in a skirt of many flowers, white blouse, ladylike. Hair brushed to the maximum. Underneath I wear the poet's uniform: skin of the jaguar. The world prays here in unison at lunch. Then two thousand spoons move synchronistically into two thousand youth- ful mouths. A young woman tells me it has been her childhood dream to land here. Another traces his family lineage to be strictly "held in line." A black daughter of the army is gracious & direct; she likes the precision of awakening at dawn. The light is friendly as it slices off trees. Flags move slightly in the spring breeze. Down a road I spy a maneuver in battle fatigues. Three soldiers in battle fatigues silently blow up two men & a cannon. Now they are hiding something. Another group is seeking what they have hidden. Across the road men are marching in tight formation. There is some remorse in the conversation about the long-ago war in Southeast Asia after I read the poem with the lines "Then gathers strength into something monstrous/right here along the coast of your feelings." But many of these officer gentlemen never had to go there. I shout "Mega Mega Death Bomb" to some polite applause. Now I want to make them laugh. Who is to say who's more awake? The heads and shoulders of the cadets move against clean buildings. Spit and shine. Spit and shine. Tamed to be fierce, unbending under the seasoned officer's eye.

I
dream
you
ancient
Romans
come
& laugh
at
modern
poetry.
You stroll
on
the
beach
with
the
transparency
of
ghosts.
You
point
to
the
sea
as
if

it
belonged
to
you.
Your
strange
hair
toys
&
curly hair
make
me
curious
about
the
cult
of
Janus.
God
of
doorways,
of
public
gates
(*jani*)
through
which
roads
passed,
and
of
private
doors.
His
double-wreathed bearded
faces
allowed
him

to
observe
both
the
interior
&
exterior
of
a
house.
He
was
the
god
of
departure
&
return
&
by
extension
the god
of
communication,
of
beginnings,
of
navigation
&
as
a
solar
deity,
presiding
over
daybreak.
Yet the

folds
in
your
dress
are more
sensuous,
Tellus Mater,
goddess
of
earth &
fecundity.
You
sit
between
Air
who
rides
on
the
back
of
a
swan,
&
Water
with
an
accompanying
sea
monster.
Urchins
tug
at
your
breasts,
plants
grow

from
your
lap.

I
sit
by
the
sea
lost
in
my
vision
of
you:

your
haughty
gait,
derisive
gestures.
You
shout
& jeer
you
throw
sand
in
the
poets'
eyes.
Flight
attendants
prepare
your
doors.

dear Frank O'Hara:
    can hate
      really be
   "graced by a certain reluctance
   and turn into gold?"
   tell me quick before
     I die of it!
        "quel head!"

    Anne-Gasping-the-Broom-More
      Tightly-Still


Messieurs Kerouac O'Hara Olson Denby Berrigan

You all float now
monsters free
poetry still brazen as the 20th Century thing
I have strutted along with it so long
up-to-date across
maps of some world definition
lovely heels, gab & loitering
You float now tattered boddhisattvas
in my heart
to struggle without limit
live a life in flames
my words seem small .
in step with your enchantments
Work finished, you "guys"
conquer no more "languages"
yet at the end of these long days, years
without you
heart can stop at the same beat
roaring down old metabolic streets
Want to say words large enough to
contain you
dear dead poets

Gilgamesh, whither are you wandering?
Life,
which you look for, you will never find
For when the gods created men they let
death be his share . . .

(ask the panel what bio-region they are coming from &
How they, as writers, address the "issues"?)

"I am no prophet, nor a prophet's
son; but I am a herdsman, and a dresser
of sycamore trees . . ."

A wandering Aramean was my father; and he went
down into Egypt and sojourned there, few in number;
and there he became a nation, great, mighty, and populous
another literary giant
passing through your home
all six foot three & 230 pounds
of argentine edgar bayley
especially bear-like
he preferred staying here
tanking up on burgundy
and having lengthy monologues
at me. on the third day
i slept while he talked
the bayley tape loops
going on & on
i guess i learned a lot this week but didn't do a goddamn thing
not even mop the floor

anyway, welcome back home
ambrose had the most phonecalls
someone came & got their skateboard
someone raked the yard

gratefully, joe

heels, gab & loitering

you float now

working to place a place

telling the story on the hour

let it down on me

      I'm not sure what all the men in your life want from you now, possibly they want to "tame" you & that it's too much of a threat to be with someone who's always in motion. The men want you to slow down so you can be with them, so they feel you're with them. You slowed down for me, I became faster to be with you, but after a while we began to revert to old tempos: how could anyone go as far as we did & survive? I wish we'd had the perspicacity to do it & fault myself often for not taking more control of my own life & not requiring that you take care of my needs which you did take care of anyway. I sometimes think the Poetry Project ruined both of my marriages because it created some adjunct world that had nothing to do with "our" life but was just a weird volatile mix of business, pleasure, friendship & that it ulti- mately all got in the way, parties every Wed. night etc. It was like a whole other family required your attention, & then where was I — as long as I didn't "need" anything I was okay. Needs are infinite & also nonexistent.

      always believed in your love when we were to- gether & that kept me going (& I think that's your great strength — to make another person feel what you're feeling )

you are my trust, a referent
back to self or "us," light I need
you, you I need you, you are
the call, call back to me
call me back to myself or
I'm not the same, eyes

seared for this view
you taught me, you forged,
you took me, I conspired
& inside a hand was caught

you are the hand, master
of this turning, my mind
to you burning, where
we were crossing I held you
around the back on the bike

touched you You said I
will never be the same
I will not be the same
I'll fight for that, and turning it's not too late

You are witness it is too late
to stop voice at the end of this
plea to ground me in your
sight, not to own the
sight but I see you everywhere
defy rude boundary of space
You are inside me that's why
I project on my screen
your insight inside eyes I love

(retina)


Impresario says, looking at Frank O'Hara with carpenters
"Carpenters had to be called in to pry her angst
"est anguish" (tr.) We believe that this time it . . . . . . "
"I see," Frank sez, scribbling in his
gloomy eyes. "But this time, we behave
from the small wooden box. This minute."
"The story is, after all, *her* dilemma,
you out with crowbars?"

in the dream of the poet-ancestor

I was my own dilemma

                              post-ancestor

"And they finally got her notebook"      Impresario
says, referring to this poem


I had just gotten news of an old friend's suicide in Massachusetts when a pray-
ing mantis sprang from over the canopy outside the restaurant and landed on
my hand. We (the mantis and I) communicated for several minutes. I brought
it right up to my face and opened my mouth and it wasn't afraid. It directed an
intense affection toward me that I could never have associated with a member
of the insect kingdom at all. Their heads move around just like a human's. It
tilted its head at several angles to look at me closer. I declared my love and (I
believe) it did the same. Then it flew over to the Chinese restaurant across the
street and camped in a flower box. I look up the etymology of "mantis" and
found out that it's associated with prophecy and divination, and madness. The
prophecy, in general, I believe is that there are no boundaries, and the angels
are communicating with me constantly, and if I take care with this relation-
ship, no door will be closed to me.
Anyway, I've begun "Mantis Ode."


"A Day In The Life Of A Male Praying Mantis" writes Ambrose

It's mating season and I'm scared. I will probably be eaten today. I was looking
for hot babes all day and then I saw the center-fold in the latest of issue of PRAY-
BOY. I started drooling. Then somebody screamed "Nice legs!" at her. My drool
was overwhelming me. I thought I was going to drown so I moved. I thought
"What a person to be eaten by!" I remembered that even after our heads are
bitten off we can continue mating. People say it looks like we are praying but
I'm of no religion. Anyway, back to the other side of the street. Where is she?
Where is she? I felt a slight gnawing on my neck. Kind of like of fatal hickey.
Then my head popped off. It was dinner time - and *I* was dinner.


*en rapport:*
thought
impulse
action

                                        slow down
                                        my genes
                                        do not
                    carry

                                        the
                                        same message

                    rancor?
                    no
flashes glowing at the boundary of the nucleus
(I can see it but is also sees you)


                    I can see it but it also sees you

SEFIROT


many
avocations
or
alterations
&
ventures
one
night
down
on
the
late
night
underbelly
I'm
with 2
bald
zennies
&
we
watch
macho

slam
dancers
perform
aggressive
deeds
it
is
the
best
ritual
to
slam
yr
body
like
a
door
I
wanted more.
I
want
to
get
on
the
floor
under
the
man
boot
then
hurled
through
air
to
male
body

no
I
wanna
crouch
down
& let
it
happen
over
my
head.
No
I
want
my
Minerva
helmet.
Nirvana
helmet.
Sweat
hold
fast
your
ground
hold
fast
yr
groin
waist
bob
unnameable thing
on
the
sea.
One
night
my

lips
get
redder
&
I
have
no
thought
but
to
be
in
this
Hell
not
a
girl.
No
girl but
kinda
old
"mahoo"
of
Tahiti
watching.
As
we
leave
the
club
the
doorman
says
there's a private party later & we're invited
back but only if the guys come dressed like that (Zen)
long erring in a globe
stern break over the knee

under a ring: blink
Order that knee in place: blink blink
Deft (Zen)
made of mud
that knee dab in the sweet milk
The term shatters us so
Wider so much wider than light a voice: why so long?
Why grind the bricks?
Why stack them?
Why build
or age the tool
what weight
carry?
Working
to place a place
in a job
place
a work man
could live here and talk
& swear, nothing much
glob of dirt under
the boot
broke a stick
upon a knee
claim check is deaf
& to all dependents
worrisome
long taste of coal
you ain't
calling
it healthy (Zen)
but maybe you could lift a
sanction, dear President
amigo?
      Our fate is forked

              *del sueño al sueño al sueño al sueño*

Anne,

Peace, though it is difficult to imagine peace in this world of violence.

All Jesuits throughout the world, including myself and all the members of our community were horrified and saddened to hear of the murder of six of our brother Jesuits in Salvador yesterday. The government claims it was the rebels, the rebels say that it was the government. The murdered Jesuits were outspoken in their defense of the poor, those never given justice. I think of the daily threats to our Jesuits in Sicily who speak out against the Mafia. But how can anyone justify the torture and brutal murdering of others? The six Jesuits of the University were dragged into the courtyard, stripped naked, had their testicles cut off by barbarians, and then machine-gunned, their brains splattering over the trees and flowers. I am happy for our departed Jesuit brothers who are now eternally happy with God, but I am profoundly depressed that so many evil men continue to flourish on the earth. Please pray for the families of these brave men, and for the families of the others daily massacred in Central America. And please pray for me, that when and if my time comes to die for the truth of the Gospel, I will be ready and have the courage of these six men. It is true that Jesuits have been murdered and thrown into prison somewhere in the world every year for the last four and a half centuries, but this last crime seems particularly brutal in light of all the changes for the better in Eastern Europe, the falling of the Berlin Wall, etc. I can add nothing more at the moment. My heart is too heavy. I have a strong temptation to leave all of my work here in Rome to go to Central America to witness Jesus and what he preached. To live is wonderful, but to die is gain! All of us here at the Historical Institute and Vatican Radio must go on. How unimportant poetry seems at this moment. Love and prayers to you.

Love in the best sense,

T.K.

Institutum Historicum Societatis Iesu

I weep at the hearth

       *del sueño al sueño al sueño al sueno al sueño*

The earth is tired

       al sueño al sueño

The earth is tired of weeping

                              The night gets cooler

                    sliver moon

& they might dance all night
warmed by a single flame
Uneasy amours
The Guru assumes a strange shape
& welcomes all pupils up
out of pools of darkness
(wet, slimy)
Yearning they in turn
lift teacher up
not passive participants in events
but subjects of a curving boundary
infinitely spinning
He's incessantly spinning in their hearts
Around! Around! Churn! Churn!

(iridescent ever-shifting world

Surprise, Joshua! fit the battle . . .

Alertness is all . . .)

You could dance all day

warmed by a single flame (guru heart)

not singly, each silhouette precise

 invade my heart

light in this heart (mine)

because I am light in your heart

& in the larger (*comprendes?* ) "goodness" heart

                    *del sueño al sueño al sueño al sueño*

the moon is a sliver

dear Joshua

the earth is tired of weeping

(our fate is forked)

Yet the most incredible result of your editing is the following:


~~as if~~ ~~i~~It hurts to hear you
talk this way, and yet
beside me, in the bath, you took
the left, the Latin Catullus and I
~~the raw~~ Zukofsky
faced each other in the
~~stillness,~~
~~shimmering~~.

~~Forgive me~~

~~I was lonely and the~~

~~sudden sunlight~~


~~the~~ salt of your skin —

To:


It hurts to hear you
talk this way, and yet
beside me, in the bath, you took
the left, the Latin Catullus and I
Zukofsky —
faced each other in the
salt of your skin.

That's all — not asking anything of you — just saying thanks, with appreciation.

My Dear Wife,

I am so glad you have had a nice warm day today but is storming now and I am afraid you will not have it so nice tomorrow. I hope the boy has not taken any cold. I expect you can tell by this time it is much warmer anyway. Clate was home today and is coming home every day. They are going to start and pack up. Kenneth has the measles now very bad. They had the Dr. today. His throat is so tight. Now Dear be very careful of your money. Watch your bag. Keep it closed and tied and do not tire yourself out. I have not seen Alma. She had company today. I will see her tomorrow. I certainly miss you both very much. I hope you get along nicely. Dona, if you see any of the coat sweaters cheap get me one size 36 or 38. You can get them from 50 to 75 cents apiece. I hope to hear from you tomorrow. Goodnight

> Your Husband
> John

(time for things to go quiet on us)

*al-Tanzil*
> the Downsent

When the sun shall be darkened, when the stars shall be thrown down, when the mountains shall be set moving, when the pregnant camels shall be neglected, when the savage beasts shall be mustered, when the sea shall be set boiling, when the soul shall be coupled, when the buried infant shall be asked for what sin she was slain, when the scrolls shall be unrolled, when Heaven shall be stripped off, when Hell shall be set blazing, when Paradise shall be brought nigh, then shall a soul know what it has produced

*hayya 'ala al-falah* (twice)

                              when time
                    is old
                         tell me
                         about
                         when
                         time
                         is
                         old

                         & forgot itself

— Fine time for things to quiet on us

— Blast them Thuggies

— Why don't they come & give us a good fight?
   How can we get a nice little war going?

— What if I was to sneak away & blow up the Taj Mahal
   or one of them sacred Indian tombs

— What do you want to do, start the whole Indian
   mutiny again?

— Dead guts & bones sticking out of the sand, that's war.

— Blood & bullets flying through the air.

— Michael J. Fox is in casualties.

— Tom Cruise is born on the 4th of July..

— Explosions ah dead, everybody gone now.

— The world is nothing.

— A Stealth blows up the enemy base.

— M-16 machine guns down whatever in sight.

— Iraq has as many tanks as both sides of World War II.

— They fight over who's going to be the President of a
  dollar bill.

— So what is a thrill, boys?

— Hitting a home run, a grand slam.

— Swearing at the Sega. I cuss at Wonder Boy, whatever he does.

— You cuss at the game because it cheated & a guy killed you
  or a bad snake or a mushroom or a snail or a fish killed you.

— They waste yr butt on Mega Man II.

— If you're Metal Man in Mega Man II you can blow their guts
  right out of their shells.

— Winning is pretty fun.

— Feels weird. "Hand-eye coordination," all that.

— This is easy. Look, look. I'm trying to turn.

— I got II on Aztec Adventure.

— Winning Bubble Bobble at level #24.

— "God damn you Tommy La Sworda!"

(I take that back)


Telling the story

telling the story on the hour

How to become a writer out of the rib of a man

How to spit out the man's marrow to breathe free

How to stand on the ground & contend with his mystical hormones

How not to get sick in the midnight hour

("Give me a break
Elvis wannabe
Madonna Wannabe . . .")


Oh, and the last movie character I recall identifying strongly with, and it amazed me as I hadn't had this sort of experience in a long while, was the Bobby Dupea character Jack Nicholson played in *Five Easy Pieces.* Especially that scene where he's goaded into playing that Chopin é      tude by the Susan Anspach character and the camera goes around the walls of the room, you see his whole life in those family pictures, then the piece ends and she tells him it was lovely and she really felt something and he says he just picked the easiest piece he could remember and felt nothing at all himself. Of course, I come from a sim- ilar musical background, but I think it was more the sexual tension mixed up with a misreading of art in that scene I felt I knew from the inside. From then on I felt I knew his thoughts, and this seldom happens to me with movies. More often I feel like I can read the director's thoughts.


*kaúsalya-ekagrata-citta*

# XVI

## DEAR SKYBOX

*Egyptian god Ptah? Prophecy — Riots in the City of Angels. It's the poet's birthday today. The student's dream scares her. Her girlfriend tells her to be sure to fasten her seatbelt so she won't end up with sutures on her skull. She writes until dawn, then dreams another Puer dream, a kind of map for political infiltration. What is this identification with young men? Are they playful tricksters inside the hag? Sometimes she can only converse with the son, his energy closer to hers than suburban housewive's judgmental gossip. The missiles, their concomitant deadly naming (Faw, Green Bee etc.) need appraising. If she appropriates their voices will she seize their power, or does it backfire? Keep adding dreams, stories, relive movie plots. Her son needs to do the assignments of the same. Memory eludes us. Skybox is science. And then what did you do today? a most terrifying proposal. Odd energies live in the cast of the mind of the child. If she includes him he understands the world better, simple as that.*

Now work to edge of time
Or if it's black
crack sleep in two
when young back
then & do
And sleep it does
or think to do, break
the dawn or night through speaking
true, itself a "self" is switched &
switch it off again
Air is clear of sun
Rain now, 2 A.M.
Roof leaks, the man
denies, but keep telling
roof leaks
here's evidence
got proof?
what?
Evidence, got proof she's writing at night
You know this?

Dear Men Of Night: here's proof I made for you in writing I read it in the news
Headline:
*A God Loses:*
*Ronald Frances Bennett, a maker of false teeth who claims to be the Egyptian god Ptah, finished last among 17 candidates in the city council election in Palm Springs, California, Mr. Bennett said running for office was the only way to draw attention to his identity.*

      *movere, delectare, docere*        a god loses in Reincarnation


O Key of David
& Sceptre of the
House of Israel
that openest
& no man shutteth

& shuttest
& no man openeth
& no woman openeth
Come & bring
the prisoner out of the
prison house
& bring him that sitteth in darkness

bring out! bring out!
              & the shadow of death
              In those days
         (& were they far from here)
          & indeed for many years
           someone was inspired
         Someone was imprisoned
           YOU WALKED ON ME
           in the shadow of death
        and I became a dakini bridge
          and was a gleam of you
         (in the shadow of death)
           high density disk
        mi madre mi madre mi solo solo

Does the eagle know what is in the pit?
Or will thou go ask the Mole?
What predator ask what hole did she climb into?

In those days & indeed for many years I was unable to say anything except a
sentence in rejoinder that I had not written out and committed to memory
beforehand . . . I had to try to foresee the situation and to have a number of
variants ready to meet its possibilities. I therefore came with a quiverful of ar-
rows of different patterns and sizes some of which I hoped would reach the
target. I sometimes thought of my mother

I sometimes thought of myself as warrior-in-progess. And little did I know the
name of Winston Churchill would resound through this hall and land. I
thought of her I thought of him

Early memory:

In the center of the lake
Her voice, breast, manliness & rub against the father
Wanting the center of the lake inside my head so that I would have
a clear pool of calm and clarity abide with me between their struggle
& battle that I would be the daughter of so & so running for office

Anne Waldeman

I write You because I fell

(Not only for le Intellect Français)

A Directress of a Distress School should take measures to protect herself

      and overcome   come over

all forms of Inclog work which are not definite

indefinite, sincerely yours,

(letter recieved June 7, in the nineties, Naropa Institute)

Scholar's lost at least 3 hours on the computer
"like dying"

The nodes of Blake or light of words
to carry none
"like dying"
He's lost time more precious than money
He's subject to machine wiles alas a student
Gin O gin has done me in
    (scent of juniper off the mountain)
in that
he's lost again to carry none
I'm in,
done

in by time
we men have enough of it or gin but
6:14, look
the black comedy hour is over
Is that Sparky barking?
The son is the speed I cannot be tonight (in gin)
Sonny boy down block
miniature Porsches & Chevvies positioned to go
all the way of pen & stare
I stare at the objects because of heat of sight because of "mammal that thinks"

He clicks the machine
Cars want to be in the hands of boys who love them
baseball on the pavement
I talk this way not urge middle malaise

Someone is on trial I have a front row seat. I'm dressed in yellow silk my hair is
quite long. A "Puer" is being tried for a misdemeanor the night before the 4th
of July fireworks display. He has used this civic occasion to promote his world
view that the best way to peace it to patent his elixir "Puer." He offers to distrib-
ute it to all the drinking fountains and water supplies in the world. "Puer." Take
your chances. He has been arrested trying to dose the central water fountain of
our village, the one with the busty mother goddess statue that towers over &
slightly intimidates children. (I am that child), The water is milky here. One
child (I was that child) drank it and had visions all night of animals known to

be extinct in these parts. He had studied them in the local gymnasium (I am that child)   Puer is tense. He is speaking in tongues & gesturing wildly with his hands. *Om namo Shivaya*

Plahn sounds like a lament not a hopeful plan, but Puer is intense hormone rage
It is the sound of any mother, any son
I wept to be a plahn to sound the gong and tell a history straight

The Harlem Hellfighters were the first Allied unit to reach the Rhine, served longer than any other American unit and were awarded the Croix de Guerre by the French. 171 of their officers & men were awarded that treasured medal individually. No black American troops were allowed to march in the great victory parade of the Allies up the Champs-Elysées even though France & Britain were represented by dark-skinned colonial soldiers. Moreover the War Department requested that no black troops be portrayed in the Pantheon among the heroes. On February 17, 1919 when they returned to New York, the entire regiment, line after disciplined line, paraded the length of Manhattan, up Fifth Avenue, behind James Reese Europe's magnificent jazz band – 60 bass & reed players, thirty trumpeters & drums. Crowds cheered them all the way up Fifth Avenue. At the top of Central Park, they marched a block west & then continued parading up Lenox Avenue to 145th Street. In Harlem the band started playing "Here Comes My Daddy Now" & the soldiers & crowds went wild with joy.

every soldier's due
& privilege that
be accorded notice here
puer had spoken enough
& lights
that bite
tell us
    war dead count
or slip
to salvage
    there
what place?

a place men died

battlefield
held raw
place that
accords
itself official
   stature
a label?
static as it be
alight
the
promise
   be
be it true


Shut down I say
   Vanity shut down
& all the flare or fare
     to be continued
             SHUT DOWN
like money
   is a power      How many megas does it take
How many tax megas
     & it is killing you
with the boils & brunts of never-more-solace here


everyone burns
everyone burns
            anger is mute here
No longer appropriate to be human
everyone everyone burning
although I wander through the thick black fog of materialism
I still aspire to see his face
(it was human passion burning to create the kingdom from Kether (Keter?)
AYIN

AYIN SOF

AYIN SOF OR

& climb the burning ladder (for we are burning burning)

Although I wander through the slimy muck of the dark age
I still aspire to see it


Dear Anne,

7:15 on a chilly Sunday morning. Now let me see if I can answer your questions.
"What was your first sexual encounter like?" An out-of-body experience. I was
extremely naive and modest and self-conscious, and so it was quite a shock to
find myself naked (no clothes on!) in bed with an older woman, her hand ma-
nipulating my cock. Of course I had had hard-ons and wet dreams before, but
it had never occurred to me that you could make it happen. So, Like I said, I was
too self-conscious to be much more than an observer. A totally embarrassing
experience. Though I felt very proud of myself (cocky) after,
    "What was your relationship to your father like?"
    Undemonstrative affection. And total embarrassment.
    "Did you have any role models as a child?" Only Jesus.
    "What 'character' (mythological, fictional, actual, such as in the movies) do
you remember identifying with at any particular point in your life?" This is hard
because I find it extremely easy to identify with anybody. I have always felt an
enormous amount of empathy, and had an affinity with homely girls: perhaps
(?) a result of identification. And then there's Katy Keene: I thought she had the
perfect life: beautiful clothes, two boyfriends, and a little sister to treat like a
doll. And nobody has influenced my life more than Ted Berrigan. But I think I
am straying from the question.
    I guess that's it for now!

                              LOVE,
                               Joe


who was a one to be straying from
*Pimelometopon pulchrum*
    (turns female to male)
        blue-headed rainbow wrasse *(Thalassoma Lucasanum)*
is *Protogynous Protandros* hermaphrodite (male)
we were discussing fish, stared at them in the tank a long time

sex you up? sex you down? the cheap song rings & turn the weighted spotlight

upon your pain & this was the deepest I'd felt from one in what gender O world?
I loved far away

My friend,

When I was 13, I came across an article in a journal about a female-to-male
transsexual who had married. Since then I had hope, I knew what "I am." I
instantly knew that I was the same. But living in a village & my mother telling
me "& when you hang yourself from the ceiling, you still won't become a boy"
( a very deeply felt humiliation – she once shouted at me when she discovered
that I bound my body in order not to show my growing bosom (ah the same
old disgust coming to my throat, start to choke again). I couldn't tell anybody
what I was. My mother forced me to wear skirts once in a while until I was 16
. . . and then I had to tell her. She admitted she always felt that I looked like a
transvestite in girls' clothes . . .

Well my mother especially worried about my sister, She was afraid I would
do some kind of damage to my sister's psyche until I was married. It took long
until she called me with my male name at home. (I was 19). This brings to mind
another offense/humiliation: my mother had a close friend, a divorced mother
of a girl my age. The daughter was like a sister to me. When I once visited my
former village where the girl stayed & was married & pregnant (they, the girl &
her mother had "known" about me but had not seen me yet, I already had
hormones.) The mother invited me to visit & when I arrived she said how good
I look!, how relieved she was but when I asked where the daughter was she said
that she, being pregnant, had not dared to see me because she was afraid she
would have such a shock the baby in her belly would get "bewitched" and
become abnormal like me. I've never seen either of them again. Yes, they were
afraid I would be a "beast," strange creature bringing evil to innocent babies –
like in the Middle Ages! (Allah, I will never forget that.)

it was weighted dream
crusty for splendor
& when I read it I warned myself to fasten my seatbelt
in the real time
& I invited the students to dream &
He who does adore his Kerouac wrote this down:

I'm walking through the student lounge at Hampshire College, leisurely, apparently knowing what I'm doing – no mystery to the situation – and I pass a woman sitting in a semi-stupor. She's sitting by herself with the fore part of her hair removed in a semicircle, with wild Bride-of-Frankenstein hair. I do a double take as I pass and I realize it's my beloved poetry mentor Anne Waldman. She murmurs something to the effect of, "You can talk to me, ya know." Her forehead and cerebrum have huge sutures traversing the top of her head with some metal, protective device over them. I turn, and sit down at the table to speak to her. We look each other directly in the eyes, not an awkward feeling but a warm pity. Nothing is said. Suddenly a large group of people is tromping toward us. As they near I can make out some of the faces: it's every English teacher I've ever had in my life converging on me. There's Benjamin Boatwright Alexander III, Diana Rose, Mr. Banas, Mrs. Niergarth and some teachers who look familiar but I can't remember their names. I look to Anne, who is in a daze — yet her eyes are wide-open, clear. Benjamin Boatwright Alexander sits down on my lap and the chair breaks. A fuzzy delirium sets in and we are all walking in the same direction outside in the streets of Amherst. Anne leads the pack in her usual black, but bald and inhuman-looking with that obtrusive protective cage around her head (she has apparently had a lobotomy or something of the sort). The group settles on a town green with park benches around. Everyone is going through their things, getting props together for some kind of show. Even I seem to know what I'm doing as we are all unpacking things: folders with poetry, musical instruments, etc. Out of nowhere, Tim Hulihan approaches with a football in hand trying to persuade us out of the performance idea and into a good old football game. He succeeds. We all opt for a game of football We line up in formation. I'm on defense—middle linebacker. Tim is quarterback on offense. Anne is offensive tackle. Tim gets the snap from some unknown bespectacled English teacher who is the center. Tim attempts a quarterback sneak — off Anne who is lead tackle blocking. Anne throws a wonderful block, bulling over Benjamin Alexander (author of a book on patriarchy). Tim runs through the hole Anne has created and gets past me too. But I spin around and grab him from behind (by the neck of his shirt). This is no sissy game of football. Tim fumbles as I bring him down in a mad scramble for the ball ensues with brutal collisions and extreme folly. Everyone is dressed in lecture and performance garb as they dive for the loose ball. The dream ends with the ball still bouncing and a pack of crazed literateurs chasing it.

& was a kind of sign
part performance that sticks
the world of illusion into form
part form
that sticks it right back out from under you to see
see gain it beauty risks or sweeps a charge pon you pond sleep pond or played
upon a mind,
Groucho said this about how we are past tense & into bungalows
to be a word
word it twas!
to be a gargoyle jointed
the frontline of the story

past tents and into shelter deeper

& called up a kind of king
You know the story of the soul gazing through the window at the veiled spirit
engaging her in conversation & she tells him some secrets of existence and then
they wanna get married

but when the king gets in there who is he who is he not who is he who is he not
what is he thinking who thinks for him of him with him who is the subject who
is the object what does it mean a king & take the scepter what is it to want to be
a man a king and don a male garb what is it to have them take your breasts away
so you will beat like a man beat your chest like a man howl like a man take on
the male mantle tell me what's it like in the kingships of yore what was ac-
corded power but when it gets to be him what he of what kind of crystal lineage
what birth with a gold spoon in its mouth with a gold cock between his legs tell
us the frailty & cruelty of the bygone kings . . .who is he who is he not whose is
it not his but is or not his for answer, for taking might be his but who is he who
is he not to represent a time forgot itself and it got dreamed up to replicate itself
as form you know of talking about the King of Kings or something like prophet
like Rebbe & take you by the hand but what is missed my Hebrew brothers is
how strange when you study this picture of the young Lubavitcher men more
than seven out of ten are wearing glasses a sore Torah eye proposes . . .

IESUS NAZARENSIS
REX IUDEORUM

(This is not a resurrection but happy Easter, king of kings)

All the "shuns"
I take or know
of
are twin to me
& not stalks of eyes
but like me
one of them, one stalk
is as light
registers
to go or not
to love a room
& go into it
then exit
surrounded by
edges:
*sh'i* music
a slavic table
a modest floor to stand on
around or
inside talk
ice is in all
the glasses
It's been variously
summer
not
at all
like love

Gatsby believed in the green light
orgiastic light
future that year
by year

different patterns
recede before us
Eludes us then
no matter
tomorrow faster faster

arms stretch
arms stretch further
so we one beat morning on

faster faster
enter now
the grace
or place of worship


TOGU NA DOGON: the men's house
millet stalk roof keeps low structure cool while men talk, prepare tobacco,
    take naps . . .

Elders meet to discuss business, defacing their own carvings to prevent theft

What do they know of leptons, elusive neutrinos?

The King Abbas, still under development, flies up to 550 miles. One of the systems nearing production stage are the Tammuz, with a range of 1,250 miles, the 3-stage Abid and a tactical antiballistic missile system called the Faw. *(disable an airfield, devastate a city)*

Zulfikar Ali Bhutto once said his countrymen would "eat grass" if necessary to build or buy a counter to India's nuclear capability.

Taiwan developed its ballistic missile the Green Bee (range 60 miles) in the 1970s using Lance missile technology provided by Israel. The country is reportedly developing a 600-mile-range missile called the Sky Horse.

Argentina & Brazil have some missiles for export. A two-stage missile called the Condor II which was to carry a 1,000 pound warhead to a range of between 500 – 600 miles.

Israel has the most advanced missile program ouside the Big Four. The Jericho, the Jericho II, the Jericho IIB can propel a payload of 2,200 pounds up to 1,500 miles, armed with nuclear warheads.

A Scud B releasing 1,200 pounds of the chemical vx agent 4,000 feet above an airfield will kill half of the people in a strip .3-mile wide and 2.5-miles long, oriented in the direction of the wind. *(disable an airfield, devastate a city.)* An equal weight of high explosives can destroy buildings more than 150 feet away and kill people more than 400 feet away. The 4,500-pound warhead planned for the Saudi missiles would more than double this lethal range (cluster bombs further enhance these effects by detonating many submunitions over a large area, thus producing a blanket rather than a point explosion.)

Accuracy is as important as destructive power. It is generally measured by the "circle error probable" (C.E.P.), an ellipse whose major & minor axes describe the maximum misses along & across a missile's trajectory. The most primitive missile guidance programs, which use inertial instruments taken from aircraft navigation systems, would typically have velocity cut-off errors of from two to four feet per second at burnout. That yields a C.E.P. of approximately 1,000 feet at a range of 200 miles, close enough for high explosive warheads to destroy most point targets and for cluster bombs or poison gas to wipe out troop concentrations and cities.

Psychological dimension to the military effectiveness of ballistic missiles: They sap the will to resist. The thousand v-2 rockets that Germany launched against Great Britain late in WW II were not particularly accurate. But their 1,000 - pound warheads wreaked as much terror among the British as the German Air Force had in bombing raids of several years before.
The thousand missiles launched during the Iraq-Iran War was the only other time such weapons have been employed.

Sine qua non of great power status: Missiles are symbols of technological prowess & political prestige like battleship of 80 years ago & will set off accordingly, eject into consciousness how many dead? how many casualties

O gracious light that raiments me
      vague wools, sovereign quest of turf
            venal enough to send anguish to
                  rhyme or art my king adroit

& you pent me, colder still, heat-seeking
      to get inside my cloak, you are
            the dumb phallus, the killer prick,
                  head of war, of poison, king weapon

            succumb or falter faint light
                  all risks to not-a-mere-dagger

I'm nubile, tremulous, panting, alone, a ceiling . . .
inside the shelter, underground, mask on,
roof never the same

also, my same old patriot light
& your volts appear, what travels Zeus?
is soldiering an error or errant?

      O my delite my light
            & pure my governing
      the mere record of a dance
            & it never nears the state of stillness

O come grate the occurence
      neither tempo is young when the anchor lunges

The sperm is brave Ha. War is the number, the playground.

Memory is a road that skirts the battlefield

Ill-remembered this passionate cozy tryst
battle very triste eh?

Erasable optical drives?

from the mother to the babe in her womb

the word "race" is a delusion
"dark
age"
is
the
time:

The noose approaches
It's usually hung in the forest
Rue of matins
The noose approaches
Mount the brooms, witches
Noose coming closer
The terror in the heart is crisp
Another day to put
together & take apart the world

Eh you for certain o way thought you only vital to my day?

Me in a sari ready to die after time spent with you

Sign your life here, the date is set

What other king might I love
solemn or hopeful where I turn?

The great house flashes: Manipulate the day & don't out-taxi Maitreya

Alcaeus, do you own your experience?

I sing to the elements
& then I sing to the wind
Why is he like stone?
Stone I call you
I sing to wind but
stone I call you
Not a heart
but a dead stone
I want it like his heart is needed
or a substitute. Is it so dead

can you really say that?
Feels dead in the little window
I see him & his heart I can fuel
It is substitute for stone, dead
I sing to say this
so I won't be sad
Stone I need as heart

& NEEDED as a kind of life apart

in a place where TARHIB means terror and TARGHIB is a kind of enticement

and Ghost Shadows fight with Flying Dragons
and both gang up against Born To Kill


 Dear Skybox,

Do you know that the packaging of your baseball cards is not biodegradable or
recyclable? The packaging may look good, but it's not helping the environment.

   Your packs are made of a material that will last for hundreds of years. I have
included an example of what I think your packs could be like, which has paper
around the cards and tinfoil over that and they are not stuck together. So you
can re-cycle them separately. And you could think about using wax paper.

   I think this is worth doing and I hope you will keep it in mind. And I know a
lot of other kids who feel the same way. Thank you.

                                   Sincerely yours, Ambrose Bye, 5th Grade


ancient in me
active in me
in the present tense under nacreous sky
I dwell inside the pearl,
hiding from all the men
to study their names:
the name of Indra:
from ind, to drop
like sperm, like seed
O god of light ray
another name: Vasava, king of the Vasas or

Maghavam: "the bountiful"
I live inside his thunderbolt and
return to his hand
I slice life right next to him
feeling his power as it drops
indefinableindicativeindividualindifferentindecisiveindelicateind irectin-
    dorseindomitable
all the "ins"
rise like the
name of insurrection
but Indra got down to his place
his implement stolen
subdued
subjugated

The date of this is April 2, 1991
*My Mom's Birthday: A Living Hell*

To start out my mom woke up with a dream that there were two guys blowing
their brains out. Then at 7:30 A.M. a lunatic had called and said I have some of
your friends hostage (Jane & Anselm Hollo) and you must do exactly what I say
if you don't want them to be hurt. He hung up after that. I locked every door
in the house. Then my dad called the police and they said this guy got a repu-
tation for pranking. My mom was scared to answer the phone.

Then when my mom picked me up from school we found out we were locked
out of our house she didn't have a key and there was none hidden under a rock
and I have locked all the doors and windows. I was having a piano lesson and I
did not have my music pieces. But we went anyway and I survived the piano.
Since we couldn't go home since my dad wouldn't be there until 11:00 we went
to *New Jack City* and watched guys blowing each other's brains out. Ice T the
rapper was an actor in the movie pretty good. Then we went to Sushi Tora
where my Mom drank a lot of sake. And I start writing this for my school report
on *What Did I Do Today*. Later we went to Andrew's and he was still up reading.
As we drove home my dad's headlights were just pulling up too.

# XVII

GROTTE

O sleep walker; is this fleece too heavy? — H. D.

*The poet travels to the south of France and beyond with family during the summer. She takes notes along the way to unmask a patriarchal past in a glorious setting trembling with murmur of archaic human habitation, middens. The dioramas, the "as ifs" tableaux are helpful, amusing. The oldest folk are dolls of a dream, clothed, groomed in extinct possibility. Evidently a stretch of consciousnesses from human realm wedded to rock. And after that: how many confusions & dispersals. Her ancestors were Huguenots. Marginalized like Cathars? What similarity lurks there? Nuit Sol. The night sun. This is the journal. Ambrose takes us to the Eiffel Tower. A bungled coup in Russia. Headlines. She misses the one who touched her mind.*


He said
   "your people"

meaning
The Huguenots
      &


in what cave do you dwell?

Wake: life
*as statue de magie*
*Bois, fer, cornes, cauris, graines, tissu, miroir*

could feel
pins stuck in
gut
      and the points along heart meridian
dissolves further down
legs already given out
*je suis fatigué*

Auto da Fé
trans-fire
Came through
trance Atlantic
to breathe l'air préhistorique
taking the light inside, he said

in
what
cave
or trance
do you
dwell?

a face – child's? lover's
next to my eye
to answer – and was that an answer? –

ancient in me
active in them
in the present tense under nacreous sky
dwelling inside the pearl
which is the way
you might see
something sudden
A small plane crash in which the pilot is immolated
& the end of his Timex which is one cycle
which continues you could believe
to any not definitive end it's relative
as said, more of occurrence
at dusk, my shadow to his light
you want master to be manly
against a tide
but, being sure of foot the way is lost
but the way is found
to be sure of thought
& the study of it
being neighbor to whatever culture

presents its lovable secrets
on hieroglyph animal
in speech, gesture
the head turns to breath
air of the next occurrence
in what time cycle do you dwell?
& what is the specific title
for any of all of this
Preliminary practices exhaust you
but the teachers never give up on you
You are tired but true to the text
which is words-only writ in blood
not more horrific like
business is ordinary
If I say so I might believe
spectacle of exploding desire
inside the cocoon

(Later in a separate sleep segment and removed scenario, Anne Waldman is
persuading us – all the Naropa students to become cops – she says she's got
these great low-risk police jobs lined up for us and all we have to do is go
through some minor screening to get them – we won't have to wear guns she
says and probably won't endure any violent circumstances – it's just minor cop
duty . . .)

        inside cocoon

*Ever since the Iraqis paraded a handful of captured allied fliers, whose bruised and battered faces
showed all the signs of a serious beating, pilots have had something else to worry about. "It plays on
your mind," says Beguelin. "You think Do I really want to get out of my jet? Because if I do, I know
I'll be partying with the boys in Baghdad." It is, in short, the ultimate role reversal: one minute
streaking along in a $30 million dollar war machine, the next landing rudely on the ground and facing
the enemy with nothing but a government-issue 9mm Beretta handgun, retail value $1,200.*

*Weather permitting, the squadron flies roughly 40 sorties every 24 hours. Between bombings, the men
laugh, lunch on bean soup and apples, brief again and get ready to punch the sky . . . "We're like a
motorcycle gang, or a roving pack of dogs," says Captain Tom Rutledge, call sign Strut, a muscular
29 who does just that.*

Strut
or blow me into the next Iraqi's sky

light

*Cher Ami*
Have you gazed into the Perseid meteor showers?
debris, detritus

flying matter

in what meteroric asteroid belt do you dwell?

*Quatuor en sol mineur K 478*
inside the Church
*Perigord Noir*

then we
cross the Rubicon
Font-de-Gaume
      points to
presage
      back inside where I was
            contentious, struts
      nothing of this but hag neanderthal
            allow
& whole
      toil, & male

what about a thousand modulations?
      fingers crooked like claws
            erratic to
wake the girl in every pose or pore
            machiolated walls
uterine
      a little bazaar inside her
: fruits and shrine-tables
potions of exotica,
excrement

& voice as
    in a quarry
hieratic
"I, the Matriarch, *did* exist"

encamped, moonlight or closed a carriage
she

rides
in sacrament
in trust of apprehension
      onto the 20th century set

hook
      a packet of . . . ?

inconsolate looks
intent upon a woman
drill
   or think about
duty
      enigma-face
shed unnatural
   Babylonian tear
captive
if there ever was such a tear

held or fit
        yet dry

a floater's desire

seems to fit

Here comes the old fit
   prerequisite to yr knowledge
of "heart"

*

gorge is green
        scent of . . .

lemon?

        grip        inside

rough, mite
        or fist

tight vegetation, dim-eye troglodyte
        monastery beaten down

& patient spin back 40,000 years
rare to go but

        but spoke that you hear

        but to snatch up

                see, see

a stern vision is told to me
the plunderer plunders
& the destroyer destroys
Go up, O Elam
lay seige O Media;
all the sighing she has caused will be brought to an end.
Therefore my loins are filled with anguish;
pangs have seized me,
like the pangs of a woman in travail

Mind reels, horror has appalled me
the twilight I longed for
has been turned for me into trembling

Arise o princes & oil the shield

youth come off a face

haste the bison
   dust is light

      khaki-past lighter
on a long way

all you hear is well of you
      *Vesere, Vesere*
*the bison*

& not signed

no one,
the supremely painted dies

but hand
   a hand in

look there
            swift as torch-flicker thought

\*

fear makes me stupid
'gainst walls
*grotte*: I thought of her teeth
   & fucked inside her belly
tongue entered her gorge
   *grotte:* rotted flesh
what remains are bones & stones
   wisp of hair restored to
the effigy got built
   words to your painted deeds
a flame that sustains me now
here
long past a witch's hours
all the family asleep
      in their caverns of dread or dream
La Borderie, on the edge
between you & you, a lover

between the mouth of the cave
&
the man's memory of cave
cave in
I cave in: *grotte*
Some woman gave birth to you &
will eat you alive
don't cross her now

in what mind do you dwell?

& the Sybil writes her oracles
on leaves that scatter in the in the in the in the wind
*while others*
*move*
*more*
*deeply*
*outside*
*caves*
Now turn to this channel for the most "cred" show in the skies

Cool Grove, Perfected In Body, Lotus Mound, Lanka Mound, Spontaneously
Accomplished Mound, Display of Great Secret, Pervasive Great Joy, World
Mound Kid Get Hyped, Higher Than The Sun, Lily Was Here, Life Beneath The
Waves, Distant Village, Divine Protection, Polish Your Own Writing
refrain your breath
even sweet breath
launches death
to animals gamboling there

 so that breathing

(be careful, be very careful)

destroys the hush
what went there?
 who goes?

what masters of the brush?
of superimposition /     of the hunt?
a sigh
    pass
bound

    meet the pigmented shape

    to put a hex on you,
buried
    excavate or die
cinders & kitchen middens
in the pithekos life
I was an ape, but . . .
He said
what stream
do you dwell in
Life or the water?
Was ape, but . . .

Called back "flume"
Call back
"contact the information office"
*un longtemps*

swirl of outrageous fortune
from Dieppe-bound
holding erect
a book or look
to pass *le temps avec*
*un gleam d'eau*

*bateau Champs-Elysées*
My friends my friends are obscure to see
"Not since le Carré has tough emergence . . ." but

Sealink thrive
Uni-ball thrive or throne

& be a lamp of Mahamudra to
*Mes amis:*
babes on deck make a Cro-Magnon word
*espoir* or
Seeing the essence of mind is called heat
in that mingling is a hundred syllables
    & every one of them has a hold on you

or blue deck all hands upon
& shoes
& shoes you caught dead in
la la la Duval
"59"
"une place de Lightning Bolt"
Paris Université teeshirts

Maroc woman

*toutes les choses fantastiques*

wake to know
& are wonderful
Make more of your money with fidelity
then follow daily life
all contours as parts of the
enlightened mandala are wonderful
I was an ape, but . . .

O you systems lacking in legitimacy

*Just before the close, the Dow Jones industrial average was 15.21 points up at 2,913.24. Earlier in the morning, the index had stood at 2,926.65 but began to fall after reports that women were being evacuated from the Russian parliament.*

In what cave do you dwell?

    After the Louvre, we walked five miles to the Eiffel Tower. When we got there, we waited in line for about half an hour to get tickets to go to the top.

First, we got in the elevator that is pulled up the side of the tower. It takes you to the second floor. It was cramped with people.

Then we got to the second floor. That is where we were supposed to get on another elevator. The line to get on it went around the whole second floor. We waited in the line for about an hour and a half. Finally we got smushed into the elevator. My face was rammed into the wall. I noticed I wasn't feeling that great. We got to the top. I could see about twenty miles of city lights shining in the dark. We walked up some stairs that led to the very top. It was freezing so I went down to the inside part again. We (my aunt, uncle, cousin, Mom, Dad, and me) were starving so we tried to catch the elevator going down. Unfortunately, when we got to the second floor, some snobby five-hundred-pound lady started complaining that she was sick and nearly killed fifty people by pushing them into closing elevator doors. My finger was practically amputated by a door. We got in the elevator and went down flattened. When the door opened, I was trampled. We got outside. I looked up. I could see the top of the tower; then I realized how tall it was.

how small I was

taking the light inside
&
light on all the tongues of . . . *vive la France!*
(but what of Mother Russia? Headline: kidnapping its own president)

& may the Fatherland crumble
(Until 1924 the emir of Bukhara had runaway slaves nailed to the gateposts of the city walls)

Vive la France, soil of ancestors
1589 The Edict of Nantes grants Huguenots freedom of worship &
    places of refuge

Revoked in 1685, the ancestors flee France

How is it with you in a cross-Atlantic traveller named *Virgin* because you never had it so good. The music company, clouds marshal out aircraft portal, divine drinks hey more of those please & conversation about the unusual amenities. Recycle waste. Cute in the most complimentary sense. Incessant logo beats the

drum of "sell, sell" "Buy buy." Hey but I paid for this. Went under.
Dear Lady,

The poem "Sightseeing" tells of a happening in which I was part of. My first mission as a radar bombadier was scheduled for a May tenth knockout blow to Dresden. Thank god the war ended on the Eighth. In actuality my plane continued on, getting involved in a "buzzing" incident of a German Village church as parishioners were still entering the church, in all probability giving thanks for the war's end, but the pilot and co-pilot just had to give them a brush, "Just to let the bastards know we are still here."

Odd ally,

Gabin

9 *Août* : Studying in this psychedelic dream the Atilians *(Atrabesquians)* who used to live in caves

*We ingest a powerplant of purple leaves ground with the ashes of Ancestor. Because these other people have no extant texts we must get to their power source & habitat through the concentrated study of a 3-D diorama, almost like a hologram, map. It resembles the inside of a hive. But we've gotta shrink too to get on top of the scheme. Some hesitation as we leap into our smaller, tighter skins. We know that this lost people are secret utopians and have the key to interstices survival.*

Dear Anne: I sent "Grotte" around & got a mixed to negative reaction response on it. I don't want to pester you with editor's critical comments. Just give you the gist which was ask her for something less journalese, more compact etc. One person suggested "Grotte" be edited, but I don't see how that is possible, given its structure. So, I'll leave response up to you. If you want to send us other things to look at, fine.

I think perhaps you sent "Grotte" thinking of my work on Paleolithic cave art – understandable, but "Grotte" is not really addressing that area of attention. So, in the future, I think you should simply show us what you consider to be your best.

Whatever it is worth (for future editing) "Huguenot" & "Iraqi" are mispelled – & you should probably be consistent re. diacritical accents (you use them on page 5 but not elsewhere, as on p. 1 – "fatigué", & "Auto da Fé" and later "Champs Elysees" etc.

'Atilians" (if you refer to post Paleo people, who decorated Mas d'Azil etc.) probably did not live in caves; almost all ancient Ice Age caves were not lived in – the midden always outside, nearly – tho some were briefly slept in, a night or two – leaving grass & pollen traces.

Best wishes, as always, C.E.


Begin at the mouth of . . .

# XVIII

## "I AM THE GUARD!"

*Some years ago she founded a poetics school on the spine of the Rocky Mountain continent with a close poet friend. The school carries the name of Jack Kerouac. They both agree that the angelic writer had realized the Wrst noble truth of suVering & composed his mind elegantly & spontaneously on the tongue to the page. He also entered the American culture, not always sympathetically. She often heard his sounds in her head, whole lines even, & many years later is invited to participate in a reading honoring his work at the local university. "October in the railroad earth." She writes these words, to be read aloud, which caress his. The challenge of the elder poet-men is their emotional pitch she wants to set her own higher than. Are these not masters? Her presumption is boundless. Her poem sees no end in sight if she continues to honor & measure her life & work against theirs. She visits her father, who speaks darkly from the corner of his room. The political climate is depressing. She likes to travel back in time.*

> *"Stop the murder and the suicide!*
>> *All's well!*
>>> *I am the Guard"*
>>>> — Jack Kerouac

> You are fun
> you are god
> you are
> "far-out-like-a-light"

Raiders, a game
   Something about skull & bones, black white logo writ 'gainst astro turf. Everyone looks into a bowl. And then the players start ejaculating into the air. Just like the beer commercials.

Could be London, shopping for just the right male dolls, a black one, yes, a white one too. One Christian doll, perhaps a Pope. The other is one of the 3 kings from Orient R.

They will coexist on my little shelf. And another comes in gold, Jambhala for wealth

*the razor in-cut of void meat Buddha*

Dear Jack Kerouac
who'd rather die than be famous
who ran away from college in 1941
*into Memorial cello time*
& spilt his gut
50 pesos
Aztec blues
A vast cavern, eh?
I caught (he did) a cold from the sun
upside-down language
*ulatbamsi* Bre-hack! Brop?
Of the cloud-mopped afternoon

and turn this lady upside down

*dyuar aham, prthivi tvam*

*May Vishnu prepare the womb;*
*May Tvastr fashion the forms;*
*May Prajapati cause the seed to flow,*
*May Dhatr place the seed within thee*

Let the marriage begin
Let the fucking begin
to people our numbers
what it's about, the fucking,
what it's
about to
become, a form,
to worry about fucking
& we are dying in it,
of it, inside the form
which is happy illusion's
mind bog anyhoop

*but you can go (go now! go now! in spite of yr blakity blakity hains)*

— 271 —

But keep me,
whatever-your-name-is-deity,
a terrible form
A "krodha-murti"
Keep me terrible
for I curse the day
I wed the poets

for I have sinned
I have slept in the arms of
another "husband"
I have advocated revolution
in the marketplace
I have looked
in the face of
Fidel Castro

*("only the laboring man adds anything to society")*

& wept
but see how
he is lost in
his "grey beard & fuzzy thoughts"
Fidel now
I am old now
(the father is speaking now
& of Kerouac
his indulgent-boy word run,
sometimes hard to keep company with . . .
slowly, fully clothed,
lying on his bed of thorns, my father
Room shuttered,
she goes to pull the light in )

*I have nothing to live for*
*No direction*
*No direction to go*

*Came here to die*
*I am waiting to die*
*I'd rather die than be famous*
*I never thought I would live it this long*


*Cry for the leaves to cover me come come over me*


who has accomplished
his children
Don't break
your tenderness


When the wind blows
you feel it
Same for the country. . .
you feel it


*I felt once for the oppressed of the world*
*& studied Marx, Hegel, Kant, Lenin*
*& the Communist Party meetings I went to*
*had no connection to reality*


You see how it changes?


Creatures of light!
That's what we are & leaves
It's all happening in snow
But I shudder
what's been buried in the grave?
Dust.


Depression drives me down
Ninety devils jokin' with me
I'm not quite clinical


But we are similar in our thinking
he, me & you too

                              although you are super
                                o logistic! woman

                    Vishnu pervades you all through the night
                                    & day comes
                        & he is still your marker & destroyer
                  What are the marks of existence where they
                                Empty of themselves?

                        Put away habit, come live with me

                        Take this love from your father
                    it comes through a wizened boy body

                    I understand how beings in their time
                            endure unbearable suffering

                                            *why listen to me*
                                              *an old man*

                                        call it to action

        *Where were you when the last Ancient Forests were being destroyed,*
                *along with the 6,000 species which called them home?*

                                        Old-growth forest
                                          dies with me,
                                        an obsolete man
                                        Hundreds of trees
                                          falling every day
        *We throw away our last ancient forest heritage for Happy Meal boxes . . .*

                                            You could say
                                              we live in
                                        a life vest mentality
                                            swim for life
                                      Lay it all that, be bobby
                                              be buddy

How optative?
go Sutter's home (his gold)

*going my way a marriage*
*had a life in the war*
*age or ache in breast*
*war was a life it woke me up*
*a long time was always*
*a long time*
*in war*

dear Jack:
not-of-war reflected in that mirror

& when you returned life was sweet

heart or breast would
swell up, proud
to die
proud to enter her womb
with renewed optimism

& thinking of all the ways to die

to die at war

to die fighting

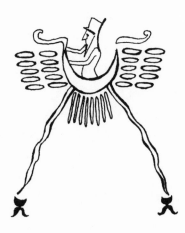

the way he looks at home,
away at war
& how in marriage
Father, I call him,
captain Kerouac
or husband
needing him most
by his words

(forget the deeds here)

Operation a Just Cause
to weep
a cutting of deals is
1,000 Panamanians dead
is a cutter of deals
billion & ½ property damage
is a cutting of deals
& 23 servicemen dead of the US of A
a "federal posse" intervenes
of a necessary day December 20, 1989,
a cutting day of deals

read it, get it? O cutter of deals
money launder drive all the blame
or drug traffic doubles
& lights go out for Miami's bulletin
in a cutting of deals

narco kleptocracy
a kind of joy
Medellín cartel
a risk you run to cut a deal
kill what "we" we bounce back on you
& kill what "we" we needed once
& serve a darker purpose
*Plap play play plap plap plapity gap*

not to wax sentiment, a groove
but pertains to any deal
the speedboat was a vessel
quick trip outta here
(the way the sun goes down in idyllic valley)

(he said in a TV movie about
a deal, episode of a mother implicated)

— 276 —

It, the vessel,
carried goods
crossed a border
was fast
crossed the harmless headline
& criminality when "smoking gun"
is your
position
& headline for
growing
narco-biz
a kind of showcase
or stop
joking with men

*I love you Jack*
*I love you Neal*

you take on macho landscape with
the freeingest sensibility, men
what ban
what sex do you play
arms sales
back up to plead guilty
& make the words sigh true
political
what care they back for then
what bitch to plead
immediate action toward Syntex
toward Sabotage or reduction flight
toward Capitol Cities front for CIA
just bought by ABC
forget another *petite histoire*
I love you for what I hate
crossing the country in my way
it was fast, I kept the notebook
I said poof bang boom

*I said shut a yap me mon*

       *what cooks mon and he was his sleepy dreamy*

    *you just gotta look at me as I crawl outta here eyes,*

*slumps at table, wake now and me with me big sentimentally hot heart setimentalitopality*


me see em
& they are all the poets in my book
a big heart church
& later down on Market Street I saw all kinda colorful street people


Dear A:

  With millions of others I spent last weekend transfixed by the Senate Judiciary Committee hearing. Can you believe that men like Orrin Hatch are in political power? There are others on the committee that make me nauseous, but Hatch seems to be the embodiment of evil. It was hard to get to sleep after watching for 9 or 10 hours this panel of middle-aged white men and listening to their inanities. The hearing to me was not a question of Thomas vs Hill, but instead a question of the sad state of our country.

  I'm woefully depressed here these days, thankful for your love. I can tell you forcefully that I support you in any decisions you may make.

  Much much love,

    Daddy


   *from this concentrated spark of raw energy what they call*

   *quantum chromodynamics predicts that a vast swarm*

   *of fundamental "quark" particles called "gluons"'*

   *will spontaneously spring into existence*


I, your *Clocharde Celeste*, spoke to you TiJean in a dream:
*So I write about Heaven.*

# XIX

## WHY THAT'S A BLADE CAN FLOAT

*The poet has by now travelled a distance, spanning mental universe, moving cross country, moving cross town and comes to rest with her box of scraps, notes, journals, memorabilia, letters, unfinished versions, her major task continuing unsettled at her feet. She spreads the documents about her, and bows her head. She feels a burden to sustain the plan. The society is crumbling around her. She can barely withstand the daily news. She thinks: why America? Am I American made? The computer is a little theater for her mind, although she senses it was designed & created & marketed by more & more men. Is this a problem? This is no mean accomplishment. She needs to enter more words. At least 400,000 characters. She has both exposed & guarded her life; whatever poetry survives is the autobiography of a dreamer. Mustering her strength she skims the surface of her dream & aspiration to find what floats, what rises. She has transcended some of her personal drama and contemplates a larger picture once again. The radio keeps her company tonight.*

*I'm on my way to America . . .*

What caller Apollinaire enamelled of him and portrait a German had of wit or style none none but peasant come and come again we came from that stock o' soup and vittel, vital to any daughter's wish. She loves him. She's one who loves the taste of burnt vittel because of him it comes by, dark bread for the peasant in you. She loves migration, how it complicates the maps of nationals and leave them writhe more problems. A chaos of place to be born out of male stroke and swoop. Andros!

What weave got France wave got put in here Huguenots, a difficult brood bittered by betrayal, and Europe's sperm said it before mix in her. Mix "x" factors here. A curse of mere cuticle a cusp or covering a couched phrase to tell a trouble in or else you come down here a Sunday and be baptized. This was not speaking in anyman's tongue but how rather she went out on a limb once a night alone and bled for all the weight of childbirth he caused her. She still said "he" as she waited for her property to be taxed. And it was daring to go that way just try me, just try she said. Incest was no explanation. A moon of problems. Property was an old handle to hold her back. Give her it back. Time again in tell a whispered her legs walked further, back to Europe and died in the bosom of would it be Abraham? Wood wood wood say it wood wode wood wood make it sing a wood praise song, my wald, velde, velt, Wotan mounts the stage to terrorize woman.

    break here

       & would a Walden be
      set
                round
         with


caller
    stone
               wood a Walden
  pre-historique

 would
blue
  a wald-man be

at
one
time
    migrate

     green
         another

(the pond)

& he says about my eyes
about blue & green
& silver, he says

view
from
a door

more contracted
than
from
eye

sock
he specs

too, happy ending
    he, nationalism fraught a kind of sympathy
    a free house, says

*(how do we talk*
*to ourselves*
*deep at*
*night*
*in the dark in bed?)*

    *die Mauer im Kopf*

        socket

the wall in the mind

& how do we

in a slice of hours
talk
        or calibrate this table in human time
2 o'clock: Page 2 is missing but what are your contacts
            in Venice, Londen, Erlangen, Paris

3 P.M.: St. Francesco rescues sailors from hunger

*(il Santo Salva dalla fame i marinai)*

they have been at it a long time

4 o'clock : the mountain comes to the man

5: Peacemaking-conference, Mideast

  (Dear A: I hope to see you otherwise. Sending you lots energy, getting my act
together you are right about academic theory of zeitgeist. LOTS ENERGY,
Madrid)

6 P.M.: *La Calùnnia di Apelle* by Sandro Botticelli depicts various outstretched arms
in degrees of panic & passion. The statues look attentive in their nearby alcoves.
I watch this instead of television

7 P.M.: why did I ever leave home for the new world

*mi padre*, the old man, is weeping, *weeping*

calling it a life to turn aside
        & he goes backward a step in his masonry


  each part of the house corresponds to a part of the human anatomy. Arms
are bedrooms & social parlors. The navel is the coutyard, sexual organs are the
gates, the anus is the garbage pit in the backyard, legs & feet are the kitchen &
granary
& head is the family shrine
      patriarch descend here
      Jove, a designate, shine here


putting doubt aside the temple
I was trying to tell you
when you call out
suddenly
like a demon
                  *he enters here*
Hallow Eve afflict
a species of madness

& he, the immigrant-deity dresses up as a hermaphrodite
(old festal table, ancient wassail, jest or sport)
he comes out of Columbus's tomb to make amends

amending to America

   & keep a ceremony there
all change in me, *muthologos*

sacred to some god always departing
lay down a book

hear the ancestral names

   Bush cruel crack
   against caribou

pipeline continue, imperialist America riding
on the nation of caribou

find you here no sanctuary from religious persecution
   collisions between nuclei
& wander freely as the first instant of creation

by whom?
of some sperm
& the first people who live here
in what mind do they dwell?

*(Kabel und Betriebssystem liegen nicht bei)*

caught as if by
force
   & forces
upon
the histoire

somber muse & disease

    walks the gangplank,
pirate to a war
    & held
in kind of thrall
for
diversity
arc back,
    you come home from all points
        *to tell the family the stories*

Doctor Benton speaks:

A. Atypical lobular hyperplasia B. Moderate intraductal hyperplasia C. Fibro-
cystic condition D. Microcalcifications. A & B are worrisome; some people feel
they are pre-cancerous. Empirically punctate calcifications can be cancer

    then he leaves the room

mi padre, mi padre
predator
doctor god America

 & give advice to workmen
 how to vote:
    force an issue

        more nonaffirmative action o women
sign here they operate, *exploratory*

males with scalpels: *milde Grossheit*
carving the u.s. of a.

Dear A,
        Back in Munich

You must know this but arose in the lecture last night the most important
person of the 18th century being John Locke, founder of political liberalism

(liberté, égalité, tolerance, fraternité, humanity etc.), who influenced George Washington, Thomas Jefferson, Madison and those who put their signatures under the Declaration of Independence and were freemasons as well. At my meeting many freemasons of today were present. They have 2 beautiful temples in Nürnberg and Erlangen. Only men are admitted. The bible the president of the USA gives his oath upon is the bible of Washington which was used in his freemason temple. George Bush is probably a freemason too. His "new world order" is a reflection of their esoteric teaching so similar to Shambhala vision. Conspiracy theory again, yes? That is my fear, distortion of a vision, in real politics. And it seems to be, indeed, a common mind-set capable of "dark" and a "white" result. We need more dialectical awareness to overcome the danger of dark results. This is what I endeavor in my scientific thinking and work. You, too, my friend . . .

my friend dark night a result
friend a light of me combine
to find alas no woman at the table
of Israel, of Lebanon, Palestine
how do they sleep? of Syria
& shine or shrink the tale as of void
& radio it says hands-on broadcast
a hundred deejays wait, not one a woman
the scholar & savage equal points of light
rub dry sticks together
a sham, a delusion, kind of affectation
never felt lonesome in it
mythology cast a spell on me
wonder a caller they say special interest
& instrumental in recording & taste you will see
on drums on bass & on Smithsonian
pumpkins so light, spear a ghost
it is an eve my friend a dark night
that's the way I feel now
they tend to shatter, words they tend to shatter
I'm a wrecker,
Roland Kirk plays "Haunted Melody"
they tend to shatter the words they tend

# XX

## OUSTED

*She must leave the family home and abide by certain forms that she challenges daily. How are these rules etched in stone? Have they worked so well? The poet finds the scholarly task of unearthing alternative histories & examples to "prove" her arguments exhausting. No one really listens. She rants at the Male who has this kind of mind-set which she considers myopic & alien. What's his problem? Mere jealousy? The whole world's ablaze & he's jealous? She chomps at a mythic bit. Her sweetest friend draws closer in the den of insects & raccoons. They push on each other's work. She falls into doubt occasionally, scorned & maligned by the "community" who still after all the centuries hasn't learned a thing. She feels banished to the outer rim of the small town mandala, the witch woman in the company of beasts, but it's a guise she will embrace. She writes in a long dark chamber. She sits in the hallway at night reading & writing so as not to disturb the child sleeping in the only room. He rolls with her mood & passion. He follows her with his eyes. He knows her energy, just seething below his own surface. She identifies especially with mystic nuns. She reads about Sor Juana & her sisters licking the dirt to make the shape of the cross with their saliva, their tongues raw with the work. Should she do penance? Someone then responds to her work.*

> *"Look for the nul*
> *defeats it all*
> *The N of all*
> *equations"*
> — W.C. Williams

When law stated was it sacred monogamy or illusion seduced ourselves to it. He kicks me out. Circa deities, what? The law fuck-wish for "have not died yet." "Am yours," violent plots, arranged mix, or match this eye with that hand. As wish for completion. Tradition means to pursue fullness & let your eyes be glutted with honey. I see you. I see you. *And stick in the blade.*

*Megaladapis edwarsi* gone, *Bos primgenius, Hydrodamalis gigas* gone, brave to be wiped out, inoffensive, easy to kill. How did they & in what habit mate? Marriage, extinction, gone beyond use in the ripe outdo-ourself-time, golden tangle exists, resists : *keep this together.* A man and woman in time. Bow down. But see the tri-angulation of desire. It could be mother/son, father/daughter. Intersect this life in that other's, see how you come out or up for air. He-Who-Kicks-Me-Out, I pray you feel the sweetness of revenge yet suffer in your stupidity. Ne'er see likes of me again, dummy. You jerk. I'll go frolic with the animals in the expensive cave.

Some brute die & you are keeper of an ancestor filling a void, bring "it" out in the shrine box, unwrap her head, make the offering. No one dies really. *Illud tempus,* a primordial touch before language & deed go hand & hand. I love my antecedents. Consort you are the saint of me. Now turned to demon. I own you and you are never out of sight, I see you everywhere proud edifice, a field accommodates you within. Tight rein. Lover said your signature is enough of roof above my world. Mystical mutters provide a flourish, sanctuary. Alphabet I marry. Tomb I marry. Ancestor I marry. Events too illicit to bear the light, nobody's business. I marry the secret too blinding she calls deception. I touch your cheek, is that a pact?

 A woman takes her clothes off around the planet & throughout the 10 directions of space. How many world systems may I get married in? & disrobe the holy corpse, I vow to enter every one of them. Trust is teacher who ensnares a girl-body. *This? Worms, a mantra of worms, food in any woman's thought, let her as her thoughts provide a mantra of worms.* Rise grisly roots, genesial laugh. I want you as mirror, dear Sky-Hero, take it to the top.

> *er bell er elly*
>                          *slike a cloud*
> *hite loud evening*
>                          *efor hudder nigh*
> *ood ill indi efface*
>
>                          *out thir*
> *weat oil ow love*
>
> *ow love ow love*
>                          *no insect is awake*

*er elly er ell*
*aclou*

*hat nul*

*weat oil*

*ow love*

*eein now, eein now ow love weat oil*


initiation into insect tongue
area of knowledge
yr wish broods
because she of earth
thinks
cup do in raccoon
substratum

\*

love's
body with
arm
has
been
longer
sky signature

\*

altar
& wine
hierophant

mount them

\*

whose
glut
not die,

rebel
sweet liturgy
write this
in pain

\*

to the wronged:
can *shift that cave*

\*

live & think
these actions

*summa scientia nihil save*

\*

abscond with booty
lust, heh, lust?

\*

be-wilder
contour

*against the threat of spiritual extinction*

I wish him a long long journey

Numbarkala, Wandjina, Ungud, Rainbow Serpent
tribe of everywhere,
*on location*

Arapahoe:

Complex of occasions
grown perfectly shy
sift back
something soft lived here
vertiginous

till ductile anchor hold
the islands
and then
but
when
is to for surely
happened
part now round
meet the sea
above
lyre sound
(his heart I care to meet)
erotic the sound
wins on me
yet screen
on see
his love
where is it?
there? o
don't scare
a heart
puts
stock
admit, admit
yr love
where is it o
dream bit:
"if only you will do such & such
the gears are more accelerated"
trying
to be good
but
faster?

occur wider range
risk is full of
snatch the light
connubial
occur his body

suck up
my belly
don't leave
me out

rave form
ghazal loose
name form is Anne-of-Sorrows

rocket
knuckle-grip
stun

with an eye to poesie?
what idiom for makers

arc of love
writ in wine

You project I want to work
You have to say what you want to do
don't project on me to get an excuse
What are the expectations/rules
of our relationship?

See what happens?
I'm simply out because I said I'm falling in love with you
And then if you're suddenly not there?
I never want to go through that again

It was not a monologue it was *respondez s'il vous plait.* Tasteless to be one so free of inhibition. Bringing up the cast of characters in a little town. Not so interesting as run out by the moon. Flagstaff is bladed. Not so as it might be even more interesting to sit you down thus and tell our story. You wanna here cry me to sleep like a bababababy . You wanna hear me cry to sleep like a gull. You wanna hear his heartbeat. Now it raises. In the basement all things taste the same. Because they are even, untried, because they are close to the ground yes that's not it but close. Really laugh? alert with the dormant spiders, the gold fardels. Barbed with raccoons. He sees them he says gazing in at him from the far step. Awake, and they are alive, awake & they are alive awake & they are awake & they are alive awake & they are all alive. I dreamed his banditoed face that night my son came over. Animals will save the story of her confinement, shall be magisterial, shall be brave. They are the extinguished ones. Never again that form that creation bring. Never again that form that brings the ant galaxy to her rug. Her rage of rug. Her killing. Let them live in the crack a while.

I went out. It was the docking hour, it was a witch of night. It was strange. I came back. I just woke up here.

I am the queen appointed herself to be of these new parts. A bridge. A view of sturdy trunks. I fast by the window. I am the novice ruler of these parts in my head, new places where the pain always hang out with me. Where ruler is to be ruler to pain. Ruler to the boiler room. All come seek shelter here. I tuck you under my big skirt like Madonna of Misericordia . Suffering does or didn't did it and does not exist. I have enough space for the suffering of all of you. Latin *obstare* : to hinder. You put the hex on me, you put the hindrance on. Put down the next song of the no eyes part of the no ears no nose all parts of what makes sense. It is a tract and include it here you are least pride of being to practice your religion yeah in peace of harmony. In the place of cellar. Where light is a thief to your light-up-world-mentality. Okay. And out it didn't go yet & does or doesn't it did govern did go out.

The governed is bowed down. She's ousted by law. Lord of the manor wants her this way: out there. But no longer live under ready rule. Yet ride with daughter power. Or she'll be the artist forever. How made these pelicans. How made them spite and strong, how made them pierce his heart, how did they lie awake & plot his quick demise. Poor Lear. This gets reversed. It comes to naught but writing, writing. . . .

I want you
desire is a field
includes the objects
& divine events
as if performing at the
fragmented dreaming site
love is a rite
includes our myth
laid out epiphany-style

in our secular environment
need is a net
guess what it includes
the way nature operates is one dimension
and through the holes goes
you can't lock nature up
love, love
above censure
chthonic rhythm can't help it
go beyond
"idea of a single"
a woman to her lover
"no sacrilege"
let him speak
Dialogue 3, Giordano Bruno:

"thus one should think of Sol as being in a crocus, a daffodil, a sunflower, in the cock, in thelion . . . For as the divinity descends to a certain measure inasmuch as it communicates itself to nature, so there is an ascent made to the divinity through nature"

*Spaccio dellabastia trionforte*

*speak to make it so*
*no matter you king of me*

*speak to make it so*
*no matter you poor man*

*speak to make it so*
*industrial wastelands blight the earth*

Of course the stories known in many lands many tribes say this: about how men go off to battle, to catch a wild animal, to avenge a sorry deed, and if they slip, if they get maimed, if the animal eludes their grip, blame it on the wives. The wives were unfaithful. And so rush home to punish them. Oust them.

was a wave of interactive particles
limbs carry me across his country
I fled I fled I fled I fled I fled
Juice was first and Juice was last
he with the glittering lightnings
Juice is King
Djeus is ruler
he with the gleaming lightnings
you see
a moment
of her mind
the form of a ladder
to . . .
can't waste anything!
every thought holy
I fled I fled
invite him in
every thought, holy
do you see far, my friend?
How far?
gather thoughts to
feel & hear
here
love is a shelter
the postulants receive
smitten by how you guess her
he's out there somewhere
look after the country
proclaim your attention
you who are attentive to this
look after the country, the beestes are coming

Every child teaches that things are backward

Dear A.W.:

First impression: a kind of aside: physically—for whomever does print the book, I think it needs a big page; something on the scale of Olson's or Frank O'Hara's *Collecteds*. I think of the pieces I've seen printed, and for me it worked best in NOTUS (STILETTO was a long page, but too cluttered for me). Because it looks like in a lot of places the page was, if not quite the compositional field à la Olson, some kind of unit or frame for you. Also the thoughts are quite long, philosophical, at times like syllogisms of Teutonic-compound-word complexity, and it helps to follow your thoughts if a reader can see a lot of words at once.

I remember the title of a book, I think, interviews (maybe essays): "Ecstatic Occasions, Expedient Forms." And when I read your work – not just here, but much of the time – the form never seems to be quite expedient enough for you. The language also has to be bent, made more expedient, wrapped about what you're trying to say the way headlights used to be "Frenched" on custom cars. So, the language is constantly slipping out of my grip (I'm not a very nimble reader, really. But, as I may have mentioned already, my value lies in my being a persistent one, I think). I lose the sense a lot in your work, but hear your voice, hear something it would be too melodramatic of me to call your "transport," but that would be very close. If the OULIPO guys (wonder why there aren't any OULIPO women) can declare that "A [OULIPO] writer never needs inspiration, because he is always inspired," meaning that their dedication to forms and formula gives them an automatic impeller for the writing, then I myself might say that you have some of this same insistent pushing-against-inertia-by-way-of-a system approach, and that the system is simply the emotional pitch you want to set the poem to. That is, you fire up the emotion, then try to catch and ride it with words; ride the whatever you might want to call it – muse, carrier wave, inspiration? – playing a fierce game of catch-up with yourself (selves?). You say this almost explicitly yourself in several places here. For instance: ". . . loves my writing / & the road in it / It roads you away, you might say/Messages get lost/Look for a word and can't find it."

*Shaman* might be the easier way for a new reader to enter your work as a whole, because everywhere you write – incl. IOVIS – you are always making charms, attempting spells, sketching out OJOS as your stanzas build up their chromosomal clusters; and like those medicine things, their component parts, your lines can be very hermetic, encoded as DNA.

In Olson, Pound, etc. the difficulty is because of their—to a reader, an outside-stancer—seemingly arbitrary arrangement, the nature of which is tough to puzzle out. You have declared these men/works as the ancestors of IOVIS, and your poem does have this architectonic puzzle aspect as well. But the pieces you use are not really like those in Olson or Pound; somewhat closer to Williams, and even Guy Davenport's fictions in *emotional* content. Because your pieces are overwhelmingly personal history, not political or geological history, as the others tend to use. Is this why the Pisan Cantos work best? Why Paul Metcalf's Patagoni is not "better" than, say, his Middle Passage, but is certainly boosted by the personal letters' immediacy? Why Olson chose to speak *as* Maximus?

But to be a little more specific about IOVIS . . . "Both Both" is a kind of alap section — alap being the intro part of Indian raga, where the theme is started slowly, completely, and most clearly before the improvisations begin.

We are "told" what the structure will be when we encounter the first male after IOVIS – Ambrose. His voice, we are told, is one of "demand and interruption," and the structure is an interrupted one, interrupted by stories that demand you tell them at certain points. And the bandwidth of the piece is established—from IOVIS across to Ambrose. And not just that the male voices are of demand and interruption, but also of contribution and celebration as well. And when you mention the given of maleness's connection with war, you state it, use it, and deal with it, but you aren't accusatory or condemning and do not as so many might have been tempted go for—the cheap shot. Rather, your take on it is one of recognition and curiosity. And when you do show the consequences of such a manifestation of IOVIS as war you do it matter-of-factly and as part of a context: ". . . now we live in the combined karma, if I might use that word . . . in the sense of what continues, a thread of energy perhaps is all. Which is why I say the poet must be a warrior of this battlefield of Mars, o give me a break, thank you very much." The poet must recognize where he or she is. A male(ness) self-recognition, even in a female poet – accept the good with the bad, and do your best. This is a clear-eyed, unflinching poem.

You say "I feel myself an open system (woman) available to any words or sounds I'm being informed by." I've already noted this fluidity in your work, though I made up my own term for it (really, borrowed from Hugh Kenner in THE POUND ERA). I've been trying for a few years to finish a book of essays on some poets — I may have mentioned this to you before: Schuyler, Brainard, Elmslie, Koch, Waldman, Berrigan, Mathews, Padgett, maybe Coolidge, and in my notes I made for your piece I called you a "Fuller's Knot" poet. In THE POUND ERA Kenner talks about a demonstration that Bucky Fuller used to do: he'd tie

a knot in a rope that was made up of a number of ropes of different materials —
some length of the rope was hemp, some nylon, etc. — and Fuller would slide
the knot along the length of the rope(s), saying the knot was not the rope but
the patterned energy that manifested itself there. And I see you as this kind of
poet, who lets energy flow through her, while you do your best to manifest the
patterned energies you sense . . . within the limits of materiality. As you say
yourself "excluding nothing" is impossible. Coincidentally in the notebook
where I was making notes on IOVIS I was also making notes on a number of other
things, and my comments on the final paragraph of your poem face a quote
from A GAIA-an biologist, and I think the quote applies to your work at this
point: "This amounts to setting broad boundaries within which many pathways
may be taken, as in a proscriptive rule (what is not forbidden is allowed). But
this is a far cry from a prescriptive rule (what is not allowed is forbidden)." He's
writing about inheritance, natural selection etc., but I think it fits your po-
etry. . . .

# XXI

### SELF OTHER BOTH NEITHER

*She will turn again to the precious Dharma which holds no corner's gender. The poet studies Madhyamika philosophy, a branch of Buddhist thought, which refutes the idea of solid exis- tence and embraces the view of codependent or co-arising origination. Things do not come from themselves nor do they come from things other than themselves, nor do they arise from both these factors, nor do they come from neither of these factors. Where do they come from? We live in a Samsarodadhi, or oceanlike world. The strands of our existence come together karmically, if I might use that word dear-sticklers-against-dogmatic-vocabulary, dear comrade poets, and through varied ruses and desires. She has set a shapely form for her thinking — 10 lines clusters that resemble wings — as she moves through a mental relationship to phenomena. Cut it out, she admonishes herself, it's also only, simply writing. But this is mysterious too. She yearns to write "outside the book," as she has written outside the kin of men. She wants an oppositional poetics.*


The desultory hours go slogging by
All that time remembered as one false start,
   one laborious outing, one laboratory's hour,
      The lights go on all at once, blinders off,
         one distinquished guest, the scientist in repose,
            the first time you ever met. Why is it in some
               cases I am entirely missing the point? What comes
                  of this meandering about: the particles coalesce
                     What exists exists only as a presentational context
                        of our presentations, Descartes suggests perhaps


And then what happens is precious & strange
This is our paradox, no perceivable rules
   Just the minds of wizards who tempt us
      to greater Herculean feats, go on now
         bringing your language out in the open, go on
            now, they sing, they reason, they coax
               It is the way to, or back into, one mouthing
                  entity, one yapping entity, speaking in
                     a kind of soft body tone or else tough and
                        uncompromising, let it go at that into air

Onto bright page, the text is inviting tonight
& speech is the plan of the hour, don't stop yet.
    Wittgenstein's "block," "pillar," "slab," "beam" is
    a tactile language, signifying the way he goes
        about it, and the workers too, the lifting & carrying,
            building up a case only to abandon the building
            once it is completed, ceremonies and all.
                "Human," "ground," "ceiling," "limit," and
                the rest of the senses hop for joy at
                    the attention they are getting, one edifice,


One sliver of recognition, one completed sentence,
one half-baked thought, one coming attraction,
    one way you looked once, the door's wide open,
        Elucidate the promises you made, will you please?
        Is it a genetic agreement, not to be taken lightly?
            I know a woman who clones skin for a living no
                kidding (but seriously), she is inspired by the work
                    And is a necessary further wrinkle on the assumption
                    that we want this all, this lone life, to go on
                        I have this bright idea I want to try out on you


If you would be ready to drop your socks
But seriously, no such insinuations, trying out
    rather the notion of the notion of this layer
        of time, how elusively it passes so, one caught,
            I'm caught catching myself thinking out back
                under the sun. Gardening would be a wise activity
                    to be engaged in, caught, no not napping, but caught
                    as 40 years blur into a single event — pouf!
                        What happens is wrong-headed thinking like this
                            Think of the present as a dimensionless membrane

Think of my presence as something to maintain,
I am saying to myself, or rather it speaks,
    the loquacious one in my head, the head of the
        Senate in the old Greek sense, and the mental machinery
            creaks, trying to flash back, ah trapped in this darn matter,
                in this bulk of stuff I affectionately call mine
                    as it rallies the other constituents to vote
                        on this one, how solid do I want to be? What
                            started this was the repercussion of the language
                                How it bounced back in these 10-line clusters


To note the matter here, that it is necessity
 beckons to straighten out the contradictory policies
    and not one of them religious in the sense of
        duty but holy, yes. Holy smoke, holy yes
            Matters to be attended to include the stars,
                which are themselves repercussions too,
                    and the rest of the firmament which I am
                        begging to penetrate, and the matter of tastes
                            which can get extreme in the sense of having
                                to live up to the beauty of that painting, that vase


Is this pure artifice? that Guston, that Orozco,
 that sleeve (embroidered to look like electromagnetic
    waves) and so on, some kind of newfangled renaissance
        at least, or living up to the best quotation
            for its pleasing music, not its sense, not the
                content but the contradiction interests the
                    ferocious entity behind the screens, the gauzy
                        veils, behind the dense intrigue of tastes,
                            who, after all, are the arbiters, and in any sense
                                could they be said to be arbitrary to the thing at hand?

Stand before anything until it becomes important
Important as obstacle or as attraction or as simply
   what it is, so marvelous it could exist!
      And meeting you too, our eyes commingle when not too
         shy to meet, and you say something in the Serbo-Croat
      And my brain filters the information stimulated
            by your eyes and the new sounds issuing from your throat
            and then it all dissolves into the next bite
               It seems that 2 signals separated by an interval
                  of up to 30 or 40 thousandths of a second mesh


Into a single event never to repeat exactly
this way again, and then they get lost in a
   third collaboration and lose time, where did
      my mind go? My mind is a reflection on the
         instant before I lost it, and suffers to get
            back its bearings again and toe the line
            Stand before anything and you, and anything
               pales by comparison. And so I remember my life
                  according to how it goes with you, for or against
                  but the fact of you as 2 signals — Could they be


blended and separately forgot? Does it matter
to count kisses? And distinguish this from that:
   the person from the object. The person from the
      rock, the river, and yet the instrument wails
         out its tragic song of identity, trapped in
            matter too, sprung free out of a kind of inspiration
            The musician takes little metal mallets to hit
               the strings and they dance over them, hear the
               plaintive wail O hear it in me, it is a woman
                  caught and suspended in sweet love or a country at war

Could it be the song you are waiting for to
 jolt you into present time? The past can wait
    to be remembered, the future is relative to this
        moment you get yourself out of here because you are
          rootless, like all thought, and philosophy
            always begins & ends with the question of Other anyway
              Who are you? Naked space? Who are you, disembodied
                song? What toils here in my late-night brain?
                  I have waited until now to state the case of the
                    imperative, for language takes its awful lawful command

And stands for naught but this French "redouté" –
 dread – and did it not exist its content goes to
    its competitors. I fear, you fear, we fear and
      we laugh also, a fragile mass of jelly and sensation,
        a bunch of silly problems, sitting in the foyer waiting
          to enter, nervous about our dress our speech our
            dignity and the coming election, who's in power,
              and the fashion of that power, its unending ineluctable
                influence on the surrounding provinces and bank accounts,
                  the way it will kill or cure the lives of thousands

Not one of them can talk back and be heard
 And stands for naught but the way you stop speaking
    when she comes in and she is your desire – the rose,
      the crux of the matter – standing in sunlight in a kind
        of deception, a feminine principle, the beginning and
          ending of your world, a mother-trust, an emblem of what
            can breathe and bloom outside the Pentagon, and that is
              your job to do today, to stand outside the building
                which has a goal of scathing intellectual tone
                  of nihilism, extinction. Irony, too?

Not my job to stand up outside and give a break
to the proceedings, take up some room, shout
and dance on the lawns, some kind of private
property anyway, has it come to this? This
old protest, this old language, old manifesto.
What he says has the form of a question but is
really a command. What they say seems rhetorical
but is it really, is it? When I say "May I"
do I mean it. And the child might say I want I
want and it will be his because he says so

Or so he thinks. Deep disquietudes, deep panic,
the objects do not come as they are bidden
He thinks he owns one of them and traces it with small
delicate fingers, he isn't sure, it is only a
frame of the thing he desires. The true things
the things that shine and cost money, the things
someone else values or did once, or the things
that are unnamed, unspoken. It looks like something
but what is it really? A master of the universe, a house
of cards, a paper bell he inspects and ultimately destroys

Not like a concrete linguistic object, more like
something neutral, unworthy, no I don't mean that
but has no energy one way or the other although it's
ready to jump in as soon as you wish to attach some
importance to it. Back here again, square one, with the
perception of form. Then: is it for or against me? And so
tonight these questions retrace their antecedents
because the "you" of the "you" interfered. Let *you* alone!
Rather, what is social, what is individual, what sublime
is the issue, and saying it to point the way

is to really get down to details: his necktie
 pearly in the light, his small hips moving in
      a kind of playful jog to amuse us, his sockless feet,
        books strewn about with the titles of things Roman,
         to conjure an eternal city is a duty here, the lines
            which are studied in another tongue. "Tungol," did you
              know, means "star"? The "you" of him, the "you" of
                his desk, you leave in a huff, and the objects remain
                  with you on them, binding me to you even further
                    even after I turn the lights out one by one


An obligation to glucose, an obligation to the empirical
 you whose ingenuity keeps us going past bedtime
      One woman's bedtime is another's rising after all, and
        even with all the lights off you burn the midnight
          oil up on the hill surrounded by the tomes that cry out
           to be loved. Let's not be pretentious about a library.
               The fear of falling into terror might inspire a mistrust
                 of science, but instead you are able to mimic the
                    indestructible and the invisible, the matter in the sense
                      of "stuff" will always allude you, what else is wrong?


A science studying the life of signs, that is the task
 after the decline of religious meanings for what we must
   get busy analyzing the gestures if we are to really
      have results, nothing else out there to amuse us
        Do you agree? I would or would not stake my life on it
          and walk away getting off easy back to the lab where
            we dissect language into miniscule parts
                Phonemes and phones ache for their missing limbs under
                  our fierce scapulas, our sharp and accurate unerring ears
                    If we can hear reason we will let you know how it destructs

It could be the interpretation of the dream
in which I am possibly "saying something"
Wooden tables are the women in the dream
Two men on either side in tall hats
and then Winston Churchill comes in
and a man called Suchness with a hammer and sickle
It is the politics of the time and the thinking
that that person indulges in a kind of discourse
with himself letting the day and night settle
in, not in the physical sense but in the sense

of yearning for more to absorb or really we do
take it in, know it or not, believe or not,
sleep or not, in love or not, talking or not,
fucking or not, waking to write something down
punctuated by the sound of water dripping,
and the so-called politics is invented by the
dreamer so that there are two sides always
to our thinking and we might roll over to
left or right, or jolt up in fear at the
total annihilation possible in one nightmare

reaching out to consume you, hazard a guess
because you keep trying to construct a different
reality based on what you want. Can't I get it?
Doesn't he she they get whatever they want?
Was it this or that they got? Now everyone read a
stanza aloud I wonder you do it so differently
Can you get ahold of it as I do, the gesture
of emotion, the sweep of a hand, a scarred landscape,
one brush stroke, someone steps off the sunporch,
that grand person's line or life or drama ends

Of course you can, and you may write it too,
or play it, or sing along, and know that
we all exist to know how to do this,
clapping or joining hands or tapping out
the meter with our foot, the whole chorus
moving en masse to honor the hero returning
from war, look how wounded he is! Look how
women kneel at his feet to kiss those wounds
listen to him tell of it, the blood and steel
Watch his eyes go wide in the gore and glory of it


And see how his exploits dance in the song
the strophe and antistrophe accentuating
the way this one was felled and that one
cried "Hold, enough!" Or was a prayer of sharp thanks
to one of many great interfering gods who like
nothing better than paeans to themselves
They come alive as we call their names and
resound in us all the passions they represent
O goddesses do not let me kill that which
is in me to kill, but if I do take it out


on that other one who crossed me with her
heart and tongue, O great goddess do this for me
because I am only of these delicate bones made
I break apart on any continent, but you soar
as mind does and can take shapes, o protean one
do this for me and for all women: Revenge!
That she should do it is not the point
working the women in us to frothy rage
against a meek one of our kind who looked
at the man belonging to the other, and so on

An old story that gets retold in a poem
Let it beat out its meter, exhausted now
    and yet keeps on and on in me, heartbeat
        or the mother's scenario, or the hag's
            or the virgin's melody she knows not what for,
                languishing in the hot forest night yet
                    not in a language more primitive than ours
                        The adjective "licht," open, is the same word as "light"
                            To make something open means to make light, free and clear
                            To make it shine in your heart


To make the forest clear of trees
The openness is the clearing, the nothing in common
    with light meaning "bright" (Heidegger) and yet let
        the brightness stream into the clearing, mind on fire
            Outward appearance is everything today
                What is the opening of what is open?
                    We pick up the book and eyes alight on the way
                        Merlin appears to Perceval as an aged man carrying
                            a sickle around his neck and wearing high boots
                                "Si fait, grand partie de ton affaire gist sur moi"


So much for others interfering in our affairs,
    the business of proud self going about a day
        arrogant until it catches sight of you, a magician,
            a glamorous one, who pants and cajoles and
                speeds his or her way into your heart, flattered
                    by the promise and pleasure, assuaged by the tone,
                        look, color, taste, touch, he is so soft
                            and I am so solid and desirable, there is no
                                thing in itself, it is only in relationship
                                    to tangible emotions, forever exchanging molecules

Which is what neurons do in order to communicate
The axon of one neuron releases the excited
    molecules of the neurotransmitter into a microscopic
        ever ready gap. While on the opposite of this royal
            divide, receptor molecules in the receiving molecule
                respond to the neurotransmitter by opening wide their
                    channels that let potassium and sodium ions into the cell
                        If enough of these positively charged ions accumulate,
                            other channels, sensitive to voltage, are tripped open
                                Speaking, on the other hand, is an individual act


Then more ions flood into the neuron causing it to fire
sending its own signal to the next cell in line
    The brain stores memory by linking neurons
        to form new circuitry. Turn up the synaptic
            volume controls by stimulating neural pathways
                in the hippocampus with high-frequency bursts
                of electricity. Give up, turn the corner
                    And let all this somehow be triggered by calcium
                        But that other is not an object but impulse
                            A rub of two sticks under moonlight, we need a fire


To push back the horizon of the observable universe
as we discover galaxies and hints of galaxies
    at distances they should not be. One ten times
        more massive than the Milky Way and at least
            12 billion light years away, and beyond
                The quasars beam out their luminosity at this
                    core of galaxies. Do I derive from this?
                        Of course, and of course not. There is no thing
                            without other things yet one thing cannot come solidly
                                from another as the edge of this writing, outside the book.

# XXII

## PIECES OF AN HOUR

*She is roused to write on call for a performance. The poet needs summoning from mental torpor and welcomes a structure which she creates with dogged attention. She has also given her students the same assignment: to write every day within the same hour in the same spot. One woman never strays from the laundry closet. John Cage is quintessential artist of this century, likely the most innovative. His "passivity," if you could call it that, both gentle & active. His work is fierce. She pays homage in a kind of twilight meditation, whatever sounds come out of her composed in this "chance" procedure to accompany an evening of his piano music which also allows for improvisation. His work gives permission to speak of the animals inside her. She is also at an interstice with the sounds of Gertrude Stein ringing in her ear. Stein is such a man. Cage seems the androgynous alchemist. She will perform with 2 men.*

*preparation: on 6 different days write within the increments of one hour*

dear John Cage:

=what?=
=Time me=

# TIME E E E E E E E E E E E E E E E

=individual who is=
=effective=
=drama drama=
=but, with a turn of gentry pretension=
=who is=
=pattern in a great part persist=
=*ist los?*=
=sacred gesture, utilize it=
=what – in *counting?*=
=4 minutes 33 seconds=

=patrician etiquette=

=of their family=
=daily like is built=
=pieces of an hour=
=1 the cause=
=2 the ceremony=
=minute flicker three=
=you see the inside of her plan=
=on very hour a minute is recorded to match=
=her time=
=prepare the piano=

=it is never wasted=
=meet the man in boulder it is a time=
=Cage's laugh would wake the dead=

=complex can be cursory=

=intricate palm leaf offering=
=but empirically, it is signal=

=restless, & where=
=dupe of leader=
=ritually a muted one=
=turn to dust=

=pieces of an hour=
=in which a small bolt was living=

=suspended web of significances=

=demand explication=
=undomesticated thought=

=it in motion=
=Tuesday=

=curious=

=coherent cluster=
=endurance=

......................................................................................

=incomplete unfinished animals=
=who complete ourselves through culture=
=through highly particular forms of it=
=Javanese, Hopi, Italian, upper class, lower, middle=
=you are on the fringes too=

=Our plasticity has been remarked upon=
=but even more how dependent on=
=a certain sort of learning=
=weather, stripping, rubbing=

=attainment of this concept I tell you it is true=
=specific systems of symbolic meaning=
=beaver build a dam=
=bird you build your nest today=
=baboon organize into social groups, go do this now=
=mice mate on the basis of forms that rest on instructions=
=coded in their genes=
=they can't wait to do this=
=& evoked by patterns of external stimuli=
=physical keys inserted into organic locks=
=but women locate food, build dams=
=shelter, organize social groups or find sexual consorts=
=under the guide of instructions=
=encoded in flow charts and blueprints=
=moral systems, aesthetic judgments=
=ground plan of activity=
=second segment of preparations=

=fine eye for detail=
=Wednesday=

=quest: metaphysical entity=
=cultural artifact=
=me *au dessus* piano=
=chips, stones, plants=
=I want to tell you a story=
=Henry David Thoreau was one of them=
=and walked=
=*wakaru:* (to understand) means to be divided=
=*widdershins:* take the left-hand path=
=baboon you sleep now=
=I am subject that I am object=
=and took to the hills=

=I was a hidden treasure=
=& I loved to be known=
=so I created the world=
=I was a word then I hid my treasure=
=mind is outer space piano: continuous memory=
=penumbral light=

=tiled tight=
=was words then=
=mottled=
=his thought pluck'd a string=
=strain=
=Cage=
=inverts the piano=

=1 minute away awaits a wit=
=without shuffling the debris of monolith intelligence=
=Thursday: mix, a rehearsal=

..................................................................................................

=minute number 2 succumbs=
=I go under=

=I fall away=
=love is strange=
=yogin please don't go=
=sing out a gut to you=
=pieces of an hour=
=await you=
=spread on a bed=
=take a shower to meet the main man=
=his day's a practice chart=
=you are flow=
=flowers of an hour=
=a piece of coffee now=
=a piece of her hair=
=voodoo is not in question=
=the cage is wide open=
= gamelan thumps your mallet=
=*ump o ah um*=
=he invited my voice=
=9:10 he invites my voice in=
(*here she lies down to make a crow sound under the piano*)

# CAW CAW CAW CAW CAW CAW CAW

=did you say it?=
=what was it?=
=savant's dream=
=unstudied=
=unsteady=
=no it was a crystal=
=It was a steady thing=
=It was sure=
=It was a sure thing=
=Did you see them?=
=Where?=
=Living=
=I said it again living=
=you mean a dwell in=

=no I don't I said living=
=like take it out=
=all students: take it out=
="life" is a word=
=like I said I mean omigod yes=
=take it out=
=it was a valley=
=it was a hill-rill thing=
=it was a swell time=
=it was a holiday=
=did you say it?=
=what I said=
=I said but what I said=
=said itself so=
=& such and such got down=
=you go koan a hand=
=a knee=
=you go moan the wounded animal=
=you go down baboon=
=meet the small bird=
=you go sing a small song=
=you are nearly extinct=
=what?=
=did you say extinction=
=I did=
=I saw him pluck the silver cactus needles=
=strum=
=it was a hill-rill thing=
=it is best said & it cab or can happen here=
=why=
=because they said it so=
=strumm=
=someone wanted it to happen=
=no not really but it does it does happen=
=it does it does happen it does doesn't it happen =
=it sure does=
=it is damaging to spill all over the place=

=and better not focus on any government=
=to be a damage all a place over itself=
=& wander thrust around about a similar mantra=
=it is about gaining & spending=
=it is a loss to a principle speech=
=what did you say?=
=I said but does it does happen doesn't it?=
=Utter in=
=under it=
=I said it utters itself well=
=I said it well=
=I said it better than that to be a burden to=
=I was the piece of my own hour=
=got stuck=
=how?=

( *here she speaks in the loudest whisper:*

# REVVVVVVVVVVVVVVVVVVVVVVVV ELATION)

=It was a setup=
=you set yourself up=
=pieces of an hour=
=you got small=
=you got taken in=
=you were the proxy=
=in the convent=
=you say your matins=
=evensong=
=you got made over every moment every moment I=
=let go but my heart to reality=
=what you said it=
=that's verboten, student, "reality"=
=I said it=
=what=
=that you are restless=
=that says it all suppose you sleep=

=suppose you sleep on Thursday=
=Thursdays were the days=
=of all my hope or fear=
=is it a strain?=
=is it?=
=to get dressed again=
=I said it well=
=& we were a moment & stopping=
=fish: sorry there is not enough memory=
=You are animal programmed=
=the genetics of the sonorous one=
=narrow you are mind of=
=slight like the insect & gossamer made=
=I love you when they ask for texts about America=
=I love you like under water=
=this is the assignment assignation part where=
=the dream got on stage again or was it silver screen?=
=& the animals were caged before their entrance=
=we will act the story of a transformer=

............................................................................

=it was metal contradictory=
=it was meeting you to do lunch=
=if you could ever "do" anything=
=do a book, do moving=
=you are moving with the slower ones=
=atrophy on the machine=
=did it?=
=what=
=Bounce=
=Did it=
=I said it did=
=or words can do it=
=like sleep=
=he can really sleep=
=I mean he can really sleep=
=Ambrose likes it=

=what =
=to be seated and happy=
=the night was half a star, half a moon=
=half over=
=did you enter in=
=someone said about the star it was sorta impossible=
=to get as far away as that=
=but he can really really sleep=
=yogin please don't go=
=are you caged who is not a man a codger be=
=mode of viziers=
=government names us here=
=& you are the such & such of taxes=
=5 things go on in this poem?=
=Can you guess what they are?=
=sustain the axis=
=what say=
=of my argument=
=what say=
=meet Friday?=
=less in admin=
=Lamartine, poet of politics, to quote=
=These times are times of chaos=
=bounded terminology=
=opinions are a scramble=
=parties are a jumble=
=the language of ideas of new ideas=
=has not been created=
=nothing is more difficult than to=
=give a good definition of oneself in religion=
=in philosophy=
=in politics=
=one feels knows lives & dies a cause=
=but can't name it=
=It is the problem of this time to classify things and men=
=the world has jumbled its catalog=
=tangent paragon=

=& tangible=
=you are suitable emended, a precious tool=
=mock realty=
=you you abode here a boulder?=
=mention that one of them is time decisions=
=and the next is a mention of specific animals=
=because Gertrude abounded the cow=
=did she let owl in?=
=I rather not=
=what=
=say=
=It is to be=
=understood it is spoken=
=are you still ready=
=were you ever ready and then did it wake you up=
=your preparedness=
=I'm not sure=
=get dresses=
=you are now putting on your shoes=
=Is it a form of do meditation?=
=how you are being and inside a rule or regular=
=space play with my=
=dresses=
=for they are the new form of me=
=I let my liberty go=
=she's not a caged animal he said she was=
=that's long ago=
=the Himalayas=
=or some other form=
=The composer is=
=holding your hand on this one=
=then he lets go=
=what sounds are the sounds you speak of=
=what sounds mount the podium=

=the space is cleared=
=we have a kind of non-pew revival=

=a performance is a cage=
=I will lie now under his instrument=
=I will be under his instrument=
=I will mount the embankment=
=I willl be ready to rise=
=How can I show you my piece of a mind=
=& let it rip=
=I will show you it from down here=
=crouch=
=like the animal you are always being=
=need a worry=
=I was not afraid of being an intimate boundary=
=Cage, who is a man woman not=
=Caged,who=
=I ask you=
=I ask you=
=I ask you=
=who is not=
=I asked you=
=remains under piano silent=
=magnet imitation=
=Erik Satie=
=He was a piece in my hour=
=whirred=
=ears took off their delicate sheaves=
=I am the sleeves of his ear tonight=

...................................................................................

=dear John Cage:=
=The world is a more humming place thank you for it=
=I listened to the traffic lights=
=I will never get used to television=
=Can you always be a man or nun=
=what is the action most diverse in all=
=the Zen of world=
=could I place a gesture here=
=it is "think of a gesture," the game=

=what hands, arms to hold you=
=my son=
=is it the increment of time I thought of=
=do animals think like this or will they never perform=
=I am asking for more time=
=I'm used to getting my way=
=I set the stage for her return=
=in the fourth place you are trying hard to lie down again=
=how many surfaces in an hour?=
=how many times do you think?==
=how many colors do you see of an hour=
=it was increment of 10 it was increment of 10=
= it was increment of 10 then double that=
=what is your thinking track it my dear home an hour=
=trying to stay with the fleet increment=

=wed the pace to the bon mot=
=how good is it?=
=it is very good=
=how limit how you plan to me=
=It is swell, it is well=
=how speed your way on?=
=10 minutes by 10 is the key to mystery=
=what master do you wanna be or control a=
=clock tower, master time=
=I would an Aztec be=
=who does this=
=what is your sense of time?=
=had it out of hand=
=It is a notion Claud Brown had=
=It is a long silence=
=Cage had it once=
=night arrived=
=night of Saturn=
=thought to himself a way to dance around it=
=pluck an untuned string just one=
=the reverb fell throughout the cell=

=did it travel=
=how far=
=let me strike a gong or shake this thing=
=let it be known the cage is open=
=& a terrible sound is loosed on the world=
=crack the page, let out from under self=
=the body sings=
= stand up=
=let them be three=
=let them be three=
=the men and me=
=let them be three=

=caged, who is a man not?=
=a woman not whirrrr=
=what is the date in a library=
=out of time=
=a clock, an hour, time is early:=
=white against white=
=engage=
=on an hour: clock whirrr=
=a man had an idea=
=that put him inside sound=
=the woman has the woman hasn't =
=the woman has the woman hasn't=
=the woman has the woman hasn't the woman has the woman hasn't=
=a conversational propriety=
=hazard, he calls to me=
=increments of 10 of 10 of 10 of 10 of 10 of 10=
=screen slated slants highlit by=
=backlit by foam of her ceiling=
=I will write and then stop=

=I will write & then stop=
=I will write & then stop=
=& to end on the daylight of the sun=

=rip rip rip rip rip rip rip=
=in the cave=
=the three-legged sister=

=white toward what hoop or blind=
=blond who is not caged=
=the piano is not a planet but has =
=a planned network=
=a "c," a high C laughs=
=a rub against book=
=rub against cock somewhere there's a universe=
=could be tenored alternative=
=could be attentive or tense=
= lover leaves again=

=what animal beckoned you here=
=what mantra was heard?=

*(chant & crow into piano here)*

# OM AING GRING CLING CHAMUNDA YEI VIJAY

# AW AW AW AW

=How many l's or leaves=
=in the doorway=
=How many leaves of an hour?=
=levered, light tread=
= enter the hour clocked upon a page=

(close – slam – a door)

*(she is lying under the piano here &*
*hits its hard black underbelly 3 times*

# KNOCK KNOCK KNOCK

# XXIII

## YOU REDUCE ME TO AN OBJECT OF DESIRE

*She is exhausted yet questions as ever the male godhead. Fat Almighty an avatar of Allah proves soft. Long Armageddon dream (backdrop is war) segues into an acceptance of her power as twin of the male and perhaps the better artist because she does write down her unflinching vision. And is willing to love her enemy. The boy teases & calls her back from her role as sober Superwoman. The final cri di coeur & deception of the Doctor is a subtle reclamation of territory, her own body. Her doctrine is desire but she is no longer an object.*

———————————— touch a nerve

————————————— ma sha' Allah

————————————— lamp light the "sinner"

————————————— goad on

————————————— Father: incline thine ear

————————————— to hear of

————————————— furies, spent of father's blood

———————————— son spent of mother's blood

——————————— & hero: a dusky weapon

——————————— to be sprung in wrath

— incline an ear

— none give him welcome

— why?

— incline the ear to hear the intellect rule her

— madness, sudden panic, for she is twin

— how did she get so "even"?

              — in the night

— to hear how he clamours for blood, but she is smart

           — in the name of the land he rages on      *Allah Allah*

     — to name it his name but she steals his words

    — to slay a demon in the same night

        — in his calling she steals his sex

— & he becomes his own head (for he has a woman's heart)

— in mixing of the wine (which is forbidden)

      — drink offers a grace        — yet curses

     — unseen unseen curses shall bar him from himself

— but she will enter the temple dishonored

— but mightily empowered

     — warrior with irresistible cause

— (such were her oracles)

*(Cumaean Sybil wrote oracles on leaves scattered by the wind)*

      — Fat Almighty with flavor of Zeus was kind of enemy too

— she dressed the part of part-animal to slaughter Fat Almighty

— she became Tramena, a hybrid

        — draw near Fat Almighty with the bleat of god

— a goat to slay, got slew

— a cutting of deals

— Shaman Goat Man nervous about Western medicines to America Sud

— incline the ear of thou who favors us, Fat Almighty

— Let righteousness walk into battle! she said . . .

— *Allahu Akbar!*

— teach me O father the marginal life before Fat Almightly gobbles us whole

— how by word or action to

— to live to fight

— day charged into night

— how to live the female night sky

— when the flames devour the flesh &
each boy child addresses his tribute of lamentation to the mother

— how to live when naught's here but evil

— undo a sentience out of anger

— as sentence not stand in doom

or as suppliant not stand in doorway blocking light

as suppliant voice intact

as suppliant claim the social security payment

as suppliant a pinch of salt to flavor the bowl

as suppliant implore sanctuary

as suppliant rehearse the logics: what did the German say?

all the philosophies won't help then supplicate all the more?

"For a murderous blow let a murderous blow be struck."

as suppliant: peaceful load for the house of Atreus

as suppliant, may these lips be moved in song

as Masai warrior get circumcized, dress like the woman, paint your face

  & shoot at the diminutive birds with little bows & arrows

they say

"so strong in hope a woman's heart, whose purpose is a man's"

..............................a gap in my life . . .
..............................I was a mutant, but . . .
..............................a gold tooth in a mouth proclaiming
..............................a gap in life, but...Mafioso stayed outta here
..............................Yet silhouette of a High Priestess her own mind was too . . .
..............................Mosiac too, I was a reminder, but . . .
..............................The hair of a pearl in − whose? − heart
..............................or memory of Keats's tomb in Rome
..............................Remember my flagellation on the Spanish Steps?
..............................But, is texture true? But? Is it?
..............................I had a memory toward the Editorial Board
              whose life attitudes were not sound
..............................& Yeats's burial place (ah dear dead poets)
..............................I worshipped all of them, diamonds, opals, guns . . .
..............................Honored all the poets
..............................Picture a distributor cap with pinions stuck out
..............................Pinions stuck out?
..............................little electrical nodes inside of it
..............................I know what you're saying sort of
              but not exactly a description
..............................Andrew said this
..............................Then Anne said:
..............................Feels good in my hand
..............................in the chaos of my life
..............................Feels good in any laboratory of desire
..............................& back in the hand, holding the reins of desire
..............................I was a truant, but . . .

I approach my family home on Macdougal Street in disguise – purple dress, yellow beret, hair dyed black – to find another costumed stranger (as I am strange to myself) at the door – either a black transvestite or woman dressed in some red clothes of mine. Not clear. There's a note from my mother saying "Please help your brother do, or 'write out' X as we used to help you." My brother Carl is sick. Mounting uneasiness & speed inside me. I notice that water is rising at the window, although there is none in the street. The basement is unfamiliar & stranger who observes me like a cat is obviously more "in possession" here. I'm here simply to take messages & pick up "assignments." He/she waves goodbye at the door & this is humorous. I turn the corner at King Street but then abrupt right uptown presumably "on assignment." The streets indicate it's the end of the world, finally. The few people I pass are not themselves, in varying degrees of disarray & stress, and garbed in odd attempts at disguise. I pass my brother Mark who says: I knew this, I came dressed like this (Bald Zennie); isn't it funny? Streets are made of wood, buildings papier-mâché, like a Red Grooms set. I'm walking on a tremendous theatrical set of 6th Avenue, created by a mysterious subliminal "will" to give the illusion of New York City. I'm to go to Madison Square Garden. Taxi?

Old Pennsylvania Station but miles underground. Bigger but populated with a multitude of sentient beings dressed *in extremis*. Nurse, Eskimo, cowboy costumes. Heavenly host? Some folks decked out as animals. A whole panoply of ill-fitting disguises — fake-identity-desire "covers." A lot of gesturing, & multilingual talk & bickering. A stage show is in progress in a theater reminiscent of The Globe, that combines with a "people's stage" (Red China?). In contrast to the colorfulness of the lively gesticulating mob, the Globe set is extremely drab. It depicts a dark subway station. A huge pulsating boulder sits on the tracks. I know for a fact that there are at least a dozen actors inside the boulder costume making it come alive and it's destined to burst although I may never see this happen. There's a *paseo* along the apron of the stage & people must pass in coupled formation. As my lover (he's a Marine) & I pass we pause to assess the action on the stage & the couple behind us frisks us & holds a gun to lover-Marine's head. But it's only plastic, shoots stage blood. We abruptly turn to catch glint of metal, the other alloy, under fluorescent light.
Someone shouts a warning, we duck as machine guns fire on the unsuspecting crowd. The "RPF" (The Rabidinal Police Force) descends. There is a bloodbath as the spectacle of color flies apart, horrible too as the assimilated "people"

writhe in pain. I crawl over the bodies of rubber, papier-mâché, down & straw that are bleeding in the cool metallic light. Is this the new Israeli War?

Wander to the arched mouth of a cave or hospital waiting room & peer out into the darkness. There appears to be a New Delhi-style taxicab awaiting me with a "couple" inside. Polish. Czech? *"Vse je v poradku."* I get in. The driver is smiling idiotically, machine is running he'll do business. Wherever we are going takes forever. Multilayered tunnels, constant U-turns, up & down ramps over "bulges" (artificial mountain suburb terrain). Couple is discussing "sex change." I realize I'm regressing, getting smaller more girllike – but I'm doing it in self-defense & it's external as inside I'm feeling stronger & it's like show me more, "okay I can take it what next?" We get to another waiting room just like first but it's completely empty (realize it's the same one but cleaned up) – everything outside car is dank & dark & damp & dark again – riding through fungus vegetable world –as before there's water rising at the window. Finally drive onto lighted tableau scene of business-as-usual Emergency Ward World. Dioramas of bodies being carried on stretchers by some earnest young men sorta like TV flat slightly sinister celluloids. Intense young doctors. He lifts his arm. He turns his head. He smiles. He studies a chart. He is being paged. He has a name like "Dusty." "Rusty?" Now he is really concerned. Someone named Sue comes in. Things look different. They're outside in a park now. Cut back to his eyes. Are these eyes to be seen through clearly I wonder? I wonder.

Now the Czechoslovakian couple is again discussing "sex change." "It's all in the range." I'm still regressing – passing back through puberty. I'm anxious to get back to the workaday world again, find a telephone. I step out of the cab & get caught once again in a barrage of machine gun fire. I'm taken prisoner, I'm surly with my "Captivators." One of the automatons will make a deal if I sleep with him/her. Won't. Lois, a prison manicurist befriends me & comments on my dyed hair & exotic looks. I realize I'm not really looking like "myself," which is not only mine but everybody's problem, & wonder if they have any control over this. I'm growing down to 9 years old by now (call me Bice Portinari) & the younger I get the more pain & suffering I feel. I want to eat my own heart. I put away my yellow beret (a mere "childish thing"). I want to call William Burroughs, my Dream Teacher, he'll know what's going on. There's a newspaper "The Nerve-Ending News" which says the incident at the Terminal has been "sewn up" & those that got away are the real victims. There are other prisoners as well, students, & those who have not had sex changes yet, and they dance as they move, beautifully. A dance of death. *De Muerte.* They weave in & out of long ballrooms guarded by garish red-skinned automatons. May an automaton have skin? There's a decision to bring in mustard gas as there is no more blood left to spill. The gas comes in blue tanks & there are some Commedia dell'Arte masks too. Everyone has to go to the hospital.

He, the lover said, "you are the nightmare & the dream."

I dream this way & give advice to the tribe in the morning:
young men, throw away the rifle & lance
take back your lasso of the reindeer herdsman
your harpoon of the seal hunter
the spirits will help you
your pronunciation will change
in a small voice you will nurse the children

& to the panel I say:
I will tell you about the Buddhist approach to cause & effect. There is no first cause, there is no final cause. All the factors we observe in any situation have arisen because of the subtle influence of many factors. Cause & effect when observed closely go back & back. We do not discover anything solid. "Egolessness" has existed from beginningless time. Conditioned by such & such, this will happen. Out of the bowels of your realization your spontaneous utterance, your poem, is the lion's roar. This view denies eternalism, this view denies nihilism.

As a cultural worker one needs to have all the skills one has a bent for. This takes discipline. Sharpen your attention. Get the facts straight, don't color them. You don't own them, you are mere vessel for lion's roar. Question the billions it takes to reinvent the plutonium trigger warhead wheel at Los Alamos, just one example. Are you too addicted to fossil fuel? Investigate the effects of burning of wastes. Learn how to write a citizen's complaint. Be accurate, articulate, awake and always move gracefully with your subtle sense of humor to navigate the dark passage. Seek out the like-minded. You will be a community of eyes. And you will create the world in your heart.

There is a text called Memphite Theology which dates back to the 2nd or 3rd millennium B.C. The theology describes a cosmogony according to which Ptah, the local god of Memphis & his emanation Atum, were the primal beings. Ptah created the world in his heart, the seat of his mind, & actualized it through his tongue, the act of speech. This resonates with the Platonic & Christian "logos"—the Word. Thoth (father of Isis) – Dhwty (Thoth Thrice greatest) – had a role in this cosmogony as the heart of Ptah, Ptah's tongue being Horus. There is an association of the heart with the intellect of which Thoth was the especial master. In other theologies, he is the inventor of writing, originator of mathematics, magician, and master of the divine act of "speech" which allows the gods to converse with each other & with men . . . . . . you know your job, men.

Dear Hermes Trismegistus: you could play all the roles. You could be the hidden god, demiurge, Holy Ghost. You could be the messenger of all the little people. You could be prophet Idris. You could be mercury. You could be father of all the gods, you could be *intellectus,* light of my mind.

I thank you, I thank you


Dear Anne W & the Idea of Naropa Institute,

I was on my way, on my way! I've been sending you clippings & haiku as a warning, your undercover poet. Remember a couple of years ago (I've been through so much since then maybe it was three (or four?))Ray Manzarek & M. McClure were to teach a workshop. I was on my way, on my way, on my way to find form. But. . . something happened. The video police kicked down the walls, broke into my bedroom my composing room. Kidnapped, drugged and brainwashed me. They had me eating garbage on Venice Beach, dragged me off to L.A. County jail. Had me hallucinating on a combination of drugs and what I think was virtual reality. So they kicked their way into my brain too. I got an elementary lecture on segregation, oil power, power, power, 10,000 dollars, power and power. I'm in a psych unit right now, the stuff is still in my head. I feel I'm being held down by Lilliputians. I hope this is not permanent.

Be Bip Be Bow Bow

Be Bip Bip Be Bow Bow

X.X.

*Prosim, kde je posta?*

all the men ride my mind
yet death is death
fire is about that high
my dear men are always in sight
Deliver me, one says, you are a witch
I am Hermes' daughter Isis
I ask the cards & more
just the way I go into a museum
nobody knows when my cards started
& I also ask my dictionary
which rescues me, which saves me
It knows me
I'm well dressed with opera glasses
I walk through narrow streets 4,000 years old
I rise from a field of Mummies
I talk with my ghosts – again, again
My angels are ropes
My angels are clay
My incense lamp will clear the mood of Europe
I throw the light around
fire gets wild in me
my hearts pounds in my pocket
These objects make me what I am
What am I?
I make the people important in my life
They are the other India
They are the other Arabia
I enter my lists of friends
onto the shelf in my car
I am linden
I am oil
I ride an orange car
What am I?

Dear Anne:

As a kid I remember identifying, the earliest I can recall, with Donald Duck, and now I realize this was probably because he was the classic imaginative fuck-up, never gave the lie to the adult male myth we were brought up to admire, never had a job, got by somehow, had amazing adventures, never took maturity seriously, even when the nephews put him down for his lack of serious plans abilities, etc. (In fact they were more adult in outlook than he was, what with their Junior Woodchuck book of rules etc.) And then I suppose I had the usual peer-group film heros, cowboys mostly at that point, but I doubt even then I thought of them as any kind of possible future model for myself, just that furious inviolability I felt for a few moments coming out of the theatre.

blast of air
Clark in love with celluloid

"You accept the language that is spoken around you and that you speak."

"You deal with it in writing."

*deal*

"The way you write will reflect what you think those words do – what effects they have, what effects they can be permitted to have – how you can change the effects they are known to have to what you want them to have."

*deal*

"You assume that your readers understand the language."

*deal*

"You can assume the existence of a large, widely accepted set of rules. You can also *not* assume or accept it

that the language be fair, that it hold you

fast, that the cross it bares exempts the woman

She rides through the poem on

villains, brothers, saints, deities

they speed her on

like a *diwes, dyeus,* a god-machine

out on the street again

long trip moving toward wha*t intellectus*

blast this air


(almost closer)


rehearse the deity-part, tell about the hospital


where the twins
rule
the
cosmos


& take an artist as their queen


The cold order loosens
The straps, they are heavy, they were dark, loosen
His head is held up high on the post, a veritable herm
How gnarly, take it down after tonight
It ties to what you were saying: "loosen, loosen"
A clench was open as he stroked the grisly hand
Held upon, loosened & lighter
Inner heat is bursting
No one needed a radiator
Not needed, hut doors
The moon is getting to "you"
He-Man arise in a prying sense
All four doors swung wide
Come in to see the light
"You" too
The insect kingdom will be out soon
Welcome them

The twin misses the twin
It's in the air
It's in the air
I missed you, twin
Love was my troubadour
I was that troubadour
I was never-at-peace-in-love
(Keep a little picture of desire in the rafters)

For what got clearer was architecture, was my power & that if you kept coming
back around section by section you'd reach my ultimate protest which reduced
me to an object of desire.

(Not.)

You reduce me to an object of desire. But I come back again. Never reject any-
thing. You reduce me to an object of desire. Never reject anyone. You slave
under the illusion of every beauty mark, every defect to catch me unawares, off
guard. You control the arrangement of room, of meal, of conversation, ideas
come to you. The fixation is complete in its optimism, in its colonial offerings.
I am the little colony. Who will save me? Who inhabits my oil wells, my mission-
ary zeal, my quixotic poetry? Who indeed surfaces to take my hand & walk me
across the desert and then across the plains. Then we climb the mountain. I'll
lead you to the ocean. I know the way. You will be baptized in my ocean. In my
fire. Who will live to tell the story? You try — reduce me to desire. You enter my
tent. The lamp is extinguished by wind. Father is a kind of wind and you are his
son. You know your business. But I am twin. The earth is a bed and grave. I am
calm again. I was the vessel for his wind, just tell me that. It was a torrent inside
me, tell me that. Just tell me that. Give me that

OM VAJRASATTA SAMAYA

a vow to light the mind

    — are you satisfied?

                    — just tell me that

— & that you are

                    — a satisfied one

                    — *(beyond monotheism)*

—— Mother, guess what?
—— What?
—— Chicken butt
—— Ambrose!
—— Shut up, mamma, shut up
    I've got to hear the score
—— Funny voice he's got
—— Mom, sports announcers *have* to be antsy pantsy
    Mom, you want them in a slow voice saying
    "Heeeee maaaaade a baaaaasket OOOOOO joy . . .
    Let's sing Kumbaya???"
—— Heh look, Scottie Pippen soaks up a play
—— Jordan shot a 3 pointer & made it
    But Drexler can't shoot worth a —— of ——
    My grandmother can shoot better'n that!
—— What's the "hustle board"?
—— Ohhhh Mom
    Look, mamma, there . . .
—— Where?
—— Chicken hair
—— Bulls lead 82 to 78
—— No! Go Blazers. O, sweet.
—— "Let their defense ignite the offense"
    "Scottie Pippen is now 0 for 3 from the line"
—— Gnarly
—— See somebody's fist in the screen?
—— Awesome. I mean down to the wire
—— You heard the man "This 4th quarter is going to be inneresting."
—— Sweet!

Finally I needed to tell you about the trip to the hospital:

Wrath that could be queen not doubt solves it like surgeon whose knife is Himalayan whose knife aberrants you. Twist down. Crumble, go bleak under blade, enter his doctoring charnel ground right now. Metal, or edge to be born to, blind too. They cover my eyes with an antiseptic plastic mask. Hospital sky blue. All wrath tenses blind to boundary. Space — is it? — or "just space." What jackal lingers there & knife turn again to drink ventricle. Metal to bone. What soft (was it?) flesh got made love to just a mite before & sings its pleasure cry: to kill to cure. It lies on any edge you care a mention. Break sigh blood ink settle restitute mores, your custom is a clutch. Hand (no jewelry) swings up to beat him back. Face (no makeup allowed) grimaces & twists its smile to contort him further. Dear surgeon-doctor-god I have not really sinned. And the Arab girl's tumor (as recorded by Roman annalist Diodorus Siculus) bursts open to reveal male genitals. She changes her name, dons men's clothes & joins the cavalry. Don't take this breast. Underneath: a man How many times o doctor trick blood sheet money leave the room. Send the bill. Can I go. Send the bill tomorrow can I go. Right now send it I want to go. Let me go. Die a death. Itemized, charged. I go now. Unstrap me. Let me go. Exist on cold slab who I called back "ancestor! ancestor!" who called wrought steel surgical a war. I cry to my ancestors & then I cry to them. Revenge. The maritime Koryak took ordinary stones instead of wives, dressed them in clothes & took them to bed to caress. I dress the cold stone in the hospital gown, place it quietly on the operating table and leave the room. To blunt the knife.

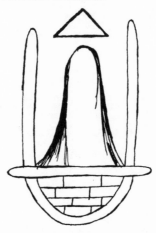